FREEING CHARLES

The New Black Studies Series

Edited by Darlene Clark Hine and Dwight A. McBride
A list of books in the series appears at the end of this book.

FREEING CHARLES

The Struggle to Free a Slave on the Eve of the Civil War

Scott Christianson

University of Illinois Press
Urbana and Chicago

© 2010 by Scott Christianson
All rights reserved
Manufactured in the United States of America
1 2 3 4 5 C P 5 4 3 2 1
∞ This book is printed on acid-free paper.

Library of Congress Cataloging-in-Publication Data
Christianson, Scott.
Freeing Charles : the struggle to free a slave on the eve of the Civil War /
Scott Christianson.
p.   cm. — (The new Black studies series)
Includes bibliographical references and index.
ISBN 978-0-252-03439-8 (cloth : alk. paper)
ISBN 978-0-252-07688-6 (pbk. : alk. paper)
1. Nalle, Charles, ca. 1821–1875. 2. Fugitive slaves—United States—
Biography. 3. Slaves—Virginia—Biography. 4. Slavery—Virginia—History—
19th century. 5. Slavery—United States—History—19th century. 6. Antislavery
movements—United States—History—19th century. 7. Underground Railroad.
8. Troy (N.Y.)—History—19th century. 9. Tubman, Harriet, 1820?–1913.
I. Title.
E450.N225C47   2010
973.7'115—dc22   2009020146

For Tamar, with love

CONTENTS

ACKNOWLEDGMENTS

Like the Underground Railroad, this book has required support from many good people from varied backgrounds, North and South, some of whom have since passed away. In my case, the journey has taken eighteen years, with many twists and turns along the way. In Culpeper and its environs, I benefited from interviews with T. O. Madden Jr., who welcomed me into his home (the historic former Madden's Tavern), shared some of his family papers and memories with me, and put me in touch with other key informants. I especially thank Ernest Brown for showing me around his Cole's Hill property. Several excellent Culpeper historians, including Eugene M. Scheel, Angus McDonald Green, and J. Newton Lindsay, provided expert guidance along the way and offered a rich lode of information about antebellum Culpeper. I benefited from many conversations with local residents, particularly Eugene E. Triplett, Adelbert Triplett, Thom Faircloth of the Germanna Foundation, Matthew J. McCarton, Dr. Hortense Hinton, Susan J. Keller, and Zann Miner. The Culpeper County Library and the Museum of Culpeper History introduced me to their marvelous collections. I also thank the Culpeper county clerk and local researchers Frances Walters and Bee Browning as well as Patricia Hurst of the Orange County Historical Association. Kathi and Steve Walker, hosts at Fountain Hall, always made me comfortable when I visited Culpeper.

Back in the 1970s I began to learn more about Virginia antebellum history from Virginius Dabney, Ruth Coder Fitzgerald, Paul Keve, and Norma Sue Wolfe. For this project, Conley Edwards, Minor Weisiger, and Bob Clay at the Virginia State Library provided assistance, and Frances S. Pollard introduced me to a bonanza of family papers and other resources at the Virginia Historical Society. I must also express my appreciation to the Thomas Balch

Library of Leesburg (especially Phyllis A. Ford); Jeanne Day at the Fauquier County Public Library in Warrenton and the staff at the Fauquier Historical Society in Warrenton; Suzanne S. Levy, Virginia Room librarian, Fairfax County Library; Gregory A. Johnson at the University of Virginia Library; and Lucious Edwards at the Virginia State University Library in Petersburg.

In Washington, I consulted staff at the Library of Congress and the National Archives, particularly Rich Gelbke and Fred Romanski, Bill Creech, Robert Ellis, and Michael Knight. Karen Blackman-Mills, chief of the Washingtoniana Division; Mohammed Jaleel, collections librarian of the Martin Luther King Jr. Library; and Matthew B. Gilmore at the District of Columbia Public Library facilitated my research about Washington, as did Gail Rodgers Redmann, vice president of the Historical Society of Washington. Judy Capurso of the Charles Sumner School Archives helped me track down some useful sources involving John and Mary Nalle. Paul E. Sluby and Hayden Wetzel helped try to locate death records and graves in Washington. Riverboat captain Clayton Embly and Ashley of Potomac Pintails, Inc., guided me along the Potomac and put me in touch with several other authorities on the river and its role in the capital area's underground railroad history. Rob Davenport and Lazarina Todorova were kind enough to put me up when I stayed in the District.

My explorations around Columbia were aided by the very knowledgeable professor Leroy Hopkins of Millersville University, professor Tracey Weis of Millersville University, Tammy Roberts and Meg Schaffer of Wright's Ferry Mansion, Ginger Shelley of the Lancaster County Historical Society, and folks at the Historical Society of Pennsylvania. In Maryland, Ray Langston of the Highland Beach Historical Commission helped me to learn more about John Nalle's death there.

My research in New York has long been facilitated by the New York State Library and Archives, especially Jim Corsaro, Stefan Bielinski, Charles Gehring, and Warren Broderick, as well as Kathleen Hulser of the New York Historical Society. Other helpful libraries included the New York Public Library, State University of New York Albany Library, University of Hawaii (Manoa) Library, Butler Library of Columbia University, Albany Institute of History and Art, Albany Public Library, and Sand Lake Town Library. I obtained vital information from several Sand Lake town historians, including Madolyn V. Carpenter, Eleanor Zaki, Mary French, and Judy Rowe. For information on Troy, I consulted with staff at the Troy Public Library; the Rensselaer County Historical Society, especially Jim Corsaro, Bob Andersen, Kathy Sheehan, Elsa Prigozy, and Ilene Frank; Thomas Phelan of Rensselaer Polytechnic Institute; the Rensselaer county clerk and Tom Carroll and Mike Barrett of the Industrial Gateway and the Civil War Roundtable; Fanny Hayes of Lansingburgh; Barbara Zuber of Troy; and professor Catherine Butler Jones of Boston University. Garry Doyle and Richard D. Ceresia granted me access to examine the former U.S. commissioner's office and vault at 5 State Street. Thanks too to Peter Shaver and Mark Peckham of New York State Historical Preservation for sharing some of their insights. For information about West Troy (Watervliet), I received some assistance from Craig Carlson, Mark Gilchrist, Tom Healey, and Tom Rocco, and also from John Swantek, Bob Pfeil, Jim Hyland, and Major Gary Mills at the Watervliet Arsenal.

My understanding of Harriet Tubman benefited from the kind assistance of two of her great biographers, Kate Clifford Larson and Jean Humez; from Mrs. Mary Gilmore, keeper of the History Room with the Ellen Jean Mahoney Collection, Seymour Library, Auburn, New York; and from Judy Bryant, a Tubman descendant, in Auburn. I was inspired by the opera based on the rescue that was composed by David Dramm of Amsterdam and first performed at the Troy Music Hall by the Albany Symphony Orchestra, and thrilled by the incomparable paintings of Mark Priest of Louisville, Kentucky. Those helping me to learn more about John Brown included professor Philip J. Schwarz of Virginia Commonwealth University, Martha Swan of John Brown Lives!, Edward N. Cotter Jr. of the John Brown Graveside, Amy Godine, Russell Banks, and the incomparable musicians and songwriters Greg Artzner and Terry Leonino of Magpie. Regarding the Underground Railroad, I especially would like to thank Paul and Mary Liz Stewart, Tom Calarco, Kate Clifford Larson, Fergus M. Bordewich, Judith Wellman, Debi Craig of the North Star Historical Project, and Christopher Densmore of the Friends Historical Library at Swarthmore College.

I have been honored to get to know some of the living descendants of several characters of this book, including my dear friends Anna Davis and Jerry Davis of Devon, Pennsylvania, as well as Vernon Tancil of Washington, D.C.; Charles Hansbrough of Washington, D.C.; Mrs. Alana C. Giles of Richmond; Thelma Wormley Hardin of Columbia, Maryland; Donald C. Nalle of Gaithersburg, Maryland; David Nalle of Washington, D.C.; Nalle Price of Marietta, Georgia; Morris Nalle of Baltimore; Talitha Z. Nalle of Washington, D.C.; Mark McKie Rigsby of South Carolina; and many others. Some of the high points of my long quest included appearances at several family reunions that were held in Virginia, involving more than three hundred mostly African American descendants of Blucher Hansbrough and their kin.

I also wish to acknowledge my appreciation to Carla Davidson of American Heritage, who assigned me to write an early article about the Nalle rescue that appeared in *American Legacy* magazine in 1997. Friends who served as a lighthouse or sounding board over the years included John Fosnot and Nancy

Brenner, Edna Goldsmith, Alice Green, Richard Jacoby, Bill Kennedy, Nikki Smith, Tom Lewis, Ed Reed, and Kenny Umina. Tom Calarco also assisted me in developing the maps and images and freely shared his knowledge of the Underground Railroad. Others who read some version of the manuscript and provided helpful comments were Tamar Gordon, Kate Larson, Jean Humez, Darlene Clark Hine, Tom Calarco, Paul Stewart, Richard Jacoby, Kelly Whitney, and many fine editors and anonymous reviewers from several august publishing houses. I am happy to have found a home at the University of Illinois Press with Joan Catapano, Rebecca McNulty Schreiber, Jennifer Clark, and their dedicated colleagues. Anne Rogers did a crackerjack job as copy editor.

Special thanks to my family, especially my parents, Keith and Joyce Christianson; my children, Kelly and her husband Scott Whitney, Emily, and Jonah; second parents Myron and Jetta Gordon; my sister Carol and her husband Tony Archambault (the printer); and all the other loved ones who have supported me on this endeavor over the years. Through it all, my beloved wife, Tamar Gordon, has always challenged me to try to understand the world and encouraged me to keep writing about it, even when the chips were down. We have lived this book together.

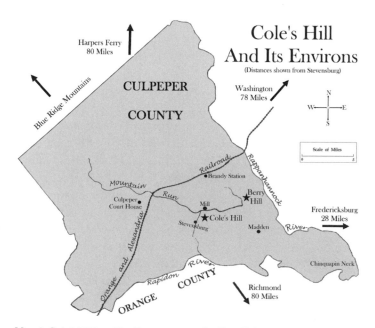

Map 1. Cole's Hill and Its Environs, map by Tom Calarco

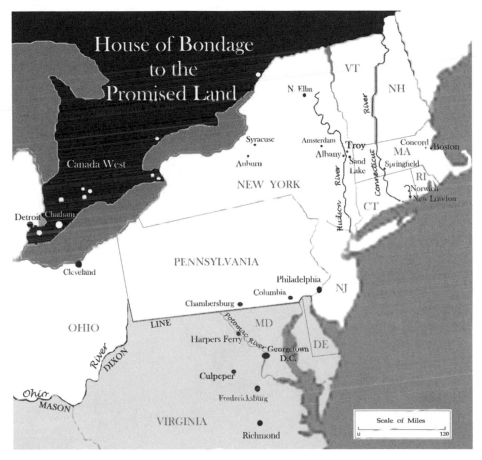

Map 2. From the House of Bondage to the Promised Land, map by Tom Calarco

Map 3. Nalle Rescue Sites, map by Tom Calarco

The following labels appear on the map:

Nalle Rescue Sites

Approx. 1/8 miles
SCALE OF MILES

North to Canada

Uri Gilbert Factory

WEST TROY

U.S. Commissioner's 1st Rescue Site

Union R.R. Station

Second Rescue Site

UGRR Headquarters

Wm. Henry Grocery

To Niskayuna

Uri Gilbert Residence

RIVER

HUDSON

ERIE CANAL

U.S. ARSENAL

Path of Charles' Flight

South to Bondage

TROY

To Sand Lake

INTRODUCTION

On August 9, 1932, several elderly African Americans stood at the corner of State and Second streets in downtown Troy, in upstate New York, eyeing the side of a stately old brick office building where a bronze plaque proclaimed:

> HERE WAS BEGUN APRIL 27, 1860
> THE RESCUE OF CHARLES NALLE
> AN ESCAPED SLAVE
> WHO HAD BEEN ARRESTED
> UNDER THE FUGITIVE SLAVE ACT

Their distinguished host, Garnet Douglass Baltimore, proudly described the epic struggle to liberate the captured runaway slave that had begun at that spot more than seventy-two years earlier, calling it "the greatest event that ever has happened in this city," and telling how hundreds of people, whites and blacks alike, had packed the streets that day.[1] Among their champions then were Harriet Tubman, the immortal Moses herself, as well as his father, Peter Baltimore, and many others from all walks of life in the community—brave people of conscience who were pitted against legions of police and hooligans that held the lawful power of the United States behind them. The ensuing battle had gone on for hours and then was repeated in a second fight across the river, where the "good mob" freed him again. Afterward, some respectable citizens of Troy and West Troy had purchased the slave's liberty for $650, finally making legal what had first to be achieved by stealth and force and finally enabling the man to live at last under the same roof with his wife and children. The actions had set an inspiring example of interracial cooperation, determination, and commitment to equal justice that remained unmatched in local memory and the episode was a significant footnote in the nation's history. Yet for Charles Nalle and his family, it marked the culmination of a long and harrowing journey toward freedom.

Information about a rescue, however, came as quite a surprise to their seventy-seven-year-old guest from out of town. John C. Nalle, the son of the former slave in question, hadn't set foot in Troy since 1865. Earlier that day, for old times' sake, he had dropped by for a brief reunion visit while en route to a little vacation in Saratoga Springs, and suddenly found himself treated as a celebrity. Somebody had even assigned a newspaper reporter to cover the occasion.[2] At the time of the rescue John had been only four years old and living far away, so there really was nothing he could add to Baltimore's account—particularly since, he was perplexed to admit, his father had never told him anything about the matter.[3]

Two months after his visit, John Nalle sent a long letter to the *Troy Times*, thanking them for their coverage of his pilgrimage. "I shall always feel a sense of gratitude towards the citizens of your city for their splendid efforts in bringing about the release of my father from the return to the horrors of slavery," he wrote, "at the same time opening an opportunity to give his children the elements of an education which was denied to the members of his race under the thralldom of slavery. . . . Just why my father never told his family of his experiences in the city of Troy at the time of his arrest I have never been able to understand. Whether it was due to his innate modesty (so that he would not appear as a hero) or his hatred of the damnable institution and those who fostered the institution, I am unable to state. Be that as it may, he had the satisfaction of giving his children the rudiments of an education (a thing that was denied to him). After living in Troy for six years, he moved his family to Washington, D.C., in 1866, where he resided until his death in 1875. Of his family of eight children only two are now living."[4]

The process of writing his letter must have awakened something in John Nalle, for afterward he kept trying to learn more about his father's life, reading everything he could find about the rescue, pulling together lists of names and dates, genealogical charts and legal documents, and bloodlines and webs of associations. When friends inquired about his progress, he said there was so much to tell he wanted to write a book about it.[5] One summer weekend he went off to visit the former home of the great abolitionist, Frederick Douglass, in Highland Beach, Maryland, on the Chesapeake Bay, a spot that had become a favorite gathering place for many of the country's most prominent African American intellectual elite.[6] There, on the night of July 29, 1934, he spent a few hours playing cards, then said he was feeling awfully tired and fell into bed. A few minutes later John Nalle suddenly stiffened, clutched his heart, and died.[7] No account based on his research was ever posthumously published. By and large, the incident passed into obscurity.

This book renews the historical investigation into one of America's greatest yet overlooked slave rescues— the protracted struggle to liberate one otherwise obscure bondsman on the eve of the Civil War. Unlike Douglass, Charles Nalle was not a famous fugitive slave who had recounted his ordeal on the lecture circuit and penned a popular narrative about his life in bondage. Nor had the Supreme Court of the United States immortalized his name in one of its most shameful decisions. Few history books have acknowledged him or his rescue. Yet the Nalle episode and reactions to it reveal a lot about the battle over slavery in the 1850s. As the only person in American history to have been rescued from slavery four times, his story conveys a sense of how terribly difficult and complicated it was to free a slave from bondage before the Great Emancipation.

Who was Charles Nalle and what were the circumstances of his slavery and escape from Virginia? How did the Underground Railroad figure in his flight and subsequent treatment in the North? What prompted persons of both races to break the law and risk so much to assist him? What was Tubman's role in the rescue? What happened as a result of the incident? Why didn't Charles Nalle tell his son about what had occurred? What would such a history consist of and what kind of historical meaning should be taken from the episode? These and many other questions have occupied this author in historical detective work on and off for more than seventeen years and they form the basis of this book.

Charles Nalle's odyssey stretched from the South to the North in a time of great cultural division and political polarization over slavery, culminating in the War Between the States. As pieced together here from many diverse sources, Nalle's dramatic journey crosses several borders: geographic, cultural, political, psychological, and intergenerational. Some of its aspects don't conform to neat historical stereotypes or reigning historiography. All told, it's a story that is intensely personal, yet it also transcends one individual's isolated ordeal. His account underscores fundamental questions about racial inequality, the rule of law, civil disobedience, and violent resistance to slavery in the antebellum North and South. Viewed today, some aspects of the historical record reveal fresh insights about the complexity of Virginia slavery, the abolitionist movement and the Underground Railroad, and the impact of slavery's aftermath.

This is a story that resonates today. As a biracial person before it was possible to be identified as such, Charles Nalle was ahead of his time insofar as he was almost white in blood and appearance but identified as a Negro and was treated accordingly. Born to a "yellow" or light-colored "mulatto" slave mother and a Caucasian father, his origins then could only be ascribed to forbidden "amalgamation," "race mixing," or "miscegenation." Yet many historical details hint at relationships that are much more intimate and reciprocal. Making his status all the more complex, he appears to have been enslaved by his biological father and later by his half-brother. His slave wife Kitty shared similar origins, involving a different master and father, and in some instances others of their forebears had also been the product of white-on-black sexual unions.

Because Charles and Kitty "belonged" to different white men, they were, despite their marriage to each other, required to live apart on neighboring farms and their relationship was subject to white control. Yet they managed to have several children together and did their best to function as a unit, until her and their children's manumission and forced relocation threatened to break up the family forever. It was their fierce determination to keep the family together that led to the dangerous plan for his escape. In mid-October of 1858 Charles Nalle left his master's farm in Stevensburg, Culpeper County, Virginia, on a pass to visit his wife and children in Washington, D.C., and ended up fleeing from Georgetown to Philadelphia on the Underground Railroad, hoping to rejoin them in the North. Assisted along the way by supporters of the abolitionist cause, he made it to upstate New York, but while learning to read and write, a local resident betrayed him as a fugitive slave for a few pieces of silver.

His arrest took place just six months after John Brown's thwarted raid on Harpers Ferry and about a year before the outbreak of the Civil War. The book shows how Brown's actions affected the climate of the day, both in Virginia and in the North, particularly in Troy, a place where Brown had strong ties and the only city after his execution where his casket was publicly displayed. It also notes the spurring effect Brown's martyrdom had, not only on many Northern intellectuals and ordinary blacks, but also specifically on his comrade Harriet Tubman, who had been expected to join in her comrade's attack but didn't. Tubman's coincidental presence in Troy at the time of Nalle's seizure spontaneously gave her a chance to redeem herself to herself by trying to forcibly free a Virginia slave from the clutches of the slave catchers and federal authorities, and she unhesitatingly responded by helping to lead one of her boldest rescue missions—up north, on the shores of the Hudson River.

Nalle's plight put others to the test as well, compelling many Trojans to take a clear, physical stand on slavery. Were they for it or against it? Would they act to support the "rule of law" that upheld slavery, or would they try to heed the "higher law" that required its defiance? Which side were they on? Although many in the streets that day doubtless were mere bystanders or provocateurs, several hundred at least answered the call according to their own core values, just as they and other countrymen would soon be compelled to decide which side to join in the Civil War. Thus the incident embodied the conscience of a community, not just at that moment, but also in the verdict of history.

Viewed today, Charles Nalle's liberation entailed what was arguably the most dramatic and hard-fought slave rescue in American history. At the moment it was taking place, the contentious 1860 Democratic National Convention was raging in Charleston and delegates were debating the party's controversial slavery platform. The slavery issue was much in the national political forefront. Within hours of the mob's action, William Lowndes Yancey, an Alabama fire-eater whose mother lived in Troy, took the convention floor to deliver an impassioned speech that lasted for two hours in which he decried the Northerners' latest assault on Southern institutions and called for the Southern states to secede from the Union—for which he received thunderous applause.[8] When news of what had happened in Troy was telegraphed to Washington, Richmond, and other places throughout the South, it prompted still more angry outcries and contributed to the sectional divisiveness that soon would culminate in the formation of the Confederate States of America and the outbreak of military conflict almost exactly one year after the rescue. This book also traces some of these reactions and examines the tumultuous impact of the resulting war in Nalle's former stomping grounds of Culpeper and Troy as another round of liberation was being played out.

The Nalle incident was briefly a significant news event that subsequently attracted limited attention from political commentators of the day and it has remained little noted by historians. One reason for this oversight may be because it happened in off-the-beaten-track Troy. At the time, neither side's propaganda machinery was as well equipped to handle it there as might have occurred in a large Northern metropolis. The nation already had witnessed previous slave rescues in Boston, Syracuse, and other locations as well as John Brown's raid a few months earlier, so many Americans may have viewed the Nalle affair as merely the latest in a series of violent outbursts over slavery. Harriet Tubman had not yet assumed her mythological stature and her involvement in the rescue would not begin to become known until a few weeks later. Unlike what had transpired in Christiana, Bloody Kansas, and Harpers Ferry, nobody had died in Troy or West Troy. There were other factors as well. Although Nalle's rescue brazenly violated the Fugitive Slave Law, to some observers the fact that his liberty was ultimately purchased may have constituted a face-saving compliance with slavery's hegemony. Afterward, the crime didn't trigger a high-profile public prosecution or political dispute on the order of the confrontation surrounding Anthony Burns, in part because it was short-circuited by the lead-up to Abraham Lincoln's election and the rush toward secession; then the matter ended up being overshadowed by the War Between the States. Yet the fact that Nalle's rescue took place between Harpers Ferry and Fort Sumter, in the percolating span when crucial battle lines were being drawn, underscores its historical significance.

The central image of the Nalle rescue looms like a harbinger of battles to come: the frozen spectacle of a black man who is being torn in conflicting directions by two mighty contestants, as if caught in some epic tug of war. One tangle of hands pulls him one way while the other tries to wrest him in another; some of the mouths are opened wide in shouts, contorted faces are flushed with exertion and wracked with rage, even as most of the eyes are oblivious to the terror and suffering the one in the middle is enduring. Ultimately, freeing Charles would not prove to be an easy task: not for his family and friends, not for the Underground Railroad, not for the mob, and least of all not for himself. The struggle to liberate a single slave on the streets of Troy would put many of the contestants, and American society itself, to a defining test, just as would later happen on the bloody battlefields of the Civil War.

1 GENESIS

Like most other slaves, Charles would never know exactly when he had come into this world—a slave didn't receive any birth certificate or celebrate his birthday—but indications are he was probably born about 1821. Slave mothers in that neck of Virginia weren't permitted to divulge who had fathered their children, and it's unlikely his mother Lucy would have told him.[1] Nevertheless, many slaves grew up to have a pretty good idea, although they had to be careful not to let on what they knew. Sometimes the physical resemblances were too obvious to ignore: in Charles's case, his exceptionally light complexion and long facial features may have offered a clue.[2]

Today the scant surviving records furnish little information about his origins and early life, offering almost as much factual confusion as they do documentation. Deed books suggest the circumstances were extremely complicated. The origins of his mother-to-be, Lucy, remain obscure, but she was apparently born into slavery about 1794 or so. In September 1805 she was described as a "mulatto girl" of unspecified age when Charles C. Allen of Culpeper mortgaged her along with "one sorrel horse one sorrel mare two feather beds and furniture [and] one cow," to William G. Allen of Orange County for $200.[3] The courthouse paper trail offers another possible clue: in February 1819, with William Allen being gravely ill, his wife Elizabeth entered into an indenture for a small parcel of land in Stevensburg that previously had been owned by William Banks; and on March 6, 1819, this transaction was certified by the acting justice of the peace, Peter Hansbrough of nearby Cole's Hill, indicating that Hansbrough was in Lucy's vicinity at about that time, though exactly how they came together remains unsubstantiated.[4] One way a white man of means could keep the knowledge of his intercourse with a slave from becoming obvious was to travel about the countryside utilizing taverns and slave women who belonged to others. It may have been in such a place that Charles was conceived, although again his mother would never discuss such a thing. As one historian has observed, for many whites "[t]he image of Jezebel excused miscegenation, the sexual exploitation of black women, and the mulatto population,"[5] but today, that view has changed.

Two years later when the Allen estate couldn't meet his debts, Allen's beleaguered wife agreed to unload some of their slaves at a sheriff's sale. Among those put on the block were "one Negro woman aged about twenty-seven by name Lucy and her four children: Harriet, Henry, Maria and an infant child" (Charles), as well as Poll and Bob.[6] At the auction, Peter Hansbrough successfully bid $875 for "Lucy a yellow woman about thirty years of age and her four children . . . together with their increase together," and Poll and Bob went to George Slaughter Thom.[7]

The new master Peter Hansbrough (born in 1769) was one of the region's wealthiest and best-known residents, a planter aristocrat whose ancestors had first come over from England in 1639. His vast land holdings spread over several counties. In 1812, he purchased the immense tract near Stevensburg called Cole's Hill, where he became "Peter of Cole's Hill," a grandee who would continue to wear knee britches and a powdered wig in the fashion of the eighteenth century until the day he died. Many people in those parts would never forget the sight of him approaching in his elegant coach with four handsomely attired outriders, and he was widely known as an avid gambler and foxhunter, a connoisseur of wine and whiskey, and a carouser, although white Culpeper society regarded him as a thoroughly respectable gentleman.[8] His wife, Frances Anne Hooe, a daughter of William Hooe of "Pine Hill" in King George County, apparently endured her husband's frequent disappearances with silent resignation as she bore him nine children. They were not the only ones he sired.

Hansbrough's world sported such playful place names as Wicked Bottom, Devil's Jump, and Brandy Station, but it was not without its hazards and scrapes. At that time, for instance, Peter Hansbrough and George Thom were neighbors, vestrymen in the same church, fellow Masons, and partners in innumerable business ventures and card games. Thom had also married Hansbrough's daughter, Ellen. But their relationship had become strained over Hansbrough's chronic debts. Thom claimed Hansbrough had promised to let him have a parcel of twelve of his Negroes, but after Hansbrough failed to deliver all of them—and with nineteenth-century Virginia planter society being very litigious—Thom commenced litigation.[9] Hansbrough ultimately won the case, but the matter continued to engender hard feelings between some of the Thoms and Hansbroughs for several years to come.

It is unclear how Peter Hansbrough's wife acted toward young Charles or his mother Lucy. The presence of a so-called "bastard" slave child who was light in color and may have appeared to bear a physical resemblance to a white woman's husband often prompted feelings of jealousy or resentment on the wife's part, just as it could generate powerful emotions among the master's other white children.[10] After Charles was born, his mother would continue to spend many more years performing many chores about the Hansbrough household, yet there is no record about how she was treated or whether she had a slave mate, though she later issued at least one more child. It's unknown whether Peter Hansbrough treated her as a concubine, or if he exhibited any sense of parental responsibility for their child Charles or any of his other mulatto progeny.

Charles's childhood as well remains uncharted. Growing up there at that time he may have heard other servants talking about what had happened to one of the Hansbrough's former slaves, named Sharper, years earlier, for Sharper's story was the kind of account that old folks passed down over the generations. (It is also preserved in court records.) An African slave from back in the days just before the American Revolution, Sharper had been kidnapped from somewhere in West Africa and sold into bondage, ending up enslaved in those parts by an earlier Peter Hansbrough. One day somebody told Hansbrough that Sharper was trying to obtain poison from an ancient slave conjurer, so Hansbrough went to a justice of the peace to have Sharper arrested. The judge ordered Sharper held in jail until they could examine him at the next quarter sessions. But snowstorms and bitter cold delayed the trial and the case kept getting put off, causing Sharper to suffer terrible frostbite. At last the old conjurer was found to be demented, resulting in the charges being dropped for lack of evidence. But by the time they got around to opening Sharper's cell, his condition was so bad that his gangrened feet literally snapped off. Upon Sharper's death, in 1773 Hansbrough petitioned the court for this "loss of his valuable property." This time the wheels of justice turned faster and the court promptly granted his request, awarding him full value.[11] Sharper's fate and others like it reminded slaves that whether it was back in colonial days or under the laws of the Commonwealth of Virginia and the United States, the legal system went to considerable lengths to preserve and protect slave owners' rights even as it denied any rights to slaves.

One thing that is known is that the second Peter Hansbrough's youngest heir, Blucher Wellington Hansbrough, had been born in 1817, making him about four years older than Charles—the baby of the family. He was named Blucher Wellington after the two generals who defeated Napoleon at Waterloo in 1815 (General Gebhard Leberecht von Blucher from Prussia and the Irish-born Arthur Wellesley, Duke of Wellington, from Britain). Two of Blucher's sisters married cousins from the Hooe clan; his elder brother William was wed to Maria Hansbrough, who was also a first cousin; and his second-oldest sister, Ellen, was the wife of George Slaughter Thom and sister-in-law of Colonel John Thom. Hence, Blucher had many relations among several prominent white families in the Culpeper area, particularly the Hooes, Nalles, and Thoms. Unlike Charles, Blucher was brought up to know every detail of his family tree—the white side, that is. On January 1, 1831, Peter Hansbrough transferred his ownership of Charles to Blucher.[12]

Later that year, in August 1831, Charles may not have been old enough to fully understand the hysteria that was sweeping Virginia, but the legacy of that event would also continue to affect him for many years to come. The Nat Turner revolt had occurred in Southampton County, 160 miles to the southeast, yet the ripples were felt in Culpeper and throughout the South. Turner was a slave preacher on a messianic mission, determined to liberate his fellow slaves. He and six of his followers systematically slaughtered fifty-five white men, women, and children in cold blood before they were stopped. After a long manhunt, Turner and sixteen others were ultimately caught and hanged and their bodies were skinned and burned; twelve more conspirators were sold out of state. The backlash was horrific: in Southampton alone, hundreds of slaves and free blacks were said to have perished to the mob. Even in Culpeper, whites had unleashed the worst wave of terror that Negroes had ever known. To prevent a reoccurrence, Virginia changed its slave codes to forbid blacks to preach, possess a book, or learn to read and write; the patrol system was bolstered; and any newly freed Negroes were forced to leave the state.[13] All of these actions had imposed tremendous restrictions on Charles and every other person of color in Virginia, determining many key aspects of their lives from that time forward. Henceforth, white society would take greater precautions against slave sabotage and rebellion.

In 1838, when Blucher turned twenty-one, he married Martinette Nalle, ninth-born child of twelve born to Martin and Elisabeth Madison Barbour Nalle of Rose Hill, a product of several leading Virginia families.[14] She was eighteen years old when they wed and she too had been named with deference to military discipline. Her father was one of Culpeper's leading citizens and a peer of the Hansbroughs. The Nalles were celebrated for hosting some of Stevensburg's gayest balls and many of those attending these splendid parties included their relatives from the Hansbroughs, Thoms, Barbours, and Hooes. Blucher and Martinette's family relations were thoroughly intertwined, making for an extremely intricate web of kinship and social connections. The couple would have three children together: a daughter, Ella Vivion, born about a year after their marriage; William Watkins Leigh, born about 1841; and Elizabeth, who followed two years later.[15] Very little history about Martinette has survived. Like his father before him, Blucher was said to have sired many mixed-race children outside his marriage.

Upon Peter Hansbrough's death on October 15, 1843, Blucher lost his father and Charles lost his former master and likely father. Each of the half-brothers had a large extended family scattered throughout the area, but only whites were allowed to signify and preserve their lineage. Nobody would ever dare to assert the two were related. Extensive laws and customs upheld the whites' blood status, just as they denied the slaves access to the key that would unlock their entry to the social ladder. Like other gentleman planters of his milieu, Blucher enjoyed many forms of entertainment.[16] For instance, one day when he was in his early twenties, he joined with his brother William in a high-stakes cockfight against several challengers in nearby Fauquier County that was famously described by a local physician with literary talents, Dr. Alban Smith Payne. Although Payne's account doesn't mention Charles, it's likely that the young coachman and personal servant, then approximately seventeen years old, would have accompanied the Hansbroughs and their chicken fighting ensemble on that trip and many others like it. Payne estimated that a crowd of fifteen hundred onlookers witnessed this epic battle of the birds.[17] It was just one match of many. Like his father before him, Blucher sometimes sustained huge losses as a result of his gambling activities. As he grew older, his heavy drinking further hampered his ability to manage his business affairs. He too became notorious for his womanizing.[18]

As he had under Peter Hansbrough, Charles continued to enjoy some advantages over many other slaves in his region. His master didn't raise a hand against them and his world stretched farther than that of most ordinary slaves.[19] As coachman, he often got to accompany his master on many trips through the countryside, including jaunts to the courthouses, local taverns and races, chicken fights, foxhunts, family functions, and other social events, thus enabling him to become better informed and more conversant in the ways of the world outside the farm. Consequently, his circle of friends and acquaintances grew larger and his tastes were more refined than those of most slaves. A Virginia gentleman's coachman was expected to take pride in his own appearance as well as the fine condition of his carriage, and riding up high made them one of the most visible and recognizable figures in that part of the world.[20] Charles was regarded as one of the best coachmen in the region, someone who had a special talent with horses—qualities that were especially prized in that part of Virginia.[21] Tending the stable may have afforded Charles a measure of privacy, since that zone was politely considered off-limits to white ladies and gentlemen.

But just because a slave enjoyed a relatively privileged position didn't mean he was contented being a slave.[22] "It's bad to belong to folks dat own you soul an' body," one former slave would explain.[23] Having them own your body was bad enough; it was quite another to let them own your soul and mind, to relinquish your own moral and mental vision, and give up your own power of reason.[24] In order to retain a spark of their humanity, slaves often felt they had to withhold something for themselves—they needed to mask their true feelings and operate more secretively, just as masters tried to conceal certain vital information from their servants in order to protect their own security and power.

From his unique vantage point, Charles was exposed to more of his master's activities than anyone else. He and Blucher had known each other intimately for practically their whole lives, and they were privy to each other's private as well as public affairs. Blucher didn't always set a good example for his children or anyone else, but he fancied himself a Southern gentleman nevertheless. Despite his drinking, gambling, and philandering, he steadfastly strove to maintain his paternalistic authority over his wife, his children, and his slaves. Charles, meanwhile, appears to have prided himself as being both a good servant and a good husband and father; by all accounts he carried himself with dignity and didn't indulge in Blucher's vices. Their connection was a complicated one that transcended even the usual master-and-slave, white-and-black relationship, since Blucher was likely his secret elder half-brother. Psychologically and emotionally, it is difficult to simply gauge what they must have thought about each other. One is left to speculate about whether there was sibling jealousy, envy, competition, guilt, like disposition, or filial loyalty and affection between them as a result of their blood relationship, and, if so, how those feelings may have played out or been suppressed is certainly also worth considering. However, the social framework that bound them was also exceedingly powerful. In the contact zone of antebellum Virginia slavery, their interactions were marked by asymmetrical intimacy; their unspoken kinship and common humanity was trumped by Blucher's masterful paternalism; and Charles's emotional needs were subordinated to his master's requirements and whims. "A central tragedy of the slave-white relationship," historian Earl F. Thorpe has written, "was that neither side could love or hate in anything like fullness of dimension."[25] In short, their relationship was highly charged, and about to become more so.

2 REVELATION

In October 1847 an event occurred that would transform Charles's life and permanently alter his relationship with Blucher. Because Charles later regarded the incident and its aftermath as so important, and also because the episode reveals so much about the nature of slavery, it warrants being examined in some detail.

The landscape that he and his community of masters and slaves inhabited was situated in rural Stevensburg, in Culpeper County, Virginia. For miles around in every direction, onlookers could see on the horizon a distinct mound, resembling a recumbent body, rising two hundred feet above the gently sloping fields and woods. Its green top was adorned with trees, the tallest of which, an ancient English poplar, towered another hundred feet above the crest's level center. Known as Hansbrough's Ridge, the hill was a prominent local landmark that offered a panoramic view of most of the Virginia piedmont, the distinctive rolling landscape that stretched from the falls of the Potomac, Rappahannock, and James rivers to the Blue Ridge Mountains. The distinctive cupola of the Culpeper Court House stood just eight miles away to the west.[1]

On the south side of the hill there stood a substantial white house, and behind it and to the sides, a large trim barn, the stables, and other outbuildings, as well as "the row"—a few tidy little cottages, one-and-a-half stories high, and some smaller, old and dilapidated log cabins that served as the plantation's slave quarters.[2] Because house servants enjoyed better accommodations than field hands, it was in one of these simple, unpainted cottages that Charles lived with some of his kin—his mother Lucy, sister Maria, and brothers Henry and John—alongside a few other crude cabins for Hansbrough's other chattel.[3]

In those days their tiny hamlet of Stevensburg numbered only twenty houses (not counting slave cabins), holding two merchants, two blacksmiths, a saddler, a wheelwright, a tailor, and a doctor, with a population of ninety-six free persons and about as many slaves.[4]

Just below the rise, Cole's Hill covered 750 handsome acres of prime timber and rolling fields of cultivated wheat and corn, with plenty of clean water available from perpetual springs and trickling streams from Mountain Run. Much of the red clay tilled soil was carefully enriched, at considerable expense, with guano, after years of tobacco growing had exhausted the land. The barnyard and pastures supported a sizeable number of horses, mules, cows, oxen, sheep, pigs, goats, chickens, and dogs, including a brace of fine blood-horses and a shed of prize fighting cocks. The vegetable gardens provided bounties of asparagus, squash, collards, green beans, peas, pumpkin, and sweet potato. Deer grazed at its edges and the woods were alive with partridge, quail, turkey, pheasant, duck, possum, hares, coons, squirrels, turtles, and honeybees. Nature delivered apples, cherries, and peaches; the bushes were thick with blueberries, blackberries, and raspberries. Mockingbirds sang from the dogwood or cedars and crickets chirped from the clover.[5]

Cole's Hill was a medium-sized plantation, of a size that required some of the more privileged "servants" (for that was what they were usually called) to perform a number of domestic chores such as cooking, washing, mending, cleaning, and greeting, or carpentry, blacksmithing, leatherwork, tending the horses, and maintaining the wood. Hansbrough's farm was so small that everyone, except the master and his family, was expected to labor in the fields when needed. Come harvest time, everyone of color had to do his or her part with the wheat. The men would scythe and cradle, the women would rake and bind, and even the little children would help to stack it into cones and load the oxen-drawn wagons.[6] Compared to a field hand, the labor of a personal servant wasn't as strenuous or unremitting, but every slave except the aged or infirm was expected to pull his or her share. Every able-bodied slave had to work hard.

Robert Bailey, a local white man of the lower grade on the social ladder who was about five years older than Charles, served as their overseer. It was not a popular position to hold, for the slaves hated their overseers and others tended to look on them with as much affection as they gave to the public hangman.[7] Overseers guarded the slaves and made them work, dispensing punishment upon those who broke the rules or didn't work hard enough. Charles and his kinfolk considered themselves fortunate for not being whipped.[8] Virginia was full of stories about slaves who were beaten to death and full of laws that compensated masters who had suffered from such a resulting loss of their "property."

By that time, Charles was about twenty-six years old. Several things about his life had changed. For one thing, unlike most other slaves, he had acquired a surname. He was now Charles Nalle, which meant that he carried the identity of one of the region's most distinguished and respectable white families. This privilege appears to have been conferred in honor of the maiden name of his mistress (Master Blucher's wife), Martinette Nalle Hansbrough, not due to any choice on Charles's part, and certainly not as an indication of who his biological father was, for indeed, his master may have selected it to draw attention elsewhere, while at the same time acknowledging another side of the family. To this day, no historian has written a definitive work explaining how slaves received their surnames, and no record regarding Charles's naming has been found. Exactly when Charles received this name also remains unclear, although the chances are that it occurred when he was married. Several years before, he had become linked to a fine local slave woman, Catherine "Kitty" Simms, from Colonel John Triplett Thom's nearby Berry Hill estate. In keeping with family custom among the Thoms and Hansbroughs, their simple wedding (or "broom-jumping") was likely performed with their masters' permission and a white preacher's blessing, although it certainly lacked the imprimatur of the state, for Virginia didn't sanction slave marriages. In fact, the Commonwealth of Virginia and the United States of America didn't recognize that slaves had any legal rights at all that whites were bound to respect.[9] No licensed Southern preacher would ever have allowed himself to say to a slave couple, "What God done jined, cain't no man pull asunder." He just said, "Now you married."[10] But Kitty and Charles had sworn to each other and God nevertheless, and the preacher had written down proof of it in his book. Now Kitty was permitted to use the Nalle name as well.

By the fall of 1847 Charles and Kitty had two young daughters, Fanny and Anne, aged about four and two years old, respectively, although circumstances beyond the couple's control required them to live apart—he at Cole's Hill, and the others with their master, Colonel Thom, about three meandering miles up the road to the northeast. Under slavery, the practice in that part of Virginia often required married couples to be separated, for practical reasons. Because the slaves tended to be spread out in small clusters far out in the countryside, appealing and eligible mates were rarely available in the same household, and besides, most masters viewed a slave husband and wife living together under their care as apt to pose thorny problems. Controlling one mate was difficult enough, especially when he or she didn't like what was being done to the other, or to their children. Some slaves found such prospects so painful that they refused to marry.[11] Others, like Charles, "married abroad, and some preferred it that way."[12]

Slave wives who lived apart generally weren't allowed to visit their husbands as often as they wished, so if the man wanted to see his wife and their children more than once a week he had to get a written pass from his master. If no such pass were available, the man sometimes would sneak out to visit them anyway. He had to be careful not to get caught by his master, the overseer, or the gang of roughneck patrollers who policed the area in darkness, harassing any Negro they could find and assaulting any who lacked a pass. Slaves grew up playing games of "hide and seck" and "all hid" that helped them to refine their powers to avoid detection and get away.[13] If stopped abroad without a pass, the wayward servant risked being found "out of place" and whipped, simply for trying to be with his spouse and children.[14]

Sometime in the early autumn of 1847, some radical changes began to occur at Cole's Hill when Blucher decided to sell off some of his slaves, thereby breaking up one of the families—something he had always said he would not do.[15] Because slaves regarded the selling away of a loved one as the ultimate evil, this drastic action must have created deep resentment among those most affected. It must have threatened the others too, for if Hansbrough could do it to some families, he could do it to them as well.

A few days after the breakup, Hansbrough's barn full of wheat suddenly and mysteriously caught fire. Despite everyone's best efforts to put out the blaze and save the contents, the inferno left a total loss, claiming not only the barn but also most of the crop they had all worked so hard to achieve. The calamity meant an economic catastrophe of the first order; the smoldering ruins smelt like burnt toast and cast a pall over the place for days. Hansbrough suspected one of his slaves had set the fire, probably in retaliation for the forced division of the family. But he couldn't prove it. Nobody would step forward to admit the crime or implicate the culprit. Thus, Charles and the others feared some sort of collective retribution, regardless of whether any slave was responsible.

Hansbrough still had some wheat stored at a mill that was owned by William Ross, a few miles away. One day Blucher summoned Charles into his study and told him to fetch five of the other "boys" and lead them over to Ross's to "fan out the wheat"—carry out the prodigious task of separating the wheat from the chaff using a portable machine and plenty of grueling physical labor. Now fanning wheat was hard work, and processing such a large quantity in a timely way necessarily required several able-bodied men. Whites considered fanning to be "slave work," but many slaves thought masters seemed to consider all labor fit only for slaves.[16] Knowing that Ross was also a slave trader and driver, however, Charles worried there was something else afoot. Yet although he and the others—his older brother, Henry, his younger sibling John, and the three others (one of whom was named Jacob)—sensed they were in imminent danger, they had no choice but to submit. Trudging near the mill, Charles spotted an unusual number of burly white men pretending to fish in the adjoining pond—an obvious Praetorian Guard, and another sign they probably were in trouble. But again, the slaves saw no way out. They had to comply.

Hansbrough came and ordered them to enter the mill, where the wheat was piled in a large heap, and he instructed them to stir it to give it air, for soon the fan mill would arrive and the real work of cleaning the wheat would commence. Charles and the others reluctantly did as they were told, knowing full well that they were putting themselves into a trap from which there would be no escape. Sure enough, as soon as they were in, the doors shut and the fishermen rushed over from the pond, brandishing clubs and guns, and started to beat them down. The slaves were quickly overpowered. The bullies handcuffed them together in pairs. Once they had been ironed, Ross and two assistant drivers started dragging and prodding them up the road. Chained to one of his brothers, Charles found himself part of a mournful coffle that clanked and shuffled along in a miserable train. There was no chance to take any possessions or say good-bye. They feared they were doomed to never see their loved ones again. The two field hands who had already been separated from their families may have felt freer to show their contempt, but Charles and his brothers were stunned, for they knew they had done nothing to deserve such treatment.[17] The sudden drastic changes that were being imposed on his previously relatively secure life underscored the precariousness of his position as a slave. Now he was completely powerless to control his fate and that of his family. There was nothing he could do to change it.

After the coffle had marched for a few hours, Charles spied a lone figure running toward them. To his surprise, he recognized Kitty, gasping and bleeding from having just raced barefooted three miles through jagged stalks and mud. Upon learning from a friend that Charles and the others were en route to being sold at the Richmond market, she had frantically rushed out to intercept them.

Kitty was one of the most trusted servants of Ross's father-in-law, Colonel Thom, and some of Ross's relatives regarded her as if she were part of the family (which she likely was, by blood as well as by ownership). Now she begged Ross not to take her husband away. But he brushed her aside, leaving her alone in the mud, and made the coffle continue on its way. After a march of more than twenty miles, they reached Fredericksburg and were directed to the depot.[18] From there the six prisoners were herded onto a boxcar that carried them swiftly to Richmond.

Richmond hugged the James River that connected it to other parts of the Commonwealth of Virginia and the lower South. The city's low skyline appeared crowned more by smokestacks than church steeples. Some of its grandest structures were made of marble or granite, but many of its squat brick buildings were grimy warehouses or tobacco factories. With a population approaching 28,000 inhabitants, of whom maybe 12,000 were "colored," Virginia's capital was considered a major commercial and manufacturing center, as well as a political and cultural place of some repute. Fashionably dressed ladies and gentlemen strolled the sidewalks and shops. Fancy carriages and lumbering wagons rolled over the streets. Blacks were everywhere.[19] Most business was done near the white pillared capitol that Thomas Jefferson had built. Visitors with means could find comfort nearby at one of the city's fine hotels.

The great slave mart was centered at Fifteenth Street between Main, Franklin, and Broad streets. Tucked away off these streets and alleys, several slave traders and agents (called "Negro traders") kept little private jails, or slave pens, designed for the convenience of owners and traders.[20] Somebody intending to sell slaves there could board them for thirty cents or so a day, knowing they would be kept secure and readied for auction. Conditions in these pens were dismal. Fredrika Bremer of Sweden, who visited one of them in 1851, reported coming across a muscular Negro who had been sent there to have his spirit broken by the fetters he was forced to wear; after being separated from his wife and children, he had cut off his own fingers on his right hand as a means of getting back at his master. In another room, Bremer saw slaves of both sexes who had been tied down and beaten with a cowhide paddle especially selected so as not to leave any cuts.[21] More often than not, the mood among the captives in the pens was one of sullen silence, although occasionally yelps of pain or shouts could be heard. Another tourist of that era described visiting Lumpkin's Jail, one of Richmond's best-known pens, located at Wall Street between Franklin and Broad, at about the time that Charles arrived. Inside the front entrance, he passed into a large open court where Robert Lumpkin himself, "a good natured fat man, with his chair tipped back," sat propped against one of the posts. The proprietor greeted his guest with utmost courtesy and seemed pleased to show off his facility. On one side of the court was a large water tank for washing, and on the other stood a long, two-story brick house that had been especially outfitted to hold male and female slaves and their traders in separate compartments. Next door as many as twenty traders from all over the South gathered around a dining table, exchanging news of the day.[22] Slaves called it the "Devil's Half-Acre."

Once incoming slaves had reached their carceral destination, an overseer brought them down to the courtyard and told them to disrobe. Then they were splashed and scrubbed, dried, and inspected. An agent scrawled a note about each of them in a log. An attendant gave them clean plains to wear, so they would make a good impression, and soon they were rechained and led off to their cells. That kind of treatment always terrified and humiliated the newly arrived prisoners. Charles and his brothers had time to mull over how Hansbrough had betrayed them and time to worry about their mother, their wives, and their children left behind. Besides being torn from everyone and everything they knew and loved, they now had to look forward to being thrust into an alien environment and expected to bow down to a new master, probably to be treated worse than they had been up at Cole's Hill. Through all the turmoil and confusion, a slave in such a situation struggled to be as alert and observant as possible, hoping that some unforeseen miracle would save him from his horrible fate—the fate of lifetime perpetual slavery, heaped upon inconsolable grief.

Traders called Virginia the "nursery of slavery" because slave breeding and marketing were so productive there. Since 1808 the United States had outlawed the international slave trade, making women suitable for childbearing especially prized. One planter boasted that his females were "uncommonly good breeders," going so far as to suppose "there was not a lot of women anywhere that bred faster" than his.[23] Although most "gentlemen of character" tended not to want to discuss the subject in polite company, a Northern journalist who looked into the matter concluded, "[T]he cash value of a slave for sale, above the cost of raising it from infancy to the age at which it commands the highest price, is generally considered among the surest elements of a planter's wealth. . . . That a slave woman is commonly esteemed least for her laboring qualities, most for those qualities which give value to a blood mare is, also, constantly made apparent."[24]

Owners ranked Richmond as the best place in the Commonwealth to market their slaves. Buyers traveled there from as far as New Orleans and Alabama to replenish their supply, making for the highest prices. Sellers appreciated the fact that Richmond's market relied on agents and brokers to handle their transactions, discreetly concealing an owner's identity to prevent any embarrassment, since gentlemen generally wished to avoid publicity about their

resort to selling their Negroes. Such sales were often interpreted as an indication that the owner's financial situation had deteriorated, and gentlemen
considered it a point of honor not to divulge their delicate internal affairs.
Hence, they tried to keep their slave trading as private as possible.[25]

A sale was announced that same morning by a small red flag hung from
the doorway of the auction place. A simple notice tacked on the wall would
proclaim the starting time and furnish a brief description of how many men,
women, boys, or girls were to be offered.[26] Most sales were held in long, dingy
brick warehouses or mills with dirt floors and very low ceilings bolstered by
large wooden beams. Barrels, chairs, benches—some of them badly whittled
or broken—were scattered throughout the area to be moved and rearranged
as the day's activities required. The focal point was a crude wooden platform,
usually three steps high, upon which the business was staged. Even when the
walls had been whitewashed, an auction room's darkness and gloom combined
with the cramped space to create a kind of compressed, claustrophobic effect
that made the scene at once intimate and repellant.[27] It was into this terrify-
ing setting that Charles and the others were thrust. After slaves were escorted
down from their cells, attendants brought them into the auction room where
spectators in the crowd began to inspect them.

Charles had been auctioned once before in his life, but he was too young to
remember what it had been like, much less to know much about all of the con-
voluted wheelings and dealings that were entailed. But now he and his brothers were about to go under the hammer for sale to strangers. Most numerous
among the crowds at the Richmond slave auction were the rawboned kind of
men who looked like horse traders or regular farmers, and who watched everything very intently as they sized up what they might want and could afford.
Then there were the idlers, who couldn't afford anything but were there to
follow whatever they could—uncouth and unkempt fellows in soiled, rumpled
clothes, who occasionally revealed their rotten teeth. Scattered throughout, a
number of gentlemen in formal attire, complete with fine high hats, long tai-
lored coats and waistcoats, expensive shirts, polished boots, and other accoutre-
ments, gazed from their perches with all the reserve that Charles had seen at
thoroughbred sales or estate auctions. Among those attending the auction that
day was none other than Kitty's master, Colonel John Triplett Thom. Given
that Kitty's mother, Fanny Simms, was Colonel Thom's favorite and exerted
special influence over the old man, Charles had reason to hope that perhaps
he had come to purchase him as a favor to his slave women. But the situation
was complicated by the history of relations between the Hansbroughs and the

Thoms; it also would have required the dour Colonel to do business with Ross, his son-in-law, whom he detested for having sunk to the level of becoming a slave trader.[28] At any rate, Thom didn't bid.

Buyers at slave auctions typically asked, "'How old are you?' 'What can you do?' 'Who raised you?' 'Why are you sold' 'Anything wrong with you?'"[29] They ordered slaves to open and close their hands, jump up and down, show their teeth and gums, and explain any lumps or deformities. They squeezed the slaves' arms and thighs to test their musculature and used a wide assortment of traditional methods, such as lifting the skin on a person's hand and watching it fall to tell his age, in order to assess the merchandise.[30] When it came time for the bidding to begin, the first slave was put on the block, and the auctioneer mounted his platform to start his performance.

That day, however, bidders were scarce. Hansbrough's two black field hands were sold, but not at very good prices, leaving the four lighter-skinned servants still up for sale.[31] Finally, the moment came when Charles was put upon the block. Somebody had him pull up his trousers so they could examine his legs. The bidders exchanged knowing looks and biting words about his good points and his bad points. Despite the auctioneer's rapid talk about his skills as a coachman and other assets, and notwithstanding all his jolly jokes and cajoling, the salesman could only get the bidding up to $640—not a very handsome sum. Charles would later recall that after their inspection, the traders said they wouldn't take him because his legs were "so white"; besides, someone added, he was a "saucy-looking nigger" and "had too much fire in his eye." Clearly his light-complexioned appearance made them too uncomfortable—he looked too much like a white man. Once again, his color provided him with an advantage.

When it was over, Charles and the three others were sent back to jail, unsold. The next day, Hansbrough came by and told them they were going to return with him to Stevensburg. He also solemnly promised them he'd never again offer them for sale.[32] Charles and his brothers returned to Cole's Hill, back to where they'd started. But things would never be the same after that ordeal of 1847. Whatever trust Charles may have had for Blucher Hansbrough had been greatly diminished. Almost exactly eleven years later it would prove one of his most indelible grievances against his master.[33]

3 MASTER AND SLAVE RELATIONS

Although Charles's orbit was limited to a small and sparsely populated geographical area that was governed by slavery's rigid constraints, by the 1850s his changing world was full of paradoxes and complexities that complicated many traditional notions of omnipotent and despotic masters and hapless, subservient slaves. His wife and children resided in relative comfort at Berry Hill, which many considered the grandest place in the area and maybe one of the finest homes in Virginia. From the Fredericksburg Plank Road, visitors entered through a large gate that ushered them onto the five-thousand-acre estate, following a wide lane bordered with lilacs that stretched, it seemed, for hundreds of yards. In the distance, at the end of a gorgeous, poplar-lined walk, rose a large hill that was crowned with an immense four-story Georgian stone house, built in the shape of a quadrangle—the residence of Kitty's master and his family. The product of a distinguished Virginia clan, who had further enhanced his status and influence by marrying well, Colonel Thom had been friendly with Thomas Jefferson, chief justice John Marshall, John Randolph, and many other preeminent men.

His mansion steps rose a full ten feet to its wide front porch, and the elegant front hall extended forty feet long and twenty-five feet wide. At the end of this hall there was a tremendous room. Anyone who glanced in would never forget it; it was so shocking and labyrinthine. All of the walls were pigeonholed and stuffed with newspapers, letters, and documents, representing every letter that Colonel Thom had ever received from his children and every newspaper published in the United States that had ever come into the house—a paper cornucopia that was crammed so tightly with aging, fluttering parchment that it almost seemed to be alive with intelligence, knowledge, alarm, and power. The large dining room and sitting parlors were exquisitely furnished. Broad steps with hand-carved banisters and hanging tapestries led up to a spacious hallway lined with large oak presses filled with bed linen and hand-knitted lace for each of the many bedrooms that took up the second floor—enough of them to comfortably accommodate as many as twenty guests at a time, as the family's innumerable reunions and parties often required.

Sometimes Colonel Thom could be felt looking down from his balcony at the cabins in back where all of the house servants and maids and carriage drivers and cooks and washerwomen and other helpers lived. There were a lot of them. Every person in the family had his or her own house servant to tend to their needs, every boy his own slave to take care of his favorite riding horse. Near the house was the big, octagonal two-story structure that housed the dairy with its thirty milch cows in straw-filled pens and its equipment for making all of the butter and cheese and cream that everyone craved. Up the stairs was a small room for valuable china and cut glass, and next to that a sprawling library that was lined with bookshelves and packed with more pigeonholes holding thousands of legal documents: deeds from the reign of Queen Anne, copies of wills and codicils, court records from Colonel Thom's days as justice of the peace, and copies of legislative bills and proclamations emanating from his thirty years' service in the Virginia Senate and other august bodies. It was there that the Colonel stored all of his important records, including, his slaves hoped, the manumission papers that would one day set them free.

Kitty Nalle lived in one of the cottages with her children when she wasn't serving in the house or doing laundry. Part of her large extended family also resided at Berry Hill and its environs, and had done so for many years. Her mother, Fanny Simms, had worked there for decades, first as a "mammy" for one of the children and eventually as Colonel Thom's head house servant upon the death of his second wife.[1] Kitty believed Colonel Thom was her father and by all indications he showed her some preferential treatment. She, her mother, and her sisters formed a tight-knit group that derived additional strength from its numbers, and their network and influence stretched way beyond the confines of their plantation. Their bondwomen's world was more organized and interdependent than the setting in which Charles had to operate.

Down below the hill, out of sight from the house, lay all the rickety quarters of the field hands, and the carpenters, blacksmiths, shoemakers, and weavers. His slaves grew, harvested, and cleaned the wheat they transported by covered wagons to Alexandria; and they caught, cleaned, and salted the herring that supplied everyone at Berry Hill all year.[2] As always existed on larger plantations, there must have been a hierarchy among the slaves at Berry Hill, and in that continuum Fanny and her daughters appear to have held the highest status. Nevertheless, the gulf between rich and poor was very wide.

A couple of miles south of Cole's Hill, at the intersection of several roads that crisscrossed the area, there was a main junction known as Maddenville that served as a popular stopping-off place where weary teamsters pulled their rigs into a three-acre yard and climbed down from their wagon seats to purchase water, hay, oats, and barley for their horses or oxen. Often these rough travelers sauntered over to the tavern porch to order food and drink.[3] Blacksmiths at the forge clanged their hammers to fix a broken wheel or shape a needed horseshoe. Closer to the buildings one might see a slave loading goods into his master's chariot, or come across a uniformed servant rubbing down a fine riding horse. Inside the way station's small but well-stocked general store a visitor could find everything from coffee and molasses to sugar, guano, fancy ribbons, sharpened knives, fine cigars, and assorted hats. Some of the most popular items included rye whiskey and Madeira. A tiny inn and dining table also catered to travelers who were on their way to Fredericksburg or Richmond, or stopping by to pick up some items and exchange intelligence.

The place also attracted a small but loyal local clientele. When he still had his health, Colonel Thom was one of these regulars. Peter Hansbrough and later Blucher Hansbrough often visited Madden's place with Charles to get supplies or play cards and drink. Gentlemen from near and far drank, smoked, and played cards there until late into the night, wagering tall stacks of coins and piles of paper against each other like opposing generals throwing their forces into the contest. At this simple wooden table some gamblers lost shocking sums of money and land, resorting at times to trading a servant or even turning over a whole parcel of slaves to satisfy their debts. Some brought along their own entertainment, or if there was something else they desired, it too might be made to appear at the bewitching hour.[4]

Maddenville was an important information clearinghouse for slaves as well. Many regarded it, like the courthouse and the plantation dining room, as a gold mine of intelligence about what whites were up to. At any one time, Madden's spread teemed with free Negroes, hired-out slaves, traveling slaves who were accompanying their masters, and all sorts of white strangers from distant places, any one of whom might serve as a crucial conduit for important news about forbidden topics. Slaves kept in touch via a surreptitious communication system they called the "grapevine," which they used to secretly transmit information by word of mouth about anything and everything of note that transpired in the surrounding countryside, passing the news from one plantation to the next with surprising accuracy and speed. Despite all of the constant watching by masters and overseers and drivers, betrayals by informers, roughshod riding of the patrollers, and severe punishments, the slaves proved extremely adept at exchanging messages and warnings using this subterranean network.[5]

Very surprisingly, Maddenville belonged to a free Negro, Willis Madden. The whole county had more than six thousand slaves but only about four hundred or so free blacks, none of whom were as prosperous as Madden, so he was a rare bird.[6] Other things about him made him even more unusual. Since the Turner rebellion, Virginia law had decreed that free Negroes couldn't be legally educated, move to another location within the state, own a gun or any military weapon even for hunting, legally attend meetings without whites being present, conduct meetings, testify in court, vote, or receive a trial by jury except in capital cases. The law also prohibited any Negro from operating a tavern. Yet Madden somehow was allowed to do many of those things: he read and wrote, hosted meetings, and ran the most popular tavern for miles around, attracting patrons that included numerous justices of the peace, senators, and other important officials.[7] (Madden's nearest competitor, Wales Tavern, was run by whites.) Madden got around the tavern restriction by providing much of his liquor and victuals for free, but obviously there was something else at work to explain why he wasn't prosecuted and run out of the state. His peculiar power added to the complexity of Charles's social world.

Willis Madden stood 5 feet 6½ inches tall with a lean build and a long angular face, deep-set eyes, and a graying moustache. He often wore a fancy coat and tie. His light-tan color and bushy but relatively straight hair made him look almost white. Born in Stevensburg in 1799, he was officially considered a mulatto, which under Virginia law meant that he was considered to be "of one-fourth part or more of Negro blood," and hence, a Negro, although the precise breakdown of his racial makeup probably actually amounted to something whiter.[8] His mother, Sarah, had worked as an indentured servant for James Madison at nearby Montpelier.[9] In 1791 she appeared in Stevensburg County, where she worked as a seamstress and laundress.[10] With connections to many of the area's finest families, and skills that were much in demand at the time, she got along rather well even though she gave birth to twelve or more children. The paternity of none of these children was ever established, but she managed to retain custody of them and supported the family as well as she could.[11]

In the 1820s Willis Madden had married Kitty Clark, a "bright" mulatto (very light-skinned) who was small in stature, pretty, and extremely energetic.[12] In 1835 he somehow managed to purchase his own land in Stevensburg.

The first piece consisted of an eighty-seven-acre parcel near the crossroads, but over the next several years he expanded this holding into more than one thousand acres. Although the poor soil had been exhausted by too much tobacco farming and its small house was in bad shape, he gradually transformed his simple homestead into a valuable property. His depot and tavern became a local institution and he became so successful that he occasionally hired local slaves to help with his farming, thereby qualifying himself for the label of slave master.[13]

Madden had to be careful not to show too much camaraderie with slaves, but over the years, he would prove one of the most useful persons in Charles's personal network, someone the slave from next door could turn to when he needed money, help with correspondence, or other assistance. Madden offered to hire him out and would even later offer to lend him a sizeable sum of money, thereby playing an important role in Charles's efforts to gain his freedom. Madden's Baptist preacher son, Samuel, occasionally returned to the area to visit his kin and hold illegal prayer meetings at Berry Hill and other local spots; he also exchanged letters and intelligence on behalf of runaways and their loved ones. Willis Madden was a liminal character of enormous complexity and skill, someone who could operate in free-world and slavery spheres alike—and he also was a friend.

The local churches, on the other hand, continued to play a central role in supporting the ideology of slavery. Culpeper County boasted twenty-six houses of worship: nine Baptist, six Methodist, five Episcopal, one Presbyterian, and five free meetinghouses, for twelve thousand white folks' souls.[14] Although most churchgoing people in that part of Virginia, including most churchgoing slaves, were Baptist, Peter and Blucher Hansbrough and most of the Nalle family were Episcopalians, and Kitty's master Colonel Thom was Presbyterian. (At some point, Charles and Kitty also became Presbyterian.)[15] The Quakers had been the only local denomination to oppose slavery, but they had left Stevensburg in 1803 after deciding that further protestations against slavery, drinking, and whoring were futile. All of the other churches either were resolutely silent on the issue of bondage or they staunchly supported it, as they did throughout the South, forming what some abolitionists called the "bulwark of slavery."[16] Culpeper's houses of worship embraced the proslavery mentality and warded off any questioning of their position as the work of "outside agitators." The nearby Crooked Run Baptist Church admonished Brother Daniel Garnett to "refrain entirely from all allusions to the subject of slavery," because it was "deeply exciting" and "calculated to subject its intermeddler to the prejudice of the community and injure or entirely destroy its usefulness as a minister." The Shiloh Baptist Association unanimously resolved that it viewed the "interference of the northern abolitionists in the question of slavery as altogether unwarrantable," and recommended to all their brethren who might receive abolition papers through the mail that they either return such literature or burn it.[17]

Although patriots proclaimed that an individual's freedom to worship as he pleased was a fundamental pillar of American Revolutionary thought and something that was clearly protected by the First Amendment of the Bill of Rights, in fact, religious freedom and rights of religious expression in Virginia were tightly restricted.[18] The impulse to strictly adhere to proslavery values trumped support for Christ's teachings. At least one minister had to leave town in Virginia because he once selected as a text, "Do unto others as ye would that others should do unto you."[19] White churches were also careful about how they incorporated blacks into their religious services. Only a white man could hold a church office. State law forbade blacks to operate their own churches or preach in white churches.[20] Slaves couldn't possess a Bible or read anything, including Scriptures. All churches except the Episcopal had separate entrance doors for men and women, although most houses permitted families to sit together once they were inside. Some masters didn't allow their slaves, particularly the field hands, to attend any church. Other whites tried to impose their particular brand of religion on their slaves and wouldn't let them stay home on Sunday, requiring all of their house servants except the cook to accompany the white family to church.[21] Masters rode in their carriage and their servants had to walk the one, two, or three miles, often not putting on their shoes until they arrived at the church, if they had any shoes.[22] If blacks were let into the church at all, they were confined to the gallery or they congregated outdoors under the shade of a tree, close to an open window, as every once in a while the preacher would lean out the window and shout something to the slaves outside.[23] Some churches permitted them to sing hymns with the whites, provided they stuck to the pastor's rules.[24]

Many members of the clergy were themselves slaveholders. Hansbrough's minister, the Reverend John Woodville, for instance, carried out his church business with the dutiful assistance of his longtime servant "Uncle Jim."[25] Willis Madden and his family worshiped at the small, white-framed Mount Pony Baptist Meeting House that was headed by Cumberland George, who had nineteen slaves.[26] Because licensed ministers could be hard to find in the countryside, most of Stevensburg's congregations relied on itinerant preachers, who wandered the land proselytizing among whites and slaves alike. Much as the slaveholders may have evinced genuine concern for their servants' spiritual well-being, they also endorsed such religious teaching as an effective tool of social control.[27]

Nowhere was this latter motivation more evident than in the person of Stevensburg's own Reverend Thornton Stringfellow of the Stevensburg Baptist Church.[28] From the 1840s until his death after the Civil War, he was regarded as one of the leading religious figures in the entire South, best known for his "scientific discourse" and commentary on the Scriptures.[29] His most heralded work, *Scriptural and Statistical Views in Favor of Slavery* (1856), offered what many considered the most erudite and most fully developed Scriptural argument in support of slavery, in which he claimed it was sanctioned by the Almighty and upheld by the United States Constitution and all prevailing law. Stringfellow called slavery a benevolent institution that was full of mercy, a great educational tool that could prepare the slaves for salvation, and an instrument of divine mercy; he regarded slave ownership as a kind of moral stewardship as righteous slave masters inculcated obedience and Christian duty. For all such assertions he claimed to cite supporting passages from the Bible, and he could recite dozens of these proslavery admonitions, chapter and verse. He was also very rich, owning two grand estates: Summerduck, which was located just south of Stevensburg, and Belair, a thousand-acre tract located along the snaking Rapidan River, near Raccoon Ford, that he had acquired from Peter Hansbrough.[30] With seventy or more slaves, Stringfellow ranked as one of the county's biggest slaveholders, and although he fashioned himself a benevolent master, his Negroes privately complained that he often whipped his servants and insisted on administering the punishments himself.[31]

At the same time, many slaves around Stevensburg and elsewhere had discovered that evangelical Christianity offered them something valuable, provided they could adapt it to suit their own needs and not simply succumb to white interpretations. Early African American Christianity in antebellum Virginia was both a symbolic system of hope and anticipation of the future as well as a protest movement, disguised as theology, that challenged the social and religious dogmas of racial inequality. Many found hope and sustenance in Old and New Testament teachings: the deliverance of the Israelites from slavery in Egypt, the commandments, and Christ's message of equality and love. They took up the theme of sin and sought their own ways to become washed clean of sin in God's eyes.[32] In forging their own theology, they introduced African worship patterns, such as singing, shouting, clapping, dancing, and even spirit possession, into their Christian practice. Although it was risky to do so, they secretly held their own prayer meetings in cabins or woods. Virginia law made it a crime for any slave to participate in such a meeting, and bands of "pattyrollers" (patrollers) prowled the night in particular search of such illegal gatherings.[33] A law provided that any free colored person who preached or conducted a religious meeting by day or night could be whipped, not exceeding thirty-nine lashes, at the discretion of a justice of the peace, and *anybody* could apprehend any such free colored person *without a warrant*. It also demanded the same penalty for any slave or free colored person who attended such preaching; any slave who listened to any *white* preacher at night was to receive the same punishment.[34] Not even these harsh measures, however, could stop the slaves from holding their secret meetings. Often they sent out a notice over the grapevine, letting everybody know about the next planned "hush harbor."

Owing to the large number of slaves in that vicinity, the woods around Berry Hill were a favorite meeting place and hush harbor spot, and slaves from miles around often came to participate. Far from the pacifying force envisioned by Stringfellow, and others, Christianity formed the foundation for alternative forms of organization and spiritual consciousness among the slaves all over the South. Unlike the stiff, restrained hymn singing heard in the white churches, the singing in the woods moved people to tears and joy, shrieks and wild clapping, stomping, shakes, and dancing. Lacking an abandoned barn or suitable cabin to host it, some worshippers pulled together thick branches with leaves or boughs to construct a camouflaged canopy with a back and sides. Women brought along old pots and pans or blankets to muffle the sounds of their shouts and singing. The slaves posted lookouts to guard against the patrollers. Once they had gathered in their cathedral, a designated black preacher would stand up on a stump and sermonize, waving a smuggled Bible as he shook and hollered out.[35] One former slave who used to attend such gatherings later recounted, "Sometimes would stick yo' haid down in de pot if you got to shout awful loud. . . . 'Member old Sister Millie Jeffries. Would stick her haid in de pot an' shout an' pray all night whilst de others was bustin' to take dere turn. Sometimes de slaves would have to pull her haid out dat pot so's de others could shout."[36] Occasionally a free black man would show up and teach people to read as well—something the slaves called "stealin' the meetin.'"[37] Willis Madden's son Samuel was one of these free black preachers who snuck back to Stevensburg from time to time to preach and teach, but he had to be careful not to get caught.[38]

By the mid-nineteenth century, whites' ability to keep their world of slavery insulated and tightly regulated was also becoming much more difficult because many old customs and beliefs in Virginia were coming under greater scrutiny from outsiders. Newspapers, magazines, plays, and books were openly describing some aspects of plantation life for everyone to see, and white Virginians in turn were also becoming more aware of different cultures and alternative views seeping in from the North and Europe.

Advances in transportation systems were an important force driving social change. By the mid-1850s, these "internal improvements" had made it much easier to travel between the Northern and Southern states. New turnpikes, faster clipper ships, relentless steamboats, and especially locomotives were "annihilating space and time" and bringing more and more strangers to gaze upon each other with wonder, horror, and contempt.[39] The Rappahannock and Hazel River canals enabled merchants to ship their wheat and lumber on flatboats that could be poled and dragged downstream at speeds approaching five miles an hour, reaching all the way to Fredericksburg. That part of the piedmont now had some passable roads, a few of them even macadamized, linking Culpeper and Stevensburg with Fredericksburg, Warrenton, and Alexandria. A new highway connected Brandy via Stevensburg to Raccoon Ford, making travel much smoother and faster. Stagecoaches carried passengers from the Culpeper Court House to Baltimore for seventy-five cents to six dollars depending on the speed and luxuriousness of the accommodations. Then came the greatest advancement of all: Construction of the Orange and Alexandria Railroad began in early 1850 and continued for more than two years, laying track through the countryside that would enable travelers to go from Alexandria to Culpeper and return for $3.50. By mid-1855 a speeding train was carrying mail to and from Washington, D.C., and Richmond in less time than it used to take some folks to walk into town.[40] The iron horse was an especially costly beast and railroad ventures were necessarily corporate, requiring a whole group of local citizens to take stock, and several of Culpeper's leading families, including the Hansbroughs, Nalles, Thoms, and W. B. Ross, all were involved as directors or investors in the Orange & Alexandria. Willis Madden's son French worked laying rails. New business establishments sprang up to cater to the influx of rail passengers hailing from faraway places such as New York, Boston, and Bangor. The slaves in the fields would pause at their hoes to listen to the train's distant whistle or wipe their brows to see the black machine as it steamed across the landscape. The overseers and drivers would fidget and bark at them to get back to work.

At least twice a year, usually in the spring and fall, many well-to-do white Southerners would use the new trains, steamships, and roads to make a pilgrimage north to shop for all of the items they craved. The trains and ships shuttled back and forth. Many Southerners of means sent their children to Northern boarding schools, put on Northern spectacles in order to be able to read Northern books, or drugged themselves with Northern physic, and when they died, as one writer observed, "our inanimate bodies, shrouded in northern cambric, are stretched upon the bier, borne to the grave in a northern carriage, entombed with a northern spade, and memorialized with a northern slab!"[41]

In keeping with this foreign commerce, residents of Culpeper and other areas of the upper South found themselves beset by white strangers who had come down from the North for various reasons. Some were businessmen buying cotton for their factories or tobacco for their stores or they were tourists visiting relatives. Others were clergymen who came as missionaries to help run the churches or bright-eyed teachers versed in classical subjects who had been hired to tutor some of the planters' children and to staff some of the new private schools that were sprouting up.

From time to time, a few of these new arrivals were actually "secret abolitionists" who had come down to assist slaves to escape. James Redpath, for example, was a young Scotsman abolitionist-journalist who often traveled the Virginia countryside in the 1850s, secretly observing the slavery system and filing dispatches for several Northern newspapers. His reporting served as an invaluable intelligence source, not only for Northern readers and abolitionists, but also for many slaves, of whom he interviewed more than a thousand.[42] Based on Redpath's personal observations, in late 1854 he predicted that a "GENERAL STAMPEDE OF THE SLAVES" could bring down the institution of slavery in Virginia, "if only the Abolitionists would send down a trustworthy Band of Liberators, provided with compasses, pistols, and a little money for the fugitives."[43]

Another stranger who later claimed to have ventured into Virginia and other parts of the South at that time was a young Canadian physician and naturalist, Dr. Alexander Milton Ross.[44] In the early 1850s Ross had moved to New York to study medicine under the direction of renowned vascular surgeon Dr. Valentine Mott—a Quaker man of conscience who was related by blood and marriage to several committed abolitionists in New York, Boston, Philadelphia, Albany, and England.[45] Ross also spent time in Nicaragua as surgeon for Dr. William Walker, the American mercenary who was trying to take over parts of Latin America using only a small band of fighters.[46] Ross later published a memoir in which he described Gerrit Smith, a wealthy abolitionist philanthropist, and Redpath as having encouraged him to enter the cause. He said he had become an underground agent for the antislavery cause, taken on a code name, and posed as a bird watcher to travel deep into Virginia and other parts of the South to spread the word of liberation so that the slaves could be instructed in how to flee their houses of bondage.[47]

Several years earlier, another intrepid abolitionist and slave rescuer whom

Gerrit Smith had supported—Seth Concklin, from West Troy, New York—had gone on a similar mission to northwest Alabama, hoping to bring out a family of four slaves. Intercepted on his way back and detained at Vincennes, Indiana, he and his companions were later identified by the slave owner, and soon afterward in 1851, Concklin's battered corpse was found floating in the Ohio River, another casualty of the battle over slavery.[48]

In Virginia the antislavery movement had been more robust in the 1820s and '30s, but Southern reaction to Nat Turner's rebellion and more militant abolitionism in the North had effectively squelched any open discussion or organizing, forcing all remaining efforts underground. By the 1850s, Northern abolitionists entering Virginia and other areas of the South had to use a cover to conceal their deeper mission, operating as a religious-oriented emissary of the Northern-based American Missionary Association, an educational group, or some other reformist organization.[49] Infiltrators such as Concklin, Redpath, and Ross were part of a tiny but growing number of true believers who were willing to lay down their lives in the struggle by going right to the front lines. Without them and the networks of courageous black allies, many slaves (especially in the Deep South) would not have become as aware of escape routes, possible collaborators, and conditions that awaited them in the Promised Land. Without fearless slave rescuers such as Harriet Tubman and other members of the Underground Railroad, the slaves' movement of resistance and rebellion would have proved even more difficult to wage. Freedom was not something simply bestowed; it required concerted and determined struggle by blacks and whites to obtain.

4 THE SHAKEUP

In May 1855 the world of Kitty and Charles became unmoored due to the death of Colonel Thom.[1] A master's death prompted apprehension and dread among his slaves because it meant that the departed person's debts to society finally would have to be paid—something that could prove ruinous in a culture kept afloat by unpaid debts. Society required that after this debt had been extracted, the deceased person's remaining property, including any land, houses, furnishings, animals, and slaves, would be distributed among the heirs.[2] Colonel Thom had left eight of them, scattered far and wide, and each was supposed to receive an equal share of the proceeds. When it came to dividing up the slaves, this meant the servants had to be inventoried, appraised, and valued like any other property. Then the slaves would be assigned proportionate to their "value," in order to ensure that each heir received the proper net worth of assets. Complicating this accounting was the fact that slaves were worth different amounts. Prime field hands in their early twenties fetched more than young children, and lame old slaves drew literally nothing at all. Under such arrangements, any distribution was apt to touch off a concatenation of unexpected and unwelcome repercussions. A large family entailed many different and often conflicting personalities. There usually were apt to be some who wouldn't hesitate to trade or sell off certain assets, based solely in their own profit or convenience—heirs, some slaves said, who "wouldn't give you sweat off a black cat's eye now that he's gone." In compliance with this coldhearted arithmetic, some slave families often ended up getting broken up in the process.

On a hot June day, Catesby Thom gathered everybody together at Berry Hill to hear his reading of the slaves' appraisal and valuation. More than one hundred men, women, and children, including some of the late patriarch's relatives, lawyers, friends, overseers and drivers, and the servants, all pressed closer to hear the news. Mothers clutched their babies to their breasts and field hands mopped their brows with rags. Old folks were stooping to hear. Fanny Simms and the other house servants huddled with her kin, Johnson Bryant, Aaron Gibbs, Abby and Kitty, and their children and the rest. These were the servants who had worked the fields, tended the animals, cleaned the house, mended the fences, fitted the clothes, nursed the babies, opened the doors, done the wash, tended the sick, managed the gardens, chopped the wood, cleaned the dishes, fixed the roofs, emptied the chamber pots, made the shoes, comforted the hurt, dug the graves, fed the fire, shoveled the snow, skinned the game, and faithfully performed all the other innumerable daily chores of domestic life of a great estate for many years. The crowd was hushed.

Colonel Thom's debts had taken a heavy toll on his estate. Eighty-eight human beings valued at a grand total of $35,088, divided by eight, equaled $4,386 apiece, or about 10.8 slaves for each heir, but the arithmetic on the human side didn't work out so well because every slave wasn't worth the same amount and no body could ever be divided into fractions (except under the Constitution's "three-fifths" rule to determine representation in Congress). In the end, the eighty-eight men, women, and children were separated into eight lots.[3] The division shattered the community and ripped families apart, scattering some of them as far away as Alabama and Louisiana, and consigning everyone to an unknown fate.

Even the nineteen servants designated for manumission came to question their supposed good fortune. Manumission was like a stone thrown into a pond, sending ripples widening in every direction. Under Virginia law, any master who freed his slave was required to provide funds from his estate to ensure the former slave would be moved out of the commonwealth to another jurisdiction.[4] (Ex-slaves were considered so threatening that legislators had constructed a mechanism forcing them to leave the commonwealth within a year, on pain of becoming reenslaved if they ever returned.[5]) But several of Colonel Thom's manumitted servants were married to slaves who lived elsewhere in Virginia. Kitty was married to Charles, who belonged to Blucher Hansbrough; her sister, Jenny Gibbs, was married to Jim Banks, who was owned by a different master in Stevensburg; their half-sister, Winna Ann Burrell, was married to Lewis Burrell, who was enslaved in Washington; and so on. This meant that if any of these wives and children were forced to leave the state, their enslaved husbands and fathers would be left behind, causing still more family schisms.

For the time being, Kitty and Charles were thrust into in a state of terrible uncertainty, for it wasn't immediately clear how much money the emancipation fund would provide to assist those affected. The prospect of freedom was every slave's dream, but Kitty had to look to the future with trepidation because she and their children would no longer be in a position to have their basic material needs met. Manumission meant they couldn't live at Berry Hill, couldn't even remain in Virginia. When she learned the fund didn't provide enough of a stipend for the wives to purchase their husbands' liberty, the reality of their predicament assumed great urgency. Kitty had to wonder: how would they survive? Who would provide for their children? She was about thirty-two years old. She and Charles then had four girls to care for—Fanny was nine, Anne was seven, Lucy was five, and Agnes was three years old—and a fifth child was due in September.[6] That made six mouths to feed, six human beings to shelter. The biggest godsend was that their children would all become free; their days as slaves were ending and their children would never have to go through things that others before them had endured. Slavery's perpetual grip was being broken. They'd be free! This meant that none of her girls would have to grow up as an object of lust for some selfish white man. They wouldn't have to bear his child. And yet, they would also be out in the cold. Everyone was being uprooted. Would there be no one to help them?

Kitty and Charles had endured many things together. The arrangement of living miles apart for several years of marriage may have hampered their ability to communicate, making some suspicions and jealousies harder to deal with at times, but it had also compelled each of them to be more independent of their mate than they might have been if they had lived together. Each had leaned more heavily on other family and friends in their household than they would otherwise have done. The foundation of Kitty's support system was female, her mother and sisters, while his was predominantly male, consisting of his brothers and friends. Still, married slaves developed not only an instinct for survival, but also a feel for dangers that might impinge on their mates, however distant their partner might be.[7]

Kitty's younger sister, Jenny, was married to Jim Banks, who was Charles's best friend and lived nearby, and they had three children: Betty, Caroline, and Aaron, ranging in age from seven years old to only three months. They too now faced separation due to the breakup of Colonel Thom's estate. Both couples were determined to stay together, however, saying they would not let slavery or freedom stand in their way. Winna, meanwhile, wasn't being freed with the others but instead was being transferred to work for Pembroke Thom. She too was married to a slave and agonized over what to do. Her husband Lewis Burrell had been held one hundred miles from Culpeper, allowed to visit her and their children Joseph and Mary only once or twice a year. His distress over their separation had finally become so great that he sought help to plot his escape. His owner was Edward M. Clark. Lewis's brother, Peter Burrell, was a slave of Benjamin Johnson Hall, and he too decided to escape. They made their break from Alexandria. Both brothers were grieved to leave behind in bondage their mother and father, three sisters, and their brother Reuben, but they felt they had no choice. A few weeks after they had escaped, Winna received word from a trusted friend that they had made it to Canada, but some of the brothers' kin had been sold south as punishment.[8]

By now Kitty was about five months pregnant. For her removal, she was to receive only $83.88 to cover all expenses for herself and her children. Jenny was to receive $55.92. But around this paltry sum, the couples devised a daring strategy. Rather than removing to a free state, where Charles and Jim would never be allowed to visit them, the wives decided instead to relocate to Washington, D.C., about seventy-five miles from Stevensburg. The nation's capital was a slave district, not a "free state" or Canada. Yet it was the only slave jurisdiction that would allow manumitted blacks to stay, provided they had their free papers, and slaves with proper passes were often allowed to visit relatives there. The women had some family contacts in town and maybe their men could get themselves hired out to Washington and they could also get to see each other—or at least, this is what they told the Thoms. In fact, there was more to their strategy than they let on.

On May 21, 1856, with all of their children in tow, Kitty and Jenny bid their tearful adieus to their husbands and boarded the train at Brandy Station to ride in the luggage car. Charles and Jim hoped to get permission to visit them at Christmastime, but the spouses didn't know if they would ever see each other again.[9] At least for now, the two families were cracked, if not broken up.

Although few details about Kitty's new situation worked their way back to Charles, she found herself in unfamiliar and uncomfortable surroundings— just as she was nearing the end of her pregnancy. Washington was a city of great distances and sharp contradictions, a place everyone said was muddy in spring, broiling in summer, and frigid in winter. Tourists saw a vast expanse of grand open avenues lined with white marble edifices and statues, fancy hotels, and monuments, while only a block away the vistas consisted of ramshackle wooden shanties, kerchiefed laundrywomen scurrying among rows of clothes-lines, and garbage-strewn alleys swarming with clusters of skinny children playing skipping games. Pigs and chickens scattered to avoid getting crushed by congressmen's coaches. Every city block seemed crammed with unfinished construction. The glaring 152-foot-high stump of the unfinished Washington Monument, with its Stars and Stripes fluttering above, was a like a metaphor for the incomplete American experiment, a visible reminder that the government still hadn't achieved what it had set out to do in its lofty Declaration of Independence. Negroes and mulattoes numbered about a quarter of the city's population. Less than a third of them were slaves. A few years before Kitty arrived, somebody described them as "a superior class; most of them house-servants, and not a few children of members of Congress, inheriting from their fathers not only a lighter complexion, but a higher degree, also, of intelligence and sensibility." But bondage in the nation's capital carried its own special burdens. As one abolitionist had put it, "The horrible danger of being separated from their families and sold to the South always hung over them like a suspended sword."[10]

For people of color, life in the District was governed by a slave code that sharply restricted everyone who wasn't white, regardless of whether they were slave or free. No free black or mulatto person was allowed to be at large in the city after ten o'clock at night, unless they had a special pass from a justice of the peace. Persons of color were prohibited from driving a wagon or other carriage after that hour. Any violation carried a fine of ten dollars and viola-tors could be locked up until the following morning. Any free Negro found drunk or using profane language was subject to a fine of three dollars. People of color were barred from the schools, public transportation, and most profes-sions and trades. They were also subject to other checking and monitoring, and were constantly watched, stopped, questioned, and barred. The agency responsible for enforcing the slave codes in the nation's capital was the U.S. Circuit Court for the District of Columbia, which maintained extensive re-cords about deeds, manumissions, emancipations, and claims of owners of fugitive slaves. Its records contained references to owners' names, addresses, businesses, and all sorts of identifying information about their slaves, their ages and descriptions, and family relationships.[11]

Under this system, the distinction between slavery and freedom could be paper-thin—as slender as the required "freedom certificate." When challenged, free blacks had to produce written, legal proof of their status; otherwise, they could be treated as fugitive slaves. Every free black or mulatto person, males from the age of sixteen and females from the age of fourteen, who resided in the District had to provide satisfactory evidence of their title of freedom, together with a list of the names, ages, and sex of all other persons of color under those ages who were his or her children, or otherwise, inhabiting his or her house. District law didn't recognize Kitty's marriage to Charles, so she was considered the head of the family.[12] It is unclear whether she and her relatives obtained such documentation, for the surviving records don't list their names. Their legal status might have been in jeopardy. The legal and bureaucratic apparatus meant that fugitive slaves couldn't simply flee to the District and attempt to blend in as they did in Northern cities, and anyone who was caught trying to help them in Washington was subject to fines and imprisonment, or worse if they were slaves. The District's jail was particularly notorious for its horrid treatment of black women and their children. Kitty didn't have the luxury of being able to rest her pregnant body during the hot summer months of 1856. To survive she too had to work as a laundrywoman, hoping that Charles would somehow acquire enough money to join them. Her new life was stressful.

When Kitty and the others arrived in Washington, D.C., the city was buzzing about what had just happened on the floor of the U.S. Senate. Senator Charles Sumner of Massachusetts, an outspoken abolitionist, had recently delivered a speech criticizing those who wanted to expand slavery into the Kansas Territory. In it he referred to one of his leading adversaries, Senator A. P. Butler of South Carolina, slipping in a rhetorical flourish that appeared to accuse Butler of being in love with the "harlot, Slavery." Two days later, Sumner was sitting at his Senate Chamber desk, writing, when two South Carolina congressmen, Preston Brooks and Lawrence Keitt, approached. Brooks angrily told the sitting Sumner he regarded the speech a libel on both South Carolina and his uncle, Judge A. P. Butler. With that he flashed his cane, striking Senator Sumner more than twenty blows over his head and body that severely injured the older man. Proslavery Southerners cheered the attack as a noble defense of their honor as well as the institution of slavery. But the viciousness of the assault prompted one horrified Republican newspaper editor to lament: "The logic of the Plantation, brute violence and might, has at last risen where it was inevitable it should rise to—the Senate of the United States."[13]

The assault on Sumner triggered an even more violent response, as violence has a way of doing. At the time, proslavery expansionists and antislavery abolitionists were vying to determine whether the huge Kansas Territory stretching from Kansas City to the Rockies would become slave or free, figuring that the way its voters decided to go would set the trend for the rest of the territories. As one Southerner put it, "If the South triumphs, abolitionism will

be defeated and shorn of its power for all time. If she is defeated, abolitionism will grow more insolent and aggressive, until the utter ruin of the South
is consummated.[14] In the face of such stakes, proslavery "border ruffians"
from Missouri and other slave states had flooded into the area, intimidat-
ing anyone who got in their way. They rigged elections, passed oppressive
laws, and assaulted or murdered settlers who opposed slavery or expressed
any sympathy for the abolitionists.[15] Some of the antislavery settlers struck
back with their own use of force. One of their self-appointed leaders—John
Brown—was a tall, sinewy, but elderly-looking man, with steel-blue eyes and
unshakable Calvinist beliefs. Born in Connecticut in 1800, Brown had ties to
radical abolitionists in Canada, Ohio, Pennsylvania, Massachusetts, and New
York, and he considered himself a fighter for the oppressed.[16] Upon learning
of the outrage against Sumner, he fumed: "Something *is going to be done now.*
We must show by actual work that there are two sides to this thing, and that
they cannot go on with impunity."[17]

On May 24, 1856, Brown and four of his sons, along with his son-in-law
and another man, conducted a late-night raid around Pottawatomie Creek,
about two miles southwest of the present town of Lane, in Kansas. They targeted several houses, roused five proslavery activists out of their beds, and
hacked them to death with swords. Brown's terrorism caused the territory to
be known as "Bloody Kansas," marking the first time that Southerners came to
fear Northerners instead of merely despising them for their liberal views.[18]

Not long after the "Pottawatomie massacre," Redpath the reporter rushed
to the territory in hopes of covering the struggle. While crossing some woods
one day he stumbled upon a camp where a dozen saddled horses were tied.
A tall, gaunt old man with a long beard, poorly clad, with his toes protruding from his boots, stood by a campfire, cooking breakfast. Once Redpath
discovered it was John Brown, and Brown learned the identity of his visitor,
they commenced a serious interview—the first that Brown had ever given.
The journalist left the encounter convinced that he had "seen the predestined
leader of the second and the holier American Revolution," and he appointed
himself as Brown's chief image maker.[19]

News of the attack on Sumner and Brown's bloody response heated up the
atmosphere in Virginia and Washington. In this climate Charles learned that
Kitty had found a place to live and was working as a laundress, and in September 1856 he received the news about the successful birth of their first son,
John Nalle. But despite his eagerness to see them, the weeks turned to months
without his getting the pass that would enable him to travel to Washington
City. Jenny's husband, Jim Banks, had also counted on getting a pass from his

master as well, but the rising political tensions over slavery made such travel more problematic.

Throughout the autumn of 1856, rumors flew among the slaveholders about a planned slave revolt that supposedly was being plotted for the Christmas holidays. The Democratic candidate for president, James Buchanan of Pennsylvania, exploited Southern fears about slaves running away to the territories, and easily won the November election.[20] But the paranoia persisted. Worried Virginians formed their own "vigilance committees" and took other measures to protect themselves. Given that more than half of Culpeper's population consisted of slaves and free Negroes, many whites there felt especially vulnerable.[21] They warned that their country was being "traversed throughout its whole by Abolitionist emissaries in the guise of peddlers and venders of patent rights, quack nostrums, etc."[22] Culpeper bolstered its slave patrols and set up roadblocks to turn away any "suspicious-looking" strangers. Negroes caught traveling about, even with valid passes, were dealt with very severely. Some whites around Stevensburg threatened to run all the free Negroes out of Virginia once and for all; others recommended making them slaves again, as the area experienced its worst crackdown in twenty-five years.[23]

This couldn't have come at a worse time for Charles, since it blocked his hoped-for Christmas travel pass. Slaves in Virginia looked forward to the Christmas holidays as the one occasion all year when they were suspended from having to work and allowed to celebrate something by themselves. But now, for reasons having more to do with politics than reality, the mounting hysteria dashed any plans for a family reunion. In the end, New Year's Day passed without incident. There wasn't any slave revolt and all the threats proved baseless. For Charles and other slaves, the arrival of 1857 brought added resentment. What had promised to be a time of happy reunion had turned out to be one of bitter separation, suspicion, and harassment.

Then, in March of 1857, the Supreme Court of the United States ruled that slavery was permitted in all of the territories, and it decreed that all Negroes—free as well as slaves—were not and couldn't ever become citizens of the United States. The decision in *Dred Scott v. Sandford* held that blacks were "unfit to associate with the white race, either in social or political relations, and so far inferior that they had no rights which the white man was bound to respect; and that the Negro might justly and lawfully be reduced to slavery for his benefit."[24] America was undergoing a conservative revolution, fueled by firebrands who went beyond being mere apologists for the South and defenders of slavery and who now stood up to champion slavery as a positive good that they wanted expanded.[25] The "fire-eaters" fashioned arguments to tear apart fundamental notions of liberalism: they called equality a fraud and freedom a hoax, and their agenda was to maintain the status quo, contain democracy, champion states' rights, reject compromise, and strictly interpret the Constitution. They vowed to smash anyone who opposed them.

For Charles, bondage was intolerable. He desperately wanted to earn money in order to purchase his freedom and also felt the need to lend support to his wife and children. The only way to be able to do that was to be hired out. The decline of plantation agriculture in Virginia and the slaves' high birth rate had produced a surplus of slave labor, prompting more masters to cut back on their number of servants. The glut on the market also reduced slave prices, so rather than sell their slaves at deflated value, more beleaguered masters took to renting out some of their servants. By "hiring out," a master would contract with someone who needed labor performed, and the contractor would assume all the expenses to maintain the slave and also pay a fee. Some contracts lasted a whole year, but most were limited to slack times for the master's farm, freeing them up to cut timber, build barns, or do other chores.[26] The wages involved were often near what would be paid for a free worker.[27] Some masters allowed their slaves to keep all or part of the money, which made hiring out very popular among the servants, provided the employer wasn't too bad.[28] Potential employers abounded around Culpeper.[29]

Willis Madden offered to hire Charles, but Hansbrough refused to allow it, thereby denying him both the ability to earn his own freedom and to provide for his family. This denied his very manhood. After failing to gain the needed permission, Charles appealed to friends for assistance in purchasing his freedom. He managed to raise $700 from various contacts, and Madden offered to put up the security for the whole amount, which would have allowed him to earn a portion of the money when he became free. But again Hansbrough resisted. Instead of agreeing on a reasonable price, he demanded $2,200—an extremely exorbitant sum considering that Charles had only been able to fetch $640 at the Richmond market a decade earlier, when the economy was better. Despite considerable efforts, his project to buy his freedom fell through.[30]

Although Charles and his Kitty managed to briefly see each other again in February 1858 (at which time they conceived another child), afterward Hansbrough suggested it was time for Charles to find himself a new woman, because his old one was too much trouble. This greatly upset Charles, but a slave in his position had to be careful not to show his true feelings for fear of angering his master. Privately, however, holding the family together and fulfilling his responsibilities as a husband and a father assumed paramount importance.

To make matters worse, the dire state of Hansbrough's finances was coming to a head. Years of drinking, gambling, and mismanagement had tipped his debts beyond the balancing point, and some of his creditors had run out of patience. These money problems had worsened due to the national economic depression that started in August 1857. In response to the failure of an Ohio insurance and trust company, as a result of major embezzlement, New York bankers tightened their transaction procedures, setting off fears of an impending financial collapse. As Great Britain withdrew its capital from U.S. banks and grain prices plummeted, the panic quickly spread to the New York Stock Exchange. With some of the railroads defaulting on their debts and Russian cotton suppliers undercutting American export prices, an event happened that caused even more financial woes: A ship transporting millions of dollars in gold from the new San Francisco mint to create a reserve for Eastern banks sank at sea in mid-September 1857. The ensuing panic triggered a severe economic depression in some parts of the country and cost many workers their jobs.[31] Hansbrough suffered further losses just when he was already dangerously strapped for cash. Charles heard rumors that some of Blucher's creditors were about to take him to court to collect their money. He also was warned that Blucher might have to sell the farm to meet his debts.[32] An informant reported he had seen a newspaper advertisement describing Hansbrough's property.[33]

Charles concluded he had to flee as soon as possible. Although he was about a decade older than the typical Virginia runaway, in other ways he generally fit the profile of a likely fugitive: he had recently been separated from part of his family and feared he was about to be sold so that he might never see his loved ones again; he was also an intelligent, self-possessed, and determined male of light complexion who had some special skills as a coachman as well as more than usual knowledge of the world beyond the outskirts of his plantation.[34]

Yet a slave's decision to abscond carried a heavy price. Running away would make him a fugitive, a criminal, for the rest of his life. If caught, he would be whipped and probably sold. Regardless of whether he got away, some of his relatives left behind would likely be penalized on his account. Running away would also constitute a breach of trust with his master, a betrayal of sorts that might even bother his conscience. Everyone knew that life on the run could prove to be miserable, even fatal.

But Charles's master had left him no choice. To remain married to Kitty and see his children grow up, he would have to take matters into his own hands and escape. Flight offered the only possible remedy. In order to pull it off, he would need assistance, he needed a plan, and he had to move fast.

5 MAKING THE BREAK

Once Charles had decided to flee, he needed to connect with someone in a position to help him get safely away to freedom. Even in the Upper South, that was no small task.

By that time in the late 1850s, the term "Underground Railroad" or "Underground Railway" had been used for several years in northern newspapers, plays, and books such as *Uncle Tom's Cabin* (1852), to describe a cadre of intrepid individuals who participated in a conspiratorial network that tried to help fugitive slaves escape from bondage.[1] Popular images in Harriet Stowe's novel and elsewhere fostered the impression of the Underground Railroad as a predominantly Quaker club of committed antislavery activists who operated primarily along the Mason and Dixon line, in a few tiny border towns of Delaware, Pennsylvania, and Ohio. Its members were depicted as disciplined secret operatives who were organized like a railroad and communicated via coded messages, conducting themselves like highly trained spies in an espionage ring. In some respects, this was accurate. But the movement to aid slaves to escape encompassed a much wider variety of people who stretched all the way from the Deep South to northern states and Canada, involving not only Quakers but also persons from other faiths and backgrounds, including many blacks. Some participants functioned as lookouts, drivers, boatmen, outfitters, carpenters, scouts, missionaries, recruiters, financiers, politicians, housing specialists, spies and counterspies, publicists, lawyers, stationmasters, couriers, guards, combatants, doctors, teachers, ministers, or propagandists. Others merely aided someone on a spontaneous basis, acting out of compassion or happenstance.

After Britain banned slavery in Canada effective on August 1, 1834, and Canadian courts generally refused to extradite fugitive slaves back to the United States, black emigration to Canada increased. Some abolitionists and members of the Underground Railroad sought to facilitate such movement to the "Promised Land," founding missions in St. Catharines in Canada West and elsewhere that would provide needed refuge to the fugitives.[2] Starting in the late 1830s, the American Anti-Slavery Society began establishing vigilance committees in New York and other cities to protect runaway slaves from slave catchers. The committees also provided temporary shelter, food, clothing, and other assistance to transient fugitive slaves, helping many of them to continue traveling beyond the border of the United States. Some Northern vigilance committees published notices of their activities in local newspapers and their leaders handed out engraved business cards proudly announcing themselves as "agents" or "conductors" of the Underground Railroad. They also recruited supporters at county fairs and other public events, and hosted former slaves and other abolitionists to give stirring speeches at fund-raisers.

After the passage of the Fugitive Slave Act in 1850, enforcement was so lax that there were fewer than about twenty legal cases per year brought in federal court, and the number of persons imprisoned or fined was accordingly very low.[3] The level of illegal kidnappings was also much lower than it had been in the 1830s. Generally speaking, law enforcement was not the dominant factor controlling runaways.

It was one thing for a vocal minority to support the Underground Railroad in the Northern states, all of which had abolished slavery. The matter was more hotly contested in the border states and territories. But in the South, where slavery still held sway, antislavery activity was simply not tolerated. White Virginians considered it extremely dangerous, subversive, and criminal to attempt to assist a slave to rebel or escape, and anyone suspected of being involved in such actions risked being killed, beaten by vigilantes, imprisoned, or sold. It was considered too perilous to even discuss such matters. Spies and informers lurked everywhere. The nature of the antislavery movement in the antebellum South remains one of the most undocumented aspects of American antislavery, and how slaves received assistance to escape from the land of bondage remains one of the most overlooked, mysterious, and intriguing aspects of slave resistance. Yet it seems that by the late 1850s, such resistance in the Upper South had again become more pervasive. Because of their isolation, many slaves had known precious little about the Underground Railroad. Based on his personal experiences and observations in the late 1830s and '40s, Frederick Douglass observed, "Its stations were better known to the slaveholders than the slaves."[4] But in the late 1850s, Redpath wrote that the "thriving condition of the Underground Railroad establishes conclusively the existence of secret communications among the slave population of the South," and he marveled how, despite all of the slave patrols, strict surveillance on the plantation, and careful watching abroad, slaves throughout the South managed to "pass freely over large tracts of country." He estimated that "hundreds of the relatives and friends of men, who have already secured their freedom, have been informed of the means of which they can obtain the liberty so eagerly desired." Redpath concluded that the grapevine not only helped many slaves escape via the Underground Railroad; he also thought it would help spread the word of insurrection. "By its operations," he wrote, "when the appropriate hour for sounding the alarm shall have come, speedily, surely and swiftly, will the news spread southward, and reach, in the silent hours of the night, thousands of eager souls now awaiting, in trembling anxiety, for the terrible day of deliverance."[5]

Sometime during the period when Kitty's manumission was unfolding, Charles had come into contact with a stranger from the North. The appearance would prove extremely propitious, for their meeting materialized just as he desperately needed more assistance to make his escape. Minot S. Crosby, twenty-six, a devout young New England missionary, had arrived in Culpeper in 1855, purportedly on an assignment to teach school. The son of a Congregational minister in Conway, Massachusetts, he was involved in gospel ministry efforts of the American Education Association, had attended Phillips Academy in Andover, and graduated from Amherst College in 1850. Shortly before striking out for Virginia he had married Margaret Anna Loraine Maltby of Bangor, Maine, whose father was also a Congregational minister. The idealistic young couple was devoted to spreading the gospel and higher learning. A few months after landing in Culpeper, Margaret Crosby gave birth to their first child, Elizabeth, on November 26, 1855.[6]

Minot Crosby worked at the new Female Institute located at the Waverly Hotel near the downtown train station. The institute's founder, Reverend J. Walker George, was the son of Reverend Cumberland George, Willis Madden's longtime pastor, who had replaced Reverend Stringfellow at the Stevensburg Baptist Church. Walker George was a pious temperance zealot, and these driving principles were strongly reflected in his classical education program for young ladies. While in the area, young Crosby supplemented his modest earnings by tutoring several local children, including Erskine Ross, the dashing eleven-year-old son of William and Betty Ross, at Bel Pre, next to Cole's Hill. (William Ross was the agent who had escorted Charles to the Richmond slave market and his wife was Colonel's Thom's daughter.) The Ross home was also located close to Berry Hill.[7] Crosby enjoyed warm relations with members of the Ross household, the Thoms, and many other families in the area, and he often came into contact with their servants as well. He also attended various social gatherings in Stevensburg that frequently required him to travel back and forth over the roads. Winna Burrell's owner, Dr. Pembroke Thom, lived part of the time at Glen Ella, located just across the road from Cole's Hill, and as one of the few physicians in the area, he may have attended to Margaret Crosby's pregnancy-related medical needs.[8]

Exactly how Charles came to know Crosby is unclear, but connect they did. Crosby also may have met Kitty, Jenny, and Lewis Burrell before they all left the region. Certainly the earnest young tutor must have encountered Winna, who was often about the Ross and Thom households at that time.

The young teacher had to be careful not to reveal his abolitionist sympathies to any untrustworthy person in Virginia, for he was closely connected to a number of prominent Northern abolitionists, including Harriet Beecher Stowe's sister, Catherine Esther Beecher, and Theodore Parker—persons who, had the relationships been known to his Southern hosts, would have aroused intense alarm.[9]

As Crosby moved about the area, he was in a good position to exchange information with slaves, and Charles needed as much support from such an ally as he could get. Somehow they gained each other's confidence and became confidantes. Crosby may or may not have been a secret agent such as Redpath or Milton Ross, but he clearly held antislavery views and had ties to some of the leading church-oriented abolitionists in the North. The evidence plainly indicates that they did collaborate, and to such an extent that both would have found themselves in deep trouble if they were detected.

Charles knew he had no other option but to try to escape as soon as possible. The hope of living in freedom with his wife and children furnished a powerful incentive. In plotting to escape, he enjoyed several advantages over other slaves. For one thing, his location put him closer to the free states and Canada than he would have been if he lived in the Deep South. For another, his very light complexion could keep him from standing out as much as darker-colored blacks and maybe even allow him to pass for white in some situations. Furthermore, his coachman background made him a more experienced traveler than other slaves and gave him a skill that could prove useful elsewhere. His wife, being a free Negro, was in a better position to assist him than she would have been as a slave—and so were some of his other relatives and friends such as Jenny Gibbs and Willis Madden. And he had established a relationship with a well-connected white Northerner who had ties to the Underground Railroad.

All these advantages were needed, because whites in Culpeper had instituted tighter security since the recent slave insurrection scare. They had bolstered their repertoire of patrols, security checks, informers, rewards, bloodhounds, slave catchers, and other measures. If Charles managed to escape, Hansbrough would undoubtedly pursue him. He would have to keep running, hiding, and watching over his shoulder.

Charles knew that was no guarantee he would evade capture. In order for a fugitive slave to become free, he usually had to escape from the United States altogether. Remaining in any so-called free state would always leave him vulnerable to rendition and reenslavement. Not even Canada was totally safe. Some slave catchers had ventured there to illegally seize their runaways, and legions of slaveholders' lawyers and judges kept doing all within their power to enact new extradition statutes or treaties that would enable them to reach beyond the U.S. border. Most runaway slaves could expect to remain fugitives until they were caught or died, unless their owner's claims were somehow satisfied.

Charles's Egypt was vast and uncharted. His knowledge of geography was limited and his ignorance of distances and directions, landmarks, and routes amounted to a serious handicap. He was unfamiliar with the other states, rivers, mountains, or ocean he might encounter along the way. As one slave had put it, "Every slaveholder seeks to impress his slave with a belief in the boundlessness of slave territory, and of his almost illimitable power. We all had vague and indistinct notions of the geography of the country."[10] On top of this, Charles knew very little about using railroads and oceangoing vessels. He was a country boy, a rube, who had spent his whole life in rural Virginia.

Perhaps his greatest handicap was his inability to read and write. In Virginia, anyone who tried to teach a slave to read and write was subject to prosecution, such as happened at Norfolk in 1854, when a woman named Margaret Douglass was jailed and fined for teaching a certain black girl named Kate to read the Bible.[11] In Charles's case, illiteracy not only kept him from being able to decipher maps, signs, or passes; it also hampered his ability to plot his escape route and arrange a rendezvous with his wife, who was also illiterate. This required both of them to rely on intermediaries for their communications. This made for an unwieldy and hazardous means of exchanging information. Whites had their newspapers, which slaves often regarded as dangerous as snakes, because the whites controlled most of them and packed the pages with lost-slave reward notices and other intelligence that was often turned on them like rattlesnakes. Whites had their United States Post Office, with all of its exclusivity and perils. But a slave had none of these tools. He had to be extremely careful when it came to sending letters through the mail, for letters could be intercepted, opened, and used to track down a runaway or his accomplices. Yet runaway slaves and those trying to help them also realized they often had no alternative but to utilize letters. Charles recognized that he would have to take special precautions to cover his tracks and try to protect others as best he could.

A slave's loved ones constituted the thorniest aspect of all. Were it not for the strong affection that bound slaves to their families, relatives, and friends, and their fear of what might happen to them in response, many more would have decided to flee.[12] "I distinctly remember the two great difficulties that stood in the way of my flight," one former slave explained. "I had a father and mother whom I dearly loved, I had also six sisters and four brothers on the plantation. The question was, shall I hide my purpose from them? Moreover, how will my flight affect them when I am gone? Will they not be suspected? Will not the whole family be sold off as a disaffected family, as is generally the case when one of its members flies?"[13]

Once Charles had made up his mind to escape, he tried to convince his mother and siblings to also go. But all of them refused. Cole's Hill was their home. His brothers didn't want to desert their loved ones, so they elected to stay.[14] This may have given him second thoughts about leaving. James W. C. Pennington, a former slave who had undergone some of the same emotions as Charles, later wrote, "Hope, fear, dread, terror, love, sorrow, and deep melancholy were mingled in my mind together; my mental state was one of the most painful distraction." Pennington said when he looked at his numerous family, his parents and siblings and all of his friends, pitted against his life as a slave and the possibility of being sold away at any moment, it seemed to him that even the loss of his life couldn't tempt him to give up his thought of flight. And then when he considered the difficulties that likely stood along the way, and the "gloomy thought, of not only losing all one's friends in one day, but of having to seek and to make new friends in a strange world," the prospect seemed even more grim. Nevertheless, as Pennington had ultimately concluded, "the hour was come, and the man must act, or forever be a slave."[15] Charles, it appears, followed a similar calculus.

Exactly how to escape was another matter. Out of impulse or necessity, some slaves simply ran off without a plan. Pennington, for example, suddenly had decided on his own one Saturday night in mid-November to flee the next day.[16] Another slave, a bright mulatto woman with straight black hair and a large goiter on her neck, just walked away in broad daylight by following the main road out of Washington.[17] One of the most dramatic spontaneous escapes of the period involved a slave who was on the auction block when he feigned an attack of epilepsy. Taken to the jail physician, he fooled the doctor as well, and was held back from sale until further consultation could determine what to do with him. After being left alone in a cell, the enterprising fugitive desperately broke out during the night and eventually made it all the way to Canada.[18]

Most unplanned escapes were doomed to fail, however, and slaves had to be careful not to press their luck. Some of the most famous escapes had entailed ingenious schemes, such as the one used by a couple of married Georgia slaves, Ellen and William Craft, who had fled from the Deep South to Philadelphia a decade earlier by donning disguises. William's dark skin color required him to pose as a slave, but his wife's very light complexion enabled her to masquerade as his master, although she had to pretend to be a man.[19] In another celebrated well-known case, a desperate Virginia slave, Henry Brown, had himself sealed within a wooden crate that was three feet one inch long, two feet six inches high, and two feet wide, smaller than a coffin. With only three tiny holes bored in the sides to allow air to enter, and a bladder of water, the box containing Henry was delivered to the Express Office, earmarked for J. Miller McKim at the Philadelphia Anti-Slavery Office on North Fifth Street. After an ordeal of twenty-seven hours, he somehow survived to tell the tale; when the box was finally opened he popped out and introduced himself to the astonished members of the Vigilance Committee by singing and saying, "How do you do, gentlemen?"[20]

With help from his friends and relatives, Charles settled on a plan of his own and set about to follow it through. It hinged on him and Jim Banks first getting valid passes from their masters to go to Washington City to visit their wives. This in itself posed a challenge, since Hansbrough had generally denied Charles's travel requests. Charles realized his prospects were now even dimmer due to Blucher's stated wish to have him end his marriage with Kitty. He had to be careful not to arouse his master's suspicion and Hansbrough in turn didn't want to set him off either.

The crucial events started in early October 1858, when Hansbrough received word through relatives in Washington that Charles's wife had taken seriously ill and there was some worry she might not recover. She was, after all, in the advanced stages of pregnancy. Because of the apparent gravity of the situation, Hansbrough agreed to issue a one-week pass that would permit him to be at her bedside; meanwhile, Hansbrough said he intended to be away in Richmond doing some business.[21] He would allow Charles to make the trip in the company of his friend Jim Banks, the Stevensburg slave whom Hansbrough knew very well and generally considered trustworthy. Equipped with the proper papers, the two servants would ride in the train's baggage car and be subject to supervision in Washington by one of Hansbrough's designees. Blucher's cousin Lucy Eleanor Hansbrough Herndon and her husband Dr. Brodie S. Herndon had a place in the District and another relative, Martinette's sister Jane, resided with her husband Edward M. Clark (master of Lewis Burrell) in nearby Alexandria.[22]

Jim was twenty-nine years old, slightly darker than Charles, and very muscular from years of blacksmithing and leatherworking. Although owned by Martinette's elder brother Philip Pendleton Nalle, Jim had recently been hired out for his shoemaking leatherworking skills to John J. Rickard, a humble saddler in his late 50s who lived between Cole's Hill and Maddenville.[23] In deciding to take part in the escape, for the sake of reuniting with his wife and two children, Jim had been forced to say good-bye to his mother, four brothers, and three sisters, and this weighed heavily on his mind.[24] Charles and Jim made their final preparations with rising anticipation, careful not to display any unusual behavior that might give away their intent.

From one of his contacts around the courthouse, Charles learned that one of Hansbrough's old unpaid notes for twelve hundred dollars was coming to a legal climax, and a creditor had gotten wind of a rumor that a "secret abolitionist," not yet identified (presumably Crosby), was planning to help some of Hansbrough's slaves to escape. Charles's informant also warned him that somebody was going to alert Hansbrough about this scenario as soon as they could find him.[25] For Charles and Jim, this meant that part of their escape plan had already been discovered.

In the South, the mere mention of "abolitionists" inspired terror in many quarters.[26] Charles realized that he and Minot Crosby were in imminent danger. A short time later, Crosby and his family abruptly left town, even though Margaret Crosby was still weak from giving birth and their baby was in a delicate state.[27] Charles and Jim had no time to waste. If caught, their penalties would be extremely severe. After saying good-bye to his mother and siblings, in such a way as to not arouse their overseer's suspicion, Charles met up with Jim and they boarded the train to Washington, the place abolitionists called the "citadel of slavery."[28]

6 THE ESCAPE

Upon reaching Washington with their bona fide travel passes, Charles and Jim were supposed to meet with their wives, under the watchful eyes of the local authorities and some of their masters' relatives. But they somehow gave their custodians the slip and vanished. To protect their wives, they would have had to conceal any proof that the women had acted as accomplices, for if there was any evidence that either of them had abetted their escape, she would find herself in serious trouble. As it was, Kitty at least was already highly vulnerable.

Operating from the nation's highest-visibility political stage, the Washington network of the Underground Railroad occupied a key position for the nation's abolitionist movement, in part because the District housed the federal government apparatus and served as a temporary home to the president, members of Congress, and the courts, as well as other top officials and their slaves. As one early abolitionist observed, the existence of slavery in the capital provided "a sort of symbol and proof of its control over the government of the country."[1] Washington was also one of the uppermost and most physically accessible cities in the South, which could facilitate efforts to rescue slaves from its control.

Since its formation twenty years earlier, the Washington network had experienced its share of spectacular successes and setbacks.[2] Some of its most courageous and resourceful leaders had included Reverend Charles T. Torrey, a Congregational minister,[3] Baptist preacher Reverend Abel Brown,[4] portrait painter Edwin W. Goodwin,[5] former Maryland slave Thomas Smallwood,[6] and Reverend William L. Chaplin, who together had rescued thousands of escaped slaves from the Washington area and transported them to Albany and Troy, New York, for the Eastern New York Anti-Slavery Society, while posing as journalists.[7] Brown, Torrey, and Goodwin all had died early deaths (Torrey in prison), and Chaplin had been caught and jailed before he skipped bail.[8] Some members of the ring had also been involved in the network's most ambitious but unsuccessful mass rescue attempt, the daring effort to smuggle seventy-six fugitives from Georgetown to Philadelphia on the schooner *Pearl* in April 1848—an incident that contributed to the passage of the 1850 Fugitive Slave Act.[9]

In recent years the network had been run by Jacob Bigelow (alias "William Penn"), a lawyer, gas company executive, and supporter of many missionary causes.[10] A devout Congregationalist from Massachusetts, Bigelow relied on a few trusted agents for help in carrying out his removals. One diminutive associate who specialized in water transport was code named "Powder Boy" because he often hauled barrels of gunpowder in his boat.[11] Another mysterious operative, known only as "Dr. H"—who some later said had been Dr. Ellwood Harvey, a Quaker professor who ran the Philadelphia Female Medical College—utilized horse-drawn vehicles.[12] Still another agent, the free Negro Anthony Bowen, often met fugitives on incoming vessels from the south at his Sixth Street SE wharf and sometimes accompanied them to his home at 85 East W Street before leading them toward their next connection.[13]

To commence some of his overland trips, "William Penn" preferred to steer his passengers to the front gate of the White House on Pennsylvania Avenue as a starting point. The slave would be directed to jump onto the driver's seat of a waiting carriage and then make like the coachman. "The faithful horse trotted off willingly," one collaborator later recalled, and Dr. H. "sat in his carriage as composed as though as he had succeeded in procuring an honorable and lucrative office from the White House and was returning home to tell his wife the good news."[14] After leaving the city, the doctor would take the reins himself. He knew where to stop to feed his horse and at what tavern or farmhouse they might pass a night or two in Maryland before heading on to Philadelphia.[15]

In August 1858, shortly before Charles and Jim arrived on the scene, somebody complained that William Penn had pocketed part of the money intended for a slave purchase, and financier Lewis Tappan admonished the sixty-eight-year-old Bigelow for sloppy bookkeeping involving some of his fugitive passengers.[16] It is unclear whether it was Bigelow or someone else who guided Charles and Jim into hiding.

In those days, the bulk of Washington's black residents were dispersed over a few areas, mostly in the southern part of the city. Cut off from the downtown and other fashionable neighborhoods, the "island" of southwest Washington was populated by members of the working poor, including many free blacks. For the preceding twenty years or so, Anthony Bowen's mission and day school (located at the present site of L'Enfant Plaza) also served as a local Underground Railroad station. Bowen often met incoming boats from the South at a nearby wharf at Sixth Street SE, and often later took his passengers to his nearby house for food and shelter.[17]

Charles and Jim's escape plan apparently called for them to be brought to the Georgetown dock, like the *Pearl* fugitives. Georgetown had a sizable black populace, but it was a racially mixed area, with a population of about 8,500 souls, of which about one-quarter were black; of those, the majority were free black and more than 550 were slaves, making for a troublesome brew as far as many whites were concerned. Linked to Washington City by a series of bridges crossing the Rock Creek, the prosperous town with its spires and mansions was spread over several small hills and included some of the best inns, shops, and schools in the capital area. A few hundred feet or less from the river's edge ran the narrow Chesapeake and Ohio Canal, bordered by towpaths and brick warehouses.[18] Residences and industrial buildings were interspersed in some of the neighborhoods. In others, the neat line of tree-shaded brick townhouses, sidewalks, and gas lamps gave way to rows of rickety shacks huddled along dirt gutters, and crooked houses tilted among tiny stores and vacant lots. Georgetown's rulers tried to maintain tight surveillance and strict policing over their black population in order to avoid a repeat of the *Pearl* incident or worse. But the crossroads remained one of the District's most active escape points. Free blacks furnished the network's eyes and ears, especially around the waterfront and other strategic locations, where they kept lookout at all hours of the day and night.

One of Georgetown's key Underground Railroad stations was situated at the Mount Zion United Methodist Church (later the Dunbarton Avenue United Methodist Church), Washington's oldest black congregation. Slave catchers closely monitored the church for suspicious activities, however, and shortly before Charles and Jim's arrival, the police had discovered a runaway who had been hiding in the church's attic for five months.[19] Fugitive slaves were also concealed in the church's burial vault set among the woods at nearby Mount Zion Cemetery. Although it was designed to store corpses that were awaiting interment, the eight-by-eight-foot brick crypt was sometimes utilized to secrete runaways who were in the process of being moved north to Philadelphia. The vault had tiny peepholes to let in enough air and light and sometimes contained food and other supplies for its huddled fugitives.[20] It also offered the advantage of being located close to the dark, dense sanctuary of Rock Creek, so that runaways could slip between the vault and the creek without being easily detected as they made their way to the nearby canal and the Potomac. Fugitives didn't relish being entombed in a cemetery, but superstition and propriety kept any slave catchers from invading such a space.

Shortly before Charles and Jim's arrival, in August 1858, William Penn and his associates had aided the escape of Rebecca Jackson, a house servant from Georgetown, and her daughter and husband. Secret Underground Railroad records described Rebecca as a "yellow-colored" woman, about thirty-seven years old, who was highly intelligent and well mannered. Her mistress in Georgetown was Mrs. Margaret Dick, a wealthy old lady who also belonged to the Presbyterian Church (as did Kitty Nalle) and was a firm believer in slavery. Rebecca's husband was free, but she was prevented from living with him, which caused him considerable irritation. Out of Rebecca's strong desire to save her daughter, she "ascertained the doings of the Underground Rail Road" and was told a thing or two about her prospects in Canada. She therefore had resolved to make a bold adventure and with help from the network had succeeded in getting away.[21] William Penn generally worried about women escapees, claiming that "none of these can walk so far or so fast as scores of *men* that are constantly leaving."[22] The agent in Philadelphia who usually was the one to receive many of the fugitives from Washington also regarded women and children as much more likely to be caught, particularly if they traveled alone, and he estimated that females carried three times the risk of failure as males.[23] But Rebecca Jackson as well as scores of other women and children had made it safely away. Charles and Jim were expected to enjoy even better odds.

There were several ways for fugitives to go. Railroads that far south were too risky and the roads required much more time and exposure, whereas maritime escapes remained the most reliable and fastest way for fugitives to travel out of Washington, despite what had happened with the *Pearl*. Steamships and sailing vessels offered more opportunities in part because their owners tended to be more sympathetic to the antislavery cause, as their crews often included blacks, and also because the ships contained many places in which a fugitive could stow away, with or without the crew's knowledge.[24] But water escapes carried risks. A few months earlier, in June 1858, Thomas Eppes, a white slaveholder in Petersburg, Virginia, had been holding his regular prayer readings for his servants when he discovered that two of his slaves, Gilbert and Sarah, were missing. Quick investigation determined that a steamer from Delaware, the *Keziah*, had just left port that day. Eppes acted with all the speed at his command by telegraphing ahead to Norfolk's harbormaster to alert him that the vessel in question might be part of a slave-stealing operation. The harbormaster responded accordingly. He got the inspector to search the ship's cargo and found in the hold, not only the two fugitives described, but three others as well. William D. Bayliss, the ship's master, at first claimed ignorance but later turned himself in to the authorities. Four days later, the head of Philadelphia's Underground Railroad office warned John Henry Hill in Ontario, Canada: "I have just got the news that our friend Capt. B has been taken Prisoner in Virginia with slaves on board of his vessel. Poor fellow if they have got him, I am sorry, sorry to my heart." As it turned out, the slaves were indeed sent back for punishment and Bayliss was convicted of kidnapping and sentenced to forty years in prison. But he refused to betray his accomplices, remaining loyal to the cause. The Philadelphia agent later regretted Bayliss's fate as a necessary price to pay for that line of work. "A disaster on the road, resulting in the capture of one or two captains, tended to damp the ardor of some of those who wanted to come, as well as that of sympathizers," he wrote. "The road was not idle, however."[25]

Agents in Washington, Philadelphia, and other cities did all they could to prevent such disasters. They were always exploring new ways to smuggle their passengers. In April 1856 William Penn wrote to his Underground Railroad contact in Philadelphia about a recent law in Virginia requiring all vessels in its waters to be searched for fugitives. He said a sagacious friend had suggested that rather than having the "Powder Boy" enter the Potomac River to service the Washington vicinity, he might find a better port along Chesapeake Bay instead. "Suppose he opens a trade with some place southwest of Annapolis, 25 or 30 miles from here, or less," Penn wrote. "He might carry wood, oysters, &c., and all his customers from this vicinity might travel in that direction without any of the suspicions that might attend their journeyings towards this city. In this way, doubtless, a good business might be carried on without interruption or competition, and provided the plan was conducted without affecting the inhabitants along that shore, no suspicion would arise as to the manner or magnitude of his business operations. How does this strike you? What does the 'powder boy' think of it?"[26]

Penn and his contacts constantly communicated about which methods and routes to use. Three weeks after his earlier letter, after receiving a reply from the Philadelphia Vigilance Committee about his latest idea, Penn wrote back to his Philadelphia contact to recommend he "take in coal for Washington and come directly here—sell his coal and go to Georgetown for freight, and wait for it. If any *fancy articles* are sent on board, I understand he has a place to put them in, and if he has I suggest that he lies still, still waiting for freight till the first anxiety is over. Vessels that have just left are the ones that will be inquired after, and perhaps chased. If he lays still a day or two all suspicion will be prevented."[27]

When Charles and Jim showed up at a rendezvous spot near the Georgetown waterfront, another fugitive, whom they didn't know, joined their escape party. Perry Clexton was about twenty-five years old and average-sized, darker and rougher than Charles and Jim, and full of grit—a different class of Negro than they were. He had just run away from his master, a large man by the name of John M. Williams, who was in the wood business and kept a wharf in Georgetown. Perry said he hadn't been "badly treated," meaning he hadn't been whipped, but he'd been worked hard and allowed few privileges. The paltry sum of twenty-five cents a week was all that was allowed him out of his hire, although Perry knew that some people considered this a relatively liberal outlay for a slave. (Charles, after all, hadn't been allowed to hire out at all.) Regardless, Perry thought that Williams, even though he was so fat, ought to be able to do his own work himself instead of relying on a slave to do it for him. While working at the wharf, Perry probably had come in contact with Underground Railroad operatives who often used ships hauling wood and other cargo on the river. He obviously knew more about boats and the river than either Charles or Jim.

Perry said the notion of leaving home and going to Canada had been uppermost in his heart for a long time, and he probably would have acted on it sooner but for the fact that his wife, Amelia, and their child rested with great weight on his mind. Finally, though, the pressure became so great he felt he had to leave despite all of the heartache and hazards, and he forsook his wife and child, master and chains. He wasn't happy about it, but he'd made his choice. Escape so often required picking between two evils.[28] Charles and Jim as well must have been feeling some of their own regrets and guilt, since they too had been compelled to leave some loved ones behind. And so, the motley trio of Charles, Jim, and Perry prepared to leave on their journey north, alert for the dangers and full of conflicted feelings.

The only vessel listed in the newspaper as scheduled to leave Georgetown for Philadelphia at about that time was the regular packet schooner *Ann Pickerel*, which was docked at the Georgetown wharf on Tuesday, October 12, and due to embark on Friday morning, the 15th.[29] Built at Baltimore in 1852, she had one deck and weighed eighty-seven tons. Her homeport was Georgetown and her usual captain was Drake.[30] But at the moment somebody named Leverton was serving as her master. The *Ann Pickerel* may or may not have been the vehicle for their transport, but the fact that Leverton was a Quaker name associated with the Underground Railroad makes it seem more likely. A branch of the Levertons were closely connected with the black abolitionist and slave rescuer Harriet Tubman; they had helped her to escape from slavery a decade earlier, and more recently some of them may have assisted her in rescuing her parents and carrying out other underground missions.[31] Assuming that it was a ship that transported them from Georgetown, whatever vessel it was, the three fugitives would have been hurried aboard, stowed below, and probably wedged into a special compartment in the hold. None of them, with the possible exception of Perry, knew enough about ships to act like a crewman; Charles and Jim had probably never been on a ship before. Most likely, none of them could swim either, although that would have been among the least of their worries.

The weather in Washington that week was cloudy and rainy with temperatures that generally ranged from the high fifties to about sixty-five degrees. By Friday morning, October 15, conditions had generally improved all up the eastern seaboard and would remain so for several days. On the one hand, it appears they would have enjoyed clear sailing; on the other, the water and wind currents may not have been running at top speed, which might have slowed their flight, had they left at that time. To their good fortune, on the morning of October 18, the Potomac River around Washington became enveloped in a thick fog that rendered the safe passage of the steamboats and other river craft extremely hazardous.[32] Such a turn in the weather could have proved fortuitous, for it might have delayed any pursuers, just as a different change in the weather had doomed the *Pearl* a decade earlier. For once in their lives, the three slaves caught some luck.

The long journey to Philadelphia always posed its hardships and worries. The discomfort they felt from being tossed on the waves while confined in the hold was bad enough, but they also had to fear getting caught. Many fugitives experienced twinges of guilt for having escaped. The three of them and the crew were all committing a crime. In Charles's case, it wasn't that he had simply absented himself for a few days to hide out in the woods, or that he was out of place. He had crossed a big line, one that separated a mere wayward servant or runaway from a fugitive. As far as the dominant society was concerned, he had "stolen himself" and that made him a criminal, always; there would never be any changing that fact. Above all, Charles and the others faced an unknown future. What would happen to them?

Somewhere, probably in the water off Delaware, he crossed another crucial invisible line—the one that took him in one moment from being in a slave state to the next when he somehow magically entered a "free state." Many fugitives found this step to be the most momentous thing they had ever experienced. Referring to her own escape, Tubman later said: "When I found I had crossed that line, I looked at my hands to see if I was the same person. There was such a glory over everything; the sun came like gold through the trees and over the fields, and I felt like I was in Heaven. I had crossed the line."[1] Abolitionists often made a point of celebrating the milestone with a whoop or a prayer. In one glorious instance, when a fugitive had crossed the final border into the Promised Land at Niagara Falls, two of his handlers posed with him on Canadian soil, their backs to the precipice, as a photographer recorded the moment for posterity.[2] But Charles's crossing of the Mason-Dixon line apparently went unrecorded.

At last they landed in Philadelphia, the birthplace of the Declaration of Independence and the Constitution. Frederick Douglass had said the City of Brotherly Love wasn't such a good place to be black, and William Wells Brown, another fugitive slave who went on to become an acclaimed orator and author, observed that "colorphobia" was more rampant there than in the "pro-slavery, negro-hating city of New York, as Philly kept its Negroes strictly segregated and treated them as second-class citizens, subjecting them to severe discrimination and racial prejudice at every turn." From time to time, some of the city's predominantly Irish immigrant mobs were known to attack blacks on the street for sport; one time they burned the Pennsylvania Anti-Slavery Society office to the ground.[3]

In terms of the Underground Railroad, Philadelphia occupied a special rank because of its strategic location up the Delaware Bay between Washington and New York, and its accessibility by sea, road, and rail. For fugitive slaves it was considered the first port of entry in the "free world," the place where the network took stock of its fleeing passengers and decided where and how to send them. For the preceding twenty years, the city's Underground Railroad activities had been supervised by a well-organized and disciplined Vigilance Committee made up of blacks and whites. Robert Purvis, a wealthy and highly literate freeborn mulatto from Charleston, South Carolina, had chaired the office for several years, with strong support from a large cast of veterans.

When Charles and his two companions were hurried into the Anti-Slavery Office on North Fifth Street, probably under cover of darkness, one of the most experienced and savvy agents, William Still, was in charge.[4] A dark and handsome mulatto, thirty-seven years old, Still was well-dressed, impeccably groomed, and carried himself with great assurance. Born free in New Jersey as the youngest of eighteen children, two of whom remained enslaved in Maryland, he had left his family home in the Pine Barrens at age twenty with little formal education to seek his fortune in Philadelphia, and he had worked his way up from nothing, landing a position in 1847 as a janitor and mail clerk of the Pennsylvania Society for Promoting the Abolition of Slavery. He rose to become secretary of the Vigilance Committee, the organization that provided financial aid; boarded fugitives with free Negroes; purchased clothing, medicine, and railroad tickets; and made other arrangements for runaways to continue their flight northward. He was also a successful coal merchant and always wore a bow tie and suit. Although he had never been enslaved himself, he hated slavery, sometimes disdaining any Negro who didn't openly express contempt for slave-keepers and everything about the institution.[5]

Still was one of the busiest Underground Railroad agents in the country, handling close to five hundred fugitives from December 1852 to February 1857, and since then his traffic had sharply increased.[6] Those he had helped included Ellen and William Craft, Henry Box Brown, and a man named Peter who turned out to be his own long-lost brother. He had also processed Charles's acquaintances, Lewis and Peter Burrell, who had arrived at the Philadelphia office on April 21, 1856, only two days before Harriet Tubman showed up with one of her rescue parties. Most recently, some of the refugees had included a plucky little fellow from Baltimore named Henry Tucker, and a redhead from Stafford County, Virginia, Peter Nelson, who looked white until he took off his hat and showed his wooly hair; Mary Jones had been hired as a domestic in Washington for the past nine years at three dollars a month; and little Susan Bell, who was just four years old and had never walked—her mother had fled to Canada two years before. There was also William Carpenter, who had fled from cruel Senator Mason of Virginia, the father of the Fugitive Slave Act; Lew Jones and Oscar Payne; Mose Wood; Dave Diggs; Jack; Hen; Bill Dade and Joe Ball from Virginny; and Robert Johns and his wife Sue Ann from Cecil County, Maryland.

Admired for his ability to coordinate complex escapes, Still worked with all the leading Underground Railroad operatives and backers along the Eastern seaboard, including Thomas Garrett in Delaware, "William Penn" in Washington, Stephen Myers in Albany, the mysterious agent known as "Ham and Eggs," the Levertons, and many others. He particularly admired and revered Tubman, referring to her as "Moses" and marveling after one of her visits: "Harriet was a woman of no pretensions, indeed, a more ordinary specimen of humanity could hardly be found among the most unfortunate-looking farmhands of the South. Yet, in point of courage, shrewdness and disinterested exertions to rescue her fellow-men, by making personal visits to Maryland among the slaves, she was without her equal."[7]

Still himself had always managed to personally stay ahead of the slave catchers and the law, barely avoiding arrest during a number of close scrapes and follow-up investigations. A few months earlier, in March 1858, John Brown had been one of his houseguests.[8]

Much of his work entailed correspondence and mail routing involving his hundreds of contacts and fugitives. Some former passengers later sent him thank-you letters letting him know they had reached Canada or asking him to relay messages to various relatives, hoping he could help them rejoin their loved ones. William Jones, for example, who (like Box Brown) had been shipped to Still's office in a crate and survived to tell the tale, sent him a crudely scrawled message from Albany.[9] Still performed many vital functions for the Underground Railroad, helping to spot infiltrators, spies, informers, weak links, and other potential problems. He maintained an elaborate information storehouse about the inner workings of the slavocracy that enabled him to orchestrate rescues and escapes, devise a constantly changing menu of escape routes and disguises, keep in touch with other agents and supporters, participate in legal strategy sessions and criminal conspiracies, and generally do everything he could to destroy the institution of slavery by helping the slaves escape. He also served as a clearinghouse and institutional memory that aided fugitives to find lost relatives.

Together with another member of the Vigilance Committee (often J. Miller McKim, the addressee for the crate containing Henry Box Brown), Still closely questioned everyone who came into his office claiming to be a fugitive. McKim, a tall and serious white man, about forty-eight years old, was an ordained Presbyterian minister who had worked in the antislavery movement and the Underground Railroad for more than twenty years and was known for being blunt and probing in his questioning. Both men considered the interrogations necessary for the good of the Underground Railroad. They remained wary of strangers in order to detect any spies or infiltrators. They also could be extremely methodical in the way they went about extracting useful intelligence about their passengers and the slavery system in general. Typically they tried to find out as much as possible. Who was the slave's master and what was his character? What was his occupation and standing in the community? To what church did he belong? What were the names of others in his family and what were they like? How did he treat his slaves? How many slaves did he hold? What were their names and occupations? Did any of them also want to escape? Did the master allow any of his slaves to be hired out and if so to whom? How old was the fugitive? Was he or she married? Were there any children and if so how many and what were their ages? Could the fugitive read and write? Did he or she have a trade or skill? Often these interview sessions lasted for hours and generated extensive notes.[10]

Still scrupulously maintained extensive records of the interviews, along with correspondence, bills, and other information, which he frequently consulted in order to manage complex situations. Because the documents were so incriminating, for himself and everyone else involved, he guarded them extremely closely to prevent them from falling into the wrong hands. Sometimes he passed on choice documents to selected abolitionists for use in the ongoing propaganda war, to create sympathy for the slaves and engender contempt for the slaveholders, but most important, he kept the records for intelligence purposes.

Soon the time came for Charles and the others to undergo their rite of passage. Still wrote about the arrival "from Georgetown, D.C." of "Perry Clexton, Jim Banks and Charles Nole." Careful not to divulge the precise manner of their escape, he simply noted: "This party found no very serious obstacles in their travels, as their plans were well arranged, and as they had at least natural ability sufficient for ordinary emergencies"—a code, perhaps to indicate that their flight had been carefully plotted and carried out reasonably well by trusted conductors, probably without an armed escort.[11]

There is no way to know all that was said during Still's interviews because the notations were so brief, and neither Charles nor his companions left their own account of the encounter. Yet in his succinct report, Still made several extremely revealing and sometimes puzzling observations about the runaway coachman from Culpeper, which merit noting here. Still and Charles were about the same age, but they had led very different lives. The gulf between them was wide. Based on his interrogation, Still later wrote that "Charles bore strong testimony in favor of his master, Blooker W. Hansborough, a farmer," and he quoted Charles as having called Hansbrough "a first-rate man to his servants."

"I was used very well, can't complain," Charles told him.

(This was by no means the first time the agents had heard a fugitive respond in this way, but they made it a practice not to share or approve of such sentiments.)

"Why did you not remain then?" a member of the committee asked.

"I left," answered C., "because I was not allowed to live with my wife. She with our six children, lived a long distance from my master's place, and he would not hire me out where I could live near my wife, so I made up my mind that I would try and do better. I could see no enjoyment that way."

Still duly noted what Charles had said about Blucher being a "first-rate man to his servants." He had encountered such reactions before, more frequently than he liked to acknowledge, but it always troubled him to hear a runaway slave speak as if he were still in bondage, still under his master's spell. After writing down his notes about what Charles had said, the veteran agent struggled to offer some possible explanation for his interviewee's disappointing response, and finally concluded: "As the secret of his master's treatment is here brought to light, it is very evident that Charles, in speaking so highly in his favor, failed to take a just view of him, as no man could really be first-rate to his servants, who would not allow a man to live with his wife and children, and who would persist in taking from another what he had no right to take. Nevertheless, as Charles thought his master 'first-rate,' he shall have the benefit of the opinion, but it was suspected that Charles was not disposed to find fault with his kin, as it was very likely that the old master claimed some of the white blood in his veins."

Still was more sympathetic regarding Jim and Perry, writing that Perry complained he had been "worked hard and allowed but few privileges." About Jim he observed he "was quite as much a white man as he was black. He was a mulatto, twenty-nine years of age, well-made, and bore a grim countenance, but a brave and manly will to keep up his courage on the way. He said that he had been used very well, had no fault to find with John J. Richards, who was possibly a near relative of his."[12]

What the three of them may have thought about William Still can only be imagined. The experience of being sharply interrogated by a well-dressed, highly literate, and discriminating Negro who was so secure in manner and holding such a position of power must have made a profound impression on them, particularly as he stood as the gatekeeper of their freedom. Analyzed today, Charles's comments underscore some of slavery's extraordinary complexities and paradoxes for many of the human beings involved. Despite his enslavement and the horror and humiliation to which Hansbrough had subjected him, Charles still called Blucher a "first-rate" master to his slaves, indicating that he identified with him and perhaps even sought to imitate his behavior in some way. He indicated that he appreciated the way Blucher had treated him, but didn't add what would have happened if he had objected, challenged, defied, or disobeyed his master. Nor did Charles admit what he himself may have done to appease the one who held him in bondage. Maybe he didn't want to go on record as being critical of his master, because he feared the possible repercussions if it became known. Charles almost seemed grateful toward him. Maybe he was still savoring the compassion Blucher had apparently shown during their last encounter when he permitted Charles to go and visit his ailing wife. Was Charles trying to navigate the treacherous shoals of slavery and liberation by exercising what measure of agency was available to him to define his own circumstances and to craft strategies of avoidance? Whatever it was, Charles's perplexing confession indicates that he still identified with his oppressor, still felt some sort of bond to the man who had held him in slavery. Charles didn't present himself as a victim. He took personal responsibility for his decision to run away, presenting it almost as a selfish decision on his part to pursue his own individual "happiness." By doing so, he may have opened himself up to more personal guilt later on, when the consequences for his running away were imposed.[13]

As was the usual procedure at that time, Still likely provided the fugitives with fresh donated clothing and a warm meal, along with three dollars for each one to help cover some of their expenses. He may also have put them up in his house to rest for a while before hustling them off to resume their journey north. Every person he aided represented another blow against slavery, another wound to the behemoth, another brother or sister sprung from the cage.

On October 25, a few days after Charles and Jim escaped, Senator William H. Seward of New York, the leading Republican presidential contender and strong abolitionist, gave one of his most notable speeches. Sooner or later, he warned, "the United States must and will . . . become either entirely a slaveholding nation, or entirely a free-labor nation." The two antagonistic systems could no longer coexist side by side. Further compromise was out of the question.[14] Charles didn't know it at the time, but Seward's prophecy would prove remarkably prescient, not only for the country's geopolitical future, but also for himself.

After their long journey from Philadelphia, Charles, Jim, and Perry set foot in Albany, located about four hundred and fifty miles north of Culpeper and midway between New York City and the Canadian border. The Albany office of the Underground Railroad was situated near roads that headed west to Utica, Syracuse, Auburn, Rochester, Buffalo, and Canada West, and rough passages that extended north to North Elba, Vermont, and Montreal. The station stood about a mile uphill from where the Hudson River connected with the Erie Canal. "Clinton's Ditch" had made Albany the nation's biggest importer of lumber, and this provided the Underground Railroad with a useful transportation cover. But soon the onset of winter would make passage on the frozen river and canals impossible for the next five months.[1]

The narrow brick house at 10 Lark Street served as the home of Stephen Myers, who called himself "Agent and Superintendent of the Underground Railroad," and his wife Harriet.[2] He was dark-skinned and dignified in appearance, wore his hair coiled outward on both sides, giving his head a shape that resembled Napoleon's hat, and always was as well-dressed as a steamboat steward, which is what he had been for many years. Although now fifty-eight years old, he remained very active in many causes related to Negro rights and was considered one of the top black abolitionists in the state.[3]

Born in 1800 in Hoosick, Rensselaer County, a town with a strong antislavery tradition, Myers had grown up as a slave in one of Albany's most prominent households, learning to read and write pretty well although his spelling could sometimes be atrocious.[4] His master had been Dr. Jonathan Eights, a prominent Albany physician, who was married to Alida Wynkoop Eights. (She was the daughter of Jacobus Wynkoop and Alida Koens Myers of Curaçao, which apparently accounted for Stephen's surname of Myers.[5]) Stephen's master, Dr. Eights, spent time in Philadelphia and Montgomery County before establishing his medical practice in Albany in 1810 at 92 North Pearl Street near the block where another young Albany patrician, Herman Melville, lived. The Eights family was closely tied to the region's patroon (feudal lord), Stephen Van Rensselaer III.[6]

New York's law for the gradual abolition of slavery, passed in 1799, had been crafted to free all children born to slave women. The females were scheduled to be emancipated at age twenty-five and the males at age twenty-eight, but slaves already in servitude before July 4, 1799, actually had to remain in service for the rest of their natural lives, although the law reclassified them as "indentured servants" instead of slaves, effective July 4, 1827.[7] Myers was freed earlier than required, when he was eighteen years old. After his manumission he worked as a grocer and steamboat steward. Because the Hudson River Railroad did not extend from Poughkeepsie to Albany until 1851, many travelers relied on steamboats as the next fastest mode of transport, and Myers served as a steward aboard one of the most audacious vessels.[8] The speedy *Armenia* made the entire trip from New York City to Albany during daylight, so its passengers could enjoy the scenery while partaking of lavish meals and listening to haunting music played by its steam calliope.[9]

By the early 1840s Myers had become involved in antislavery activities and was assisting fugitive slaves to settle in the area or to get to Canada. He later operated part of a network that was connected to Still in Philadelphia, Jermain W. Loguen in Syracuse, and many others in Delaware, Canada West, New York, Boston, Springfield, New London, and Colchester, Maryland. With his wife, he led a group called the Northern Star Association that had published an early black newspaper, the *Northern Star and Freemen's Advocate* in 1842–43.[10] He also conducted extensive lobbying at the state capitol on behalf of free blacks.[11] In recent years he had stopped working on the steamboat to work full time on his Underground Railroad and civil rights activities.

Since then, Myers and his wife had aided hundreds of runaway slaves. From September 12, 1855, to July 5, 1856, 287 fugitives passed through their office and he paid $542.36 for their passage and $76.60 for their board.[12] Between November 1857 and May 1858 the couple had helped 118 runaways reach Canada West.[13] Many ended up staying nearby, at least temporarily. The volume was so great that Myers had recently issued a circular reporting that they had "not received enough to meet the necessary expenses of the Underground Railroad," and therefore they were compelled to make a public call for subscriptions. He noted, "The hundreds of fugitives that have fallen in my care during the last twelve years have required a great deal of labor and expense to make them comfortable. They are sent to me by the Underground Railroad, south of Albany, and in many cases they come poorly clad and are greatly in want of clothes, such as coats, pants and under garments, both males and females." Myers pledged to faithfully use any clothes or money that was donated to him for the exclusive purpose of aiding his needy passengers. "We have arrivals every few days from Southern oppression," he wrote. "[W]e forward them to the next depot, and from there they are forwarded to Canada." But he added: "If there should be any farmers wanting help, either men or women in the house, they can be accommodated by sending to this office. We consider it safe for them to go into the country, and it saves expense. We have sent quite a number in the country during this season and the last, and they write to us that they make good help."[14] As recently as February 1858, Myers reported handling thirty-six "through passengers" in the first twenty-three days of the month alone, besides the usual amount of "way travel." Instead of passing through to Canada, a large proportion of emigrants from the South were deciding to stop in New York state.[15]

By the time Charles, Jim, and Perry arrived at Myers's office in the later part of October, the passage from Albany to Syracuse had risen to two dollars and fifty cents. Lodging at his home cost a shilling per night and eighteen cents per meal. Although the Albany Vigilance Committee office was known as one of the nation's best, funding was a constant struggle. In Philadelphia, Still was able to raise money through antislavery societies and fairs, but in Albany, Myers ran his operation as a business, supported largely by donations from moderate members of the Republican Party, particularly Thurlow Weed, the political boss and publisher of the *Albany Evening Journal*.[16] Myers had to collect every dollar himself, constantly seeking handouts from men of substance. After his retirement from the steam line, he depended almost entirely on the Underground Railroad for his income, which amounted to ten percent of each dollar he received. A committee of well-to-do "gentlemen" inspected his books once a month and agreed to help support him if he could not collect enough money to make his services pay $450 a year. Lately, the heavy traffic had made him even more financially strapped than usual. So Myers offered his passengers a choice: either they could head on to freedom in Canada, traveling by rail with a ticket he provided, or they could remain in the Albany area, where he would place them in employment that would enable them to earn some money to defray their expenses, help support the Underground Railroad, and start to gain some cash for themselves. Whenever he could, Myers made it his practice to send his passengers into the country to sympathetic farmers who would harbor them and employ them for a while.[17] Some fugitives ended up staying on in the area for years, even permanently.

Presented with such choices, Perry opted to continue on to Canada, but Charles and Jim decided to remain in the vicinity, hoping that would put them in a better position to reunite with their wives and children, who likely would soon come up to join them. Myers decided to send Jim a few miles north to West Troy, to work for an employer who would enable him to use his black-smithing and shoemaking skills.[18] Charles, the experienced driver, would be placed across the river in a small village called Sand Lake, situated in central Rensselaer County, about fifteen miles east of Albany and about the same distance southeast of Troy, just a day's ride from the Massachusetts line. At least for the time being, he would work there as a teamster, driving lumber wagons and performing other labor, for which he could expect to receive his room and board and a small wage. While in town he would also be placed under the care of his former benefactor from Culpeper, Minot Crosby, who had relocated there.

Prosperous Sand Lake stood at a crossroads for travelers who approached it by stagecoach or wagon. Its hills were covered with forest that produced large quantities of cordwood, charcoal, and tan bark, which teamsters hauled to the Troy and Albany markets. Some of the top wood merchants supported the Underground Railroad and the lumber industry employed a number of blacks; their wagons also furnished a cover for the transport of fugitive slaves. It was often aboard one of them that a fugitive slave first entered town. The village had numerous lakes and meandering creeks, the liveliest of which, the twisting Wynants kil, was considered one of the finest industrial resources powers in eastern New York. It rushing waters powered a foundry, Staats Tompkins Paper Mill, a flouring mill, two knitting mills, and a cotton warp factory, making the little village a modest industrial center of the sort that had made the Northeast the nation's predominant manufacturing region. Yet even Sand Lake depended on slavery to some extent. Three of its mills relied on cotton—one million pounds of it per year—to manufacture knit goods for men's underwear and warp. This cotton, of course, was a product of Negro slave labor from the Deep South. Sand Lake's share amounted to only about two thousand bales out of a national output of 3.9 million bales produced down South in 1860. But without it, the local mill workers might not have found such steady employment. As a result of this codependence, the textile industry tended to foster close collaboration between merchants in the North and planters in the South and often entailed their frequent travel back and forth, not to mention a grudging recognition of their common economic interests. Ironically, some of the same coarse, scratchy material that was used to clad field slaves on Southern plantations—so-called nigger cloth that was emblematic of slavery—had been manufactured for years in one of these very mills, tucked away on a winding country road in "free" Sand Lake, New York.[19] Abolitionist Charles Sumner decried what he called the "unhallowed union . . . between cotton planters and flesh mongers of Louisiana and Mississippi and the cotton spinners and traffickers of New England—between the lords of the lash and the lords of the loom."[20] But New York had many towns that were just as implicated, and Sand Lake was one of them.

Although the political climate there was much more mixed than in the South, the little village's links to slavery and the Democratic Party raised the danger level for Charles and others involved in the Underground Railroad. Its residents' sentiments regarding issues of slavery, abolitionism, and members of the Negro race were by no means uniform; in fact, for many economic as well as political and social reasons, both blacks and antislavery causes probably weren't regarded very warmly by most of the local population. The Sand Lake Baptist Church had a long history of involvement in antislavery activities, dating back at least to 1840, when the Reverend Abel Brown, a radical abolitionist and Underground Railroad organizer, briefly served as pastor—until he was abruptly dismissed and asked to leave town. A few doors away from the Baptist Church lived Dr. Charles H. Gregory, the physician and church deacon who had sided with Abel Brown even after his dismissal.[21] Dr. Gregory had also corresponded with slave rescuer Charles Torrey after Torrey's disastrous arrest and imprisonment in Maryland in 1844.[22] The Gregorys were strong supporters of the Underground Railroad and personally helped to assist fugitive slaves, as did some other families; two local men would soon gain national publicity for their participation in an attempted slave rescue in Oberlin, Ohio. Stephen Myers's benefactor, Thurlow Weed, had briefly lived in the village and continued to stay in touch with some residents. But many neighbors took a different view; hence, the village wasn't classified as an abolitionist center.

Years earlier, an elite school in the village known as the Rensselaer Institute had become the Sand Lake Academy, and that in turn had split into two small but well-regarded private educational institutions: Scram's Collegiate Institute and the Sand Lake Female Seminary, both of which sought to instill Christian values and classical knowledge.[23] Founded in 1852 as the first preparatory school in town, William H. Scram's Collegiate Institute consisted of a large, stately white building surrounded by a white picket fence.[24] Scram and his wife had come to the area from Syracuse. Their current enrollment of twenty-five to thirty-six teenage boys included representatives of some of the leading families in upstate New York, such as the Lansings and the Van Rensselaers, as well as a Breckenridge from Ohio, two lads from Florida, a Bush from Mississippi, and two Eckers from Georgia.[25] In some instances, the boarding pupils' mothers accompanied them for the school term, living nearby in a local hotel or apartment, thereby lending a Southern flavor to some of the local interactions.

Directly across the road from Dr. Gregory's house stood the prestigious Female Seminary, modeled after Troy's Emma Willard School and the Hartford Female Seminary. It too was a commodious and freshly painted white structure, which was not the only thing new about it, for simultaneous with Charles's arrival that fall, it had welcomed its new principal, Minot S. Crosby of Massachusetts, the adventurous young teacher whom Charles had known in Culpeper and who had aided their escape.

For Charles, Crosby's presence must have constituted Sand Lake's greatest attraction of all, for it meant that he had a powerful friend and ally in the community—somebody who could protect and assist him, and hopefully someone who might help him to reunite with his wife and children. Crosby lived by the seminary in a spacious two-and-a-half story boardinghouse that was located on the shore of crystalline Sand Lake. With him were his wife Margaret and their children (Elizabeth, who had been born in Culpeper in 1856, and little Margaret, who was born in January 1860), although Mrs. Crosby was still recovering from the death of her newborn—the little baby who tragically had expired during the frenzied flight from Culpeper.

Also living in the same apartment house were John A. Weiss, aged thirty, a well-to-do lumber merchant from Massachusetts, and his wife and three children, the second of whom had been born in Canada West in 1858. (It was Weiss who actually oversaw Charles's employment driving the lumber wagon and performing other work.) The other tenants included two young female teachers from Massachusetts, who were sisters of Crosby and his wife; a music teacher; a cook; a seamstress; Reverend John Cushman, aged thirty, of the Presbyterian Church; and Reverend Daniel Robinson of the Baptist Church and his wife and four children. Robinson, fifty-one, had arrived in town about the same time as Crosby and Nalle.

Charles lived with Crosby's family (there was a tiny cottage with a horse stall next door) and worked around the schools, hauling lumber and doing other chores.[26] He must have been concerned he would stand out in his new hiding place because Sand Lake's population was almost exclusively white and he was an outsider from the South, not the usual local servant or Irish-born maid or laborer. When the 1860 Census was taken, the whole town of 2,494 included dozens of young Irish women but only three black males and five black females. The village's population of about 1,000 inhabitants apparently included only two black households—the Tompkins and the Lavenders, whose places of origin and occupations would remain unlisted in the U.S. Census—but there may have been a few more blacks living in the area who evaded the census taker, as he was also the deputy U.S. marshal responsible for rounding up fugitive slaves.[27] Fortunately for any fugitive slave, Sand Lake had no constabulary or sheriff of its own and only a couple of justices of the peace.

Sand Lake's winter of 1858–59 proved worse than any Charles had ever experienced. The cheerless wind left snowdrifts piled to the tops of the fence posts, making the roads impassable to wagons. Everything around him was white. The snow covered everywhere, sagging the great pine branches, making sharp things round, forming lumps and mounds mysterious, hiding tracks, burying the brook except for a dark gray rivulet that continued running madly away. It and the bitter cold kept everyone closer to home and gathered more tightly around the fire, making Charles's life in Sand Lake at first prove relatively quiet, isolated, and uneventful. He missed his family and his home back in Virginia.

Figure 1. Historical plaque, First and State streets, Troy, New York.

Figure 2. John C. Nalle looks over an early class of the District of Columbia public school (courtesy Charles Sumner School Archives).

Figure 3. Cole's Hill today.

Figure 4. Culpeper wheat harvest, 1863, by Edwin Forbes (Library of Congress).

Figure 5. William Still of Philadelphia's Vigilance Committee interviewed Charles and Jim after their escape from Georgetown and didn't like some of what he heard.

Figure 6. John Brown holding the *New York Tribune* as he prepares for Harpers Ferry, 1859 (Library of Congress).

Figure 7. Horatio Averill pictured decades after he betrayed Charles Nalle and had the village named after him (Town of Sand Lake).

Figure 8. View of Troy from Congress Street looking east to Eighth Street, photographed by James Irving, c. 1860 (courtesy Rensselaer County Historical Society).

Figure 9. Industrialist and prominent Republican Uri Gilbert was one of the richest men in town when he hired Charles Nalle as his coachman in 1860 (courtesy Rensselaer County Historical Society).

Figure 10. The Reverend Henry Highland Garnet, a fugitive slave from Maryland who went on to become one of the leading black orators in the nineteenth century, had built a reputation as the most militant Negro in American when he presided over Troy's Liberty Street Church a decade before the rescue (courtesy Rensselaer County Historical Society).

Figure 11. Troy rescue site, then the office of the U.S. commissioner who administered the Fugitive Slave Law.

Figure 12. Martin I. Townsend, the Troy civil rights attorney who intervened to save Charles (Rensselaer County Historical Society).

Figure 13. Harriet Tubman, known as "Moses," as she looked about the time of her rescue of Charles Nalle in 1860. Photo by H. B. Lindsey (Library of Congress).

Figure 14. The building in West Troy (now Watervliet) where Nalle was taken after he was apprehended following the Troy rescue (City of Watervliet).

Figure 15. Refugees escaping across the Rappahannock from war-torn Culpeper, August 1862, photographed by Timothy O'Sullivan (Library of Congress).

Figure 16. African American descendents of Blucher W. Hansbrough and their kin at a family reunion in Virginia, 2004 (author's photo).

Figure 17. T. O. Madden Jr. of Stevensburg, great-grandson of Willis Madden, free black entrepreneur and grandson of Jack Wale the slave catcher, shares some of his family's papers dating back to the eighteenth century at his ancestral home, October 1, 1994 (Tamar Gordon).

Figure 18. The author researching deeds in Culpeper Court House, 1993 (Tamar Gordon).

Figure 19. Author Scott Christianson at the Troy rescue site (Tamar Gordon).

Then Charles received the first communiqué about what had happened to the others since his escape. Upon hearing its sketchy but brutal contents, he learned that two weeks after his escape, Kitty was arrested in Washington on charges of living there as an emancipated colored person contrary to law. Thrust into jail despite her poor health, she could have died but for the active intervention of a "white man" who also paid the $20 fine to gain her release. Thankfully, she and the children had managed to obtain refuge in Columbia, Pennsylvania.[1] A detailed report wasn't forthcoming at that moment.

Today it is even harder to piece together precisely what happened to Kitty. The jailing of black women in Washington at that time wasn't unusual; many suspected fugitive slaves and other prisoners were held in the District of Columbia Jail in the present-day 400 block of F Street NW, a three-story-high, remarkably ugly castle-like structure with boarded windows and a blue-gray stucco exterior that everybody called the "Blue Jug."[2] Her alleged failure to present her free papers meant that she legally could have remained locked up for months and eventually been auctioned as a slave in order to pay her jail costs, had she not been able to pay them. This practice, which Jacob Bigelow had exposed in 1857, would still be going on in December of 1861, when newspapers reported that sixty suspected fugitive slaves, males and females, were being held at the Blue Jug "in the midst of filth and vermin and contagious diseases, on a cold stone floor, many without shoes, nearly all without sufficient clothing, bedding or fire, and all in a half-starving condition . . . confined because—in the language of their commitments—they were suspected of being runaways, and no proofs had been adduced that they were not runaways."[3]

A District jail register from 1858 has survived, showing the keepers' notes about which owners, agents, or others were responsible for placing each slave in the jail, along with the name of each fugitive slave, the date he or she was committed, and when and how they were released. But Kitty's name isn't included.[4] In 1991 historian John Hope Franklin analyzed this log and concluded that most runaways remained in jail from three days to two weeks, although there were instances where some were kept for more than a year. With maintenance costs running about seventy-five cents a day, an owner or some other person who intervened could be expected to pay out as much as $100 or more. Franklin added, "A very few alleged slaves were discharged as free persons either because they proved their freedom or because no one claimed them. Some blacks were taken up for 'safekeeping,' presumably on suspicion of having run away, and they were disposed of as runaway slaves."[5] The fact that Kitty isn't identified either in the register of blacks with freedom certificates or in the jail log adds to the mystery surrounding her Washington ordeal. Clearly she was living on the edge.

The nature of her "illness" may explain why Blucher Hansbrough allowed Charles to visit her in Washington. At that time, Kitty was in the final stage of her pregnancy with their daughter Mary, so it's more likely that her medical problem was pregnancy-related, and verified as such to Blucher by one of his relatives in the city. That may also explain why Kitty didn't flee with Charles and Jim Banks when they left Georgetown, for indeed she may have been physically unable to do so.[6] Another possible clue has turned up in the accounts of Colonel Thom's emancipation fund, wherein Colonel Thom's executor, John Catesby Thom, recorded that in December 1858 he paid ten dollars for "Dr. Herndon's bill for medical services."[7] This makes sense because Kitty knew at least one Dr. Herndon who was closely connected to both the Hansbrough and Thom families, and who was often about Washington at that time. Might he have been the one who treated Kitty and bailed her out of jail? (For more about this intriguing mystery, see the appendix.)

After fleeing the capital, Kitty and the Nalle children took sanctuary in Columbia, Pennsylvania, a town perched high on the eastern bank of the mighty Susquehanna River located about one hundred and ten miles north and sixty miles west of Philadelphia, and a favorite train stop linked to Washington, D.C., and New York.[8] Its Underground Railroad history was filled with violence and intrigue.[9] Besides having a sizeable free black population, with a significant black middle class, Columbia boasted the richest Negro in America, Quaker William Whipper, who together with his partner, the Reverend Stephen Smith, had made a fortune there in the lumber business.

Their extensive investments included real estate, lumber, coal, steamboats, and railroad cars, stretching all the way to Canada—enterprises that often employed fugitive slaves and were deeply intertwined with the Underground Railroad.[10] Slave catchers continued to conduct raids into the town.[11] In 1856, as a captured fugitive slave was being escorted along Walnut Street, he dived into a cellar way and escaped through the back of the house.[12] Another time a group of residents descended on a slave catcher named Isaac Brooks, dragged him through the snow to the back of town, stripped him naked, and thrashed him with hickory withes.[13] Lancaster County was also the domain of Thaddeus Stevens, a white abolitionist lawyer who often defended fugitive slaves in court and secretly waged a spy war against the slaveholders, slave catchers, and their informers.[14] Years later it would be revealed that one of the slave catchers' local agents had actually been a double agent working for Stevens.[15]

It was in this nest of intrigue that Kitty obtained sanctuary with the children after her release from jail, living so quietly and inconspicuously she left no record of her time there. It must have taken her some time to regain her health and nurse the baby. It is also interesting to note how much the lumber industry had figured in their story since leaving Culpeper. Charles had escaped via a lumber wharf at Georgetown and then received aid from William Still, the coal-and-lumber merchant in Philadelphia, and from Stephen Myers at Albany's lumber-district Underground Railroad office. Then he had moved to haul lumber at Sand Lake, while his family hid out in the lumber town of Columbia. The wood business had served them well.[16]

But demons often haunted a fugitive slave who had left his or her family behind. Charles's brother-in-law, Lewis Burrell (who was married to Kitty's half-sister Winna Ann) had escaped to Canada in April of 1856, but almost three years later he still was tortured by his separation from his loved ones. From his sorrowful exile in Toronto, Lewis appealed to Still for help in rescuing his wife. Lewis wrote that he had received a letter from a friend in Washington the previous night telling him that his wife was in Baltimore and would come away if she could find a friend to assist her, so he asked if Still could help him contact someone trustworthy. Lewis suggested Still could write to Noah Davis in Baltimore, who was well acquainted with his wife, but he didn't think Davis was a true friend, or the agent could contact Reverend Samuel Madden (Willis Madden's son from Stevensburg, who was then a Baptist preacher in Baltimore); however, he was afraid that a letter coming from Canada might be detected. Therefore, Lewis asked if Still would write to someone he knew instead to get them to see Samuel Madden to obtain the necessary information. "[N]ow Mr Still will you attend to this thing for me, fourthwith," Lewis pleaded. "[I]f you will I will pay you four your truble, if we can dow any thing it must be don now, as she will leave theare in the spring, and if you will take the matter in hand, you mous writ me on to reseption of this letter, whether you will or not."

Unfortunately for Lewis and Winna Ann, his poignant entreaty didn't produce the desired result, and a discouraged Still later wrote in his notes: "As in the case of many others, the way was so completely blocked that nothing could be done for the wife's deliverance. Until the day when the millions of fetters were broken, nothing gave so much pain to husbands and wives as these heart-breaking separations."[17] (In fact, it would be four more years before Winna could escape, and their children would not be so lucky.)

Harriet Tubman was another runaway slave who knew how it felt to have left loved ones behind. Born about the same time as William Still and Charles, she had worked as a field hand in Dorchester County, Maryland, later saying, "I grew up like a neglected weed, ignorant of liberty, having no experience of it."[18] After her master died in 1849, the heirs had attempted to sell her and some of her kin, but the transaction at first fell through. Faced again by an imminent breakup of the family, she and her brothers Ben and Henry had run away from home but later disagreed about how to proceed and glumly returned home. Shortly afterward, Harriet had left home alone and without her husband, traveling at night. By following the North Star and with guidance supplied by blacks and white Quakers (including the Levertons), she made it to Philadelphia, but discovered she was neither legally free nor free of the longing she felt for her loved ones left behind. "I was a stranger in a strange land," she later recalled, "and my home, after all, was down in Maryland; because my father, my mother, my brothers, and sisters, and friends were there. But I was free and *they* should be free."[19] Tortured by their continued bondage, she toiled as much as she could for wages, saved every penny she could get, and dreamed about carrying out her loved ones' liberation.

Tubman, however, had managed to act on her dreams in ways that other fugitive slaves could only imagine. When, in December 1850, she learned that her niece Kessiah was about to be sold at Baltimore, she rushed back into the land of slavery, went to the scene, and made contacts on the waterfront through some of her Underground Railroad friends. She and Kessiah's husband, John Bowley, devised a scheme to rescue the young woman and her two children, James Alfred and Araminta, directly from the slave auction. Incredibly, they managed to succeed and get the three away by boat.[20]

Tubman also struggled to save her other kin from slavery. Over the next year, she went back and rescued her brother Moses and two other men. Then she tried to bring away her husband, only to find out that he had married another woman and that he refused to leave.[21] A few months later she returned to Maryland again to bring out of bondage another brother and his wife and nine others.[22] En route to Canada, she passed through Philadelphia, New York, and Troy or Albany before receiving shelter in Rochester from Frederick Douglass.[23]

On Christmas Day in 1854, Tubman went down and rescued her three other brothers.[24] On their way out of the plantation, she had glimpsed from a hiding place to see their mother, Rit, step from her cabin, shading her eyes with her hand as she took a long look down the road to see if her children were coming, and then they "could almost hear her sigh as she turned into the house, disappointed."[25] Unable to rescue her mother, she led the others to St. Catharines. Interviewed in Canada, Tubman explained that whenever she had seen a white person, she was "afraid of being carried away."

But after liberating herself, her worldview had changed. "Now I've been free," she said, "I know what a dreadful condition slavery is. I have seen hundreds of escaped slaves, but I never saw one who was willing to go back and be a slave. . . . I think slavery is the next thing to hell. If a person would send another into bondage, he would, it appears to me, be bad enough to send him into hell, if he could.[26]

Over the next few years she made several more trips to the Eastern Shore, bringing away her sister and her sister's children, and finally in 1857 her aged parents.[27] She also made other trips to bring away groups of fugitives who weren't related to her, but whom she nevertheless risked her life to save. Still was amazed by Tubman's fierce determination to aid her family, and he marveled at her unblemished success at guiding fugitives north to freedom. He and others in the movement glorified "Moses" for her exploits in leading their people out of the wilderness.

For Charles, however, the letter informing him about what had happened to Kitty was mild compared to the other cryptic news he received from Culpeper about what had befallen his kin back at Cole's Hill. For it was then that he belatedly learned the most horrible results of all: following his escape, Blucher Hansbrough had taken his two brothers and another mulatto slave to the Richmond market and sold them off to a plantation in Alabama—one of the worst fates any slave from Virginia could ever contemplate, the equivalent, many said, of a death sentence.[28] In reality, the victims had done nothing to aid his escape. The guilt Charles felt would haunt him for a lifetime, especially since it appeared they had been punished for something he had done. Rightly or wrongly, he would always feel responsible.

Early in the morning of August 11, 1859, the heavens unleashed a freakish explosion over Sand Lake. "About seven o'clock in the morning," one observer wrote, "while the sky was perfectly cloudless, while hardly a breath of air was stirring, while not a single indication prevailed of a natural commotion of any sort whatever, there was a terrific, shocking, detonating report, accompanied apparently by two sharp echoes." The force of the concussion was so great that houses were shaken and persons walking along the road could feel the ground vibrate underneath them. Men dropped their tools and craned their necks to scan the horizon, little children started to cry and call for their mothers. "It was as if the sound had come from the sky, but there were no clouds, not a single indication of the prevalence of electricity, and that explanation could not be entertained." Fifteen miles to the north, the county clerk had just finished his breakfast and was standing in his yard when he spied "a bright light in a southerly direction from his house" that was descending very rapidly to earth. When it appeared to have fallen to within half a mile or so of the ground, it suddenly disappeared and the sky gave forth a very loud explosion, like thunder, then another, and another, three strong explosions in all. The clerk saw "three distinct clouds of smoke in the track of the meteor" that "looked like a large sized sky rocket." Fifteen miles away, in Albany, a stone fell from the sky and struck a barn.[1]

Some saw its appearance as an omen, a metaphor. Writing a few months later about the cataclysmic events to come, Brooklyn journalist, transcendentalist, and poet Walt Whitman described 1859 as the brooding "year of meteors." The comet, he said, had come "unannounced out of the north flaring in heaven" and left everyone full of forebodings. "What am I myself but one of your meteors?" he asked.[2]

Nine days after the meteor shower appeared over Sand Lake, Frederick Douglass was in southwestern Pennsylvania for a rendezvous with the radical outlaw who would inspire Whitman's poem. The two had known each other for twelve years. Twenty months earlier, Captain John Brown, traveling under the alias of Nelson Hawkins, had made an extended stay at Douglass's elegant Rochester home while en route to visit Gerrit Smith at Peterboro. It was on Douglass's writing table that Brown had penned a model constitution for the new political state for runaway slaves he intended to establish in the mountains of western Virginia—a constitution that in many ways was superior to the American one insofar as it prohibited slavery and included other protections for equal rights.[3] Brown had discussed with Douglass his vision of an armed assault on a slavery stronghold in Virginia, carried out by a combined force of whites and blacks. He claimed his rescue would arouse the slaves and set off a massive slave rebellion that would spread throughout the South. Douglass, however, had responded by opining that such a scheme was doomed to fail, in part because it overestimated the likelihood that slaves would join his rebellion—not because they didn't want to be free, but because they weren't suicidal.

At the time of Brown's visit, Douglass had been hosting in his household a fugitive slave from Charleston, South Carolina, who called himself Emperor, or Shields Green. Although Green was a man of few words and had trouble expressing himself in speech, he exhibited such dignity and courage that Brown readily confided to him his plans and purposes. Green in turn vowed to join Brown when the critical time came. So in the summer of 1859, when Douglass received a coded letter from Brown, urgently asking him to meet him at an old stone quarry near Chambersburg, Pennsylvania, and to bring along any money he could raise along with Shields Green, Douglass obeyed the old man's summons, and Green the runaway slave went with him.[4]

On their way south, the pair stopped over in Brooklyn to call upon two trusted members of the Underground Railroad, the Reverend James Newton Gloucester, a pioneering African Presbyterian church minister, and his wife Elizabeth, a Richmond native, who were Brown supporters. (Brown too had recently visited their home on Bridge Street, prayed with them in their tiny kitchen, and shared some of his initial plans for an attempted slave insurrection.) As Douglass was leaving Gloucester's home, Mrs. Gloucester gave him twenty-five dollars and asked him to put it into Brown's hand with their best wishes.[5]

On his travels through several states, Brown had tried to recruit blacks and whites to join his grand slave rescue. While visiting the colony of runaway slaves in St. Catharines, Ontario, on April 8, 1858, one of those he had especially sought out was Harriet Tubman, a fugitive slave who already had made a name for herself among abolitionists for her fearless missions into the South. The Reverend Jermain W. Loguen of Syracuse accompanied Brown and made the introduction. Tubman impressed Brown so much that he called her "General" and "he." Hours later, Brown wrote an excited letter to his son, John, reporting, "I am succeeding to all appearances beyond my expectations. Harriet Tubman hooked on his whole team at once. He Harriet is the most of man naturally; that I ever met with. There is the most abundant material; & of the right quality; in this quarter; beyond all doubt."[6] Brown left their meeting expecting that Tubman would join him as a comrade in arms.

Brown also believed he had succeeded in convincing distinguished black editor Dr. Martin R. Delany to help him recruit blacks to an upcoming anti-slavery convention in Chatham that Brown was planning. Delany was inspired by Brown's commitment to an effort, led by blacks and whites together, to attempt to overthrow slavery by violence. When Delany confided he was surprised Brown hadn't been able to win more support for his militant approach, Brown replied: "Why should you be surprised? Sir, the people of the northern states are cowards; slavery has made cowards of them all. The whites are afraid of each other, and the blacks are afraid of the whites. You can effect nothing among such people. . . . It is men I want, and not money. . . . Men are afraid of identification with me, though they favor my measures. They are cowards, sir! Cowards."[7]

But as it turned out, when the time came for Brown to commence his military action, very few blacks or whites had actually signed up to participate in the attack. For some reason (possibly illness), Harriet Tubman had not joined. Nor had several others Brown had expected. One who did enlist was Danger-field Newby, a free black man from Culpeper County who was about the same age as Charles Nalle. After being manumitted by his white master, who was also his father, Newby had struggled in vain to purchase the freedom of his enslaved wife and their seven children.[8] Some other black members of Brown's army included Lewis Sheridan Leary, a fugitive slave, and his nephew, John A. Copeland Jr., both of whom had participated in the Oberlin slave rescue the previous year.

After his stay with the Gloucesters in Brooklyn, Douglass arrived in Chambersburg and called upon the local barber (Henry Watson) whom Brown had designated to guide him and Shields Green to the rendezvous spot. Shortly before sunrise on Friday, August 19, the party ended up in an abandoned stone quarry, which Douglass approached "very cautiously," for he knew that Brown was always well armed and wanted for murders in Kansas. Sure enough, Brown followed his approaching visitors with suspicion, from behind a rifle. But once he recognized them, he received them cordially. He had disguised himself as a fisherman, and looked as comfortable in the area as any local farmer, but in keeping with his study of guerilla warfare, he'd carefully selected his clothing to blend in with the quarry stone (camouflage). Brown and his white companion, John Kagi, sat down with Douglass and Green among the rocks to talk.

Brown described in detail his planned slave insurrection that was soon to be aimed at the federal arsenal at Harpers Ferry, Virginia. His strategic selection of that specific target was directed at both the institution of slavery and the federal government that upheld and protected it. The idea called for his small force to first take over a neighboring large plantation and liberate its slaves, many of whom would then join his army, and then they would seize the arsenal and take control of its arms. Some of the army would fan out in different directions, distributing weapons, spreading word of the insurrection, and gaining more recruits. If necessary, they could take refuge in the nearby Alleghenies while others of his allies demanded political concessions. Douglass argued against the plan on numerous grounds. But the old man retorted that he thought it was just what the nation needed. Brown, Douglass later wrote, said "the capture of Harpers Ferry would serve as notice to the slaves that their friends had come, and as a trumpet to rally them to his standard." Douglass, who was one of the great talkers of his era, tried to convince him otherwise, but Brown wouldn't reconsider. Douglass warned he would be "going into a perfect steel-trap"—once in, he would never make it out alive, he would be surrounded at once and denied escape. Brown listened respectfully, but wouldn't budge. After arguing for several hours without reaching agreement, Douglass headed back to Chambersburg for a lecture engagement, but he returned the next morning to resume their debate. "Our talk was long and earnest," Douglass would write; "we spent the most of Saturday and a part of Sunday in this debate—Brown for Harpers Ferry, and I against it; he for striking a blow which should instantly rouse the country, and I for the policy of gradually and unaccountably drawing off the slaves to the mountains, as at first suggested and proposed by him."

Finally, Brown embraced Douglass and said: "Come with me, Douglass; I will defend you with my life. I want you for a special purpose. When I strike, the bees will begin to swarm, and I shall want you to help hive them." But Douglass refused. At last, when it was clear that neither Brown nor Douglass would change his mind, Douglass turned to Shields Green and asked him what he intended to do. To his surprise, the fugitive slave replied, "I b'leve I'll go wid de ole man."⁹

Word of Brown's plan or general rumors about an upcoming insurrection already were circulating among abolitionists and members of the Underground Railroad. William Still and others in Philadelphia knew something was brewing. A few days after Brown's meeting with Douglass, a colored military company in the city, known as the Frank Johnson Guards, was preparing to hold a public street parade and picnic at Haddington on August 16 to proudly display their eighty-man contingent of strong, uniformed, armed forces—something that was bound to raise white alarm. (An account of the episode was later published by William Henry Johnson, a free black man from Philadelphia, via Albany and Alexandria, Virginia, who at the time had been twenty-six years old and a member of both the Guards and Still's Underground Railroad office.) According to Johnson, writing in his little-noted autobiography published in 1900, when John Brown heard about the group's scheduled parade, Brown rushed to Philadelphia to try to get them to lower their profile, out of fear that their actions would put the authorities on alert and frustrate his plans. But as Johnson would later recall, "On the evening before the parade, General J. J. Sim[m]ons, of New York City, one of Brown's lieutenants, at a public meeting held in Shiloh Presbyterian Church, Lombard Street, Philadelphia, made a speech in which he commended the Negroes of Philadelphia for organizing the military company and stated there was a grand project afoot to invade the South with an army of armed Northern Negroes and free the slaves. Simmons called for recruits for this invading army from the Negroes of Philadelphia." Unbeknownst to most members of the audience, one of their number included Brown himself, who was sitting there shocked as he heard Simmons utterly destroying any surprise element in his carefully hatched plans.

Later that night, Johnson said he was roused from his bed and summoned to an urgent meeting of top antislavery leaders in Philadelphia. He arrived to find Frederick Douglass and about a dozen others, including a wiry old man he didn't recognize. Somebody told him it was John Brown. "I thought Brown, of whom I had heard before, a most striking man in appearance and I was surprised to see that Douglass, who always took the lead, seemed to look up and defer to him," Johnson later wrote. "John Brown spoke of his great project and said that Si[m]mons' speech had ruined all his plans, but something should be done to offset the effect of the publication of Si[m]mons' incendiary utterances in the newspapers." Efforts were made to mend the mischief, but the damage had been done. According to Johnson, the government and the slaveholders had been placed on alert and Brown's invasion was doomed from the start.

In his autobiography, Johnson also claimed that he was present at another meeting held at the Philadelphia home of Thomas Dorsey, a leader of the city's antislavery movement. Douglass and John Brown were also there. Brown was accompanied by one of his men, Captain Aaron Stevens. "He told us that he was about to make a raid in Virginia," Johnson later remembered. "But, said he, it will be a failure. Our little band will be but the forlorn hope of what might have been a grand expedition, but blood will be shed or the bonds of the colored men will never be broken." Douglass presented a list of colored men from Philadelphia whom he said were willing to join Brown's raid. Upon examining the likely recruits, Brown turned to Johnson and asked, "Are you married?" Johnson replied he'd been married seven years.

"Have you children?" the old man asked. Johnson replied that he had not, but expected to be a father in a few weeks.

"Then you can't go," he said with a sad smile. Johnson later recalled, "I did not go, but would have done so if I could."[10]

On the evening of October 16, 1859, John Brown and his twenty-one-man Army of Liberation, made up of whites and blacks, launched their raid on Harpers Ferry (located about fifty-five miles from the nation's capital and less than fifty miles north of Culpeper). Brown's band quickly seized several hostages, including Colonel Lewis Washington, the great-grand-nephew of George Washington, and Brown personally took control of the founding father's precious sword as a further symbol of his liberationist goals. But just as Douglass and others had warned, only a few slaves in the vicinity joined in the uprising, and Brown and his men were soon cornered in the arsenal's engine house. An alert resident telegraphed warnings to the authorities in Virginia and Washington, prompting President James Buchanan to immediately dispatch a force of U.S. Marines under Colonel Robert E. Lee and J. E. B. Stuart. After the brief shootout, ten raiders, including two of Brown's sons, ended up dead; seven, including Brown and Shields Green, had been captured, and five had escaped.[11] Angry whites mutilated the slain body of Dangerfield Newby and left the bloody corpse lying in the gutter for dogs to eat. The vigilantes also had to be restrained from lynching the dazed survivors from the nearest tree.

The bloodshed proved to be only the first response to the attempted insurrection. Within hours, the authorities raided Brown's former safe house in Maryland to find bushels of incriminating documents, including voluminous letters between Brown and dozens of radical abolitionists. Soon the attention focused on a core group of financial backers called the "Secret Six"—Gerrit Smith, Reverend Thomas Wentworth Higginson, Theodore Parker, George Luther Stearns, Samuel Gridley Howe, and Franklin Sanborn—all of them illustrious Northerners, men of letters and high standing in their communities, who apparently had supported Brown's plot. But in fact there were many more than six prominent individuals who faced possible prosecution. Contents of some of their communiqués started appearing in the newspapers, causing a panic throughout the abolitionist community. Many of Brown's contacts burned any records or correspondence that might implicate them in the conspiracy and William Still quickly hid his Underground Railroad records in a church loft. Several plotters fled the country, and Gerrit Smith's family had him committed to the Utica State Hospital for treatment, possibly to avoid arrest.[12] Brooklyn's Reverend James Gloucester hurriedly moved with his wife to Troy, fearing that he too might become entangled in Brown's demise.

In Virginia, an editorial in the *Richmond Enquirer* condemned the federal government for not protecting the institution of slavery, and claimed that the problem went deeper than the attempted insurrection at Harpers Ferry, to a failure to properly enforce the Fugitive Slave Law. Brown, fugitive slaves, and the Underground Railroad were all seen as related. "Non-intervention has practically liberated the slaves of one entire tier of counties in Virginia," the editor roared. The nation's failure to uphold the Fugitive Slave Law, he wrote, "poisons the very life-blood of slavery in Virginia, and unless arrested, will eat, like a loathsome cancer, into the very vitals of Southern slavery."[13]

At first, the public reaction to Brown's action was uniformly critical in the North as well. The press condemned him as an insane fanatic and even many antislavery leaders scorned his resort to violence. But blacks were astonished by Brown's commitment to their cause. Radical white abolitionists privately applauded Brown's action. James Redpath and some other hard-line supporters considered mounting a jailbreak. Ralph Waldo Emerson began exploring a possible clemency plea to Governor Henry Wise. But Brown, who somehow had survived his injuries, refused to cooperate with anyone who was seeking leniency. He said he didn't wish to cause any trouble for his kind jailer, John Avis.[14]

Starting in late October, Henry David Thoreau, the author of the great "Essay on the Duty of Civil Disobedience" and other works, stepped forward to publicly defend Brown's actions.[15] "I hear many condemn these men because they were so few," said Thoreau. "When were the good and the brave ever in a majority? . . . He is not Old Brown any longer; he is an angel of light."[16] Then Emerson, whose voice as America's leading intellectual carried special weight, also joined in, calling Brown a saint and comparing him to Christ.[17] Hundreds of persons wrote admiring letters to Brown and dozens of visitors flocked to the jail in an effort to see their newfound hero. A Boston-based sculptor, Edwin A. Brackett, sat outside Brown's cell making sketches he would later use for a haunting marble bust.[18]

Brown was charged with conspiracy to incite a slave insurrection, treason against the Commonwealth of Virginia, and first-degree murder. His trial had all of the earmarks of a backwoods tribunal, until he stood up after his conviction and delivered remarks that Emerson later called the greatest American speech ever made to that point. "Had I so interfered in behalf of the rich, the powerful, the intelligent, the so-called great, or in behalf of any of their friends," said Brown, "it would have been all right. Every man in this Court would have deemed it an act worthy of reward rather than punishment. . . . Now, if it is deemed necessary that I should forfeit my life for the furtherance of the ends of justice, and mingle my blood further with the blood of millions in this slave country whose rights are disregarded by wicked, cruel, and unjust enactments, I say, let it be done."[19]

Brown's hanging on December 2, 1859, at Charles Town became a national event—the first such execution case in American history, but not the last. Many people, North and South, celebrated the occasion. En route to the gallows, the unrepentant abolitionist passed a folded note to one of his captors that said, "I John Brown am now quite certain that the crimes of this guilty, land: will never be purged away; but with Blood. I had as I now think: vainly flattered myself that without very much bloodshed; it might be done."[20] His body swung and dangled from the gallows for several minutes until the officer in charge called out, "So perish all such enemies of Virginia! All such enemies of the Union! All such foes of the human race!"[21]

Poet Henry Wordsworth Longfellow wrote in his diary: "This will be a great day in our history; the date of a new Revolution—quite as much needed as the old one."[22] Public prayer meetings were held throughout the Northeast and Middle West, drawing many Negroes and whites donning black armbands. New York's governor ordered a 100–gun salute that echoed seven miles away, where mourners had packed Troy's Liberty Street Church to hear Reverend Gloucester commemorate Brown's sacrifice.[23] The *Troy Daily Arena* later reported, "The heavens hung out a black flag yesterday—even the sky was Africanized. Dull and sombre clouds, weeping with rain, obscured the light of day and cast a gloom upon the very air."[24]

America's deep preoccupation with John Brown's body was also just beginning. Virginia authorities permitted Brown's widow, Mary, to remove his corpse for burial, but the remains of two of her sons—Oliver and Watson—were withheld for dissection. She found her husband's face had turned so deep a crimson it was almost black. At Philadelphia, enraged medical students broke up a public prayer meeting and gangs of white toughs prowled the streets looking for Brown sympathizers. The night of the execution, as the train bearing Brown's body and some of his supporters stopped at the depot to allow an undertaker to do his work, one of the young black men appointed to guard the corpse was William Henry Johnson, the Philadelphia black self-defense enthusiast who had met Brown with Douglass the previous summer. "I laid my hand on his upturned brow," Johnson would later recall, "and in that presence, I registered a vow never to be false to my God, my country or my race."[25] After Philadelphia's mayor ordered them to leave the city to avoid a riot, some of the widow's protectors led her to safety while others sent away an empty hearse to draw off some of the mob so they could transfer the real casket to a furniture car that took it to the Walnut Street Wharf. At 2:30 p.m. the body was slipped safely out of Philadelphia by boat, bound for Amboy and then New York, in the charge of Reverend J. Miller McKim of the Philadelphia Vigilance Committee, while Mary followed later in another train.[26]

More threats in New York required the abolitionists to take elaborate precautions. On Saturday night McKim arranged to have the body snuck into Manhattan by boat and brought to an undertaker, who removed it from its wooden shipping crate, dressed and iced it to improve its looks, and put it into a special "northern" casket to continue its journey north by rail. For added protection, Brown's body lay inside a steel container that was encased by a simple pine box.

On December 5, John Brown's body reached Troy by the 2 p.m. train, accompanied by Mary; her youngest son, McKim; Wendell Phillips, the famous abolitionist orator from Boston; a few other supporters; and numerous reporters.[27] The itinerary called for the party to make a brief stopover where Captain Brown had often visited as he had shuttled back and forth between North Elba.

Word of their scheduled arrival spread fast and soon a huge crowd flocked to the scene. Brown had many supporters in Troy, and plenty of detractors too. Southern students from the university shook their fists and cotton merchants sneered at the welcoming committee that was gathering to greet their martyred hero. The throng included a large segment of the black population, many of the city's white civic leaders, and curiosity seekers. Also present were scores of journalists, among them an editor with strong antislavery leanings, Charles MacArthur, and one of his employees, Horatio Averill, who had been horrified by what John Brown had done. Given his Underground Railroad contacts and wood-hauling duties between Sand Lake and Troy, there is a good chance that Charles Nalle was also there to witness the historic occasion.

As soon as the train arrived, a delegation of the colored people stood with bowed heads, awaiting the black-clad widow. They watched as Mary Brown parted her veil, revealing some of her sad, drawn face so lined with suffering; then she came down from the train and walked calmly and steadily past them through the icy slush, astonishing everyone by her strength of nerve. John Brown had recommended the American House at Third and Fulton as a suitable place for his widow to stop on her journey home. Besides being a temperance hotel, it was the place where their son, Oliver, had taken his final leave of his new bride just before setting off to meet his fate at Harpers Ferry. The hotel owner proudly pointed to several pages in his register where her illustrious husband had signed his name.[28]

Meanwhile, back at Union Station, onlookers gasped as attendants carried the heavy pine box into the depot and put it on display in a roped-off section of the lobby. The family wanted it to remain there to allow admirers to pay their respects. Passions ran high and some mourners wailed or shouted. After excited relic-seekers took to slicing off slivers from the box, a squadron of policemen removed the box with the body inside to a glass-enclosed baggage room, so that Brown's party could continue to display it without danger of mutilation.

Hours later, Mary Brown and her escort, along with the casket containing her martyred husband's remains, resumed their journey. That night and next morning they headed up the Troy and Boston Road, through Saratoga, Burlington, Rutland, and Vergennes, over to Otter Creek, Westport, and Elizabethtown. Next morning the funeral party resumed their labors, trudging through the slush and snow until in the pitch black they reached North Elba. At Brown's desolate farm, people holding lanterns rushed out to greet them and there were many anguished cries and embraces.[29]

The next morning, abolitionist Wendell Phillips, his ruddy face even pinker from the cold and the surge of his emotion, delivered a bitter eulogy. "John Brown violated the law," he said. But "George Washington, had he been caught before 1783, would have died on the gibbet, for breaking the laws of his sovereign. . . . It is honorable then to break bad laws, and such lawbreaking history God loves and blesses!"[30]

Conducting correspondence through the U.S. mails was difficult and dangerous for a fugitive slave, even more so in the hysterical months following Harpers Ferry. Anything put down on paper could prove incriminating if it fell into the wrong hands, so any fugitive or fugitive's correspondent had to be especially careful not to inadvertently divulge any secrets. Letters often had to be sent through intermediaries and sometimes rely on multiple postings to throw the slave catchers off track. Even in calmer times, it was an unwieldy and time-consuming way to communicate.[1]

As soon as he was able, Charles set out to pursue one of his foremost goals, learning how to read and write, something that as a slave had always been barred to him. Charles was fortunate to be working around fine schools, sheltered under the wing of a good teacher, and surrounded by a small community of highly literate persons, all of which increased his appetite for literacy. But unfortunately, it was through this pursuit of education that he would suffer a major setback. For in his hunger to learn to read and write, his need to rely on Crosby to help him with his personal correspondence, and his efforts to communicate with his family, he came to the attention of someone who was not inclined to be sympathetic to his plight—someone who was willing and eager to hold it all against him.

Charles's Judas was Horatio F. Averill, the former attaché for the *Budget* newspaper who had been among those witnessing Brown's funeral party in Troy. Averill, who was twenty-five years old, came from an old Sand Lake family and counted himself as a fifth-generation descendant of a Massachusetts Puritan. The Averills lived across the street from the Gregorys and next door to the Female Seminary, which was convenient for his twin sisters, Ellen and Emily, four years his junior, who taught pupils at the academy under Minot Crosby. His family also had connections to Scram's Collegiate Institute where Charles was employed. Their kid brother, James, aged thirteen, was a pupil there and the Averills had at least two boarders in their household who were associated with the school—Mrs. Margaret Ecker of Georgia and her six-year-old son, who were staying in the area while the older Ecker boy attended the academy.[2] The Averills must have encountered Charles about that vicinity on numerous occasions, as they occupied virtually the same spot.

Horatio had graduated from Scram's before going on to study law in Troy under David L. Seymour and Judge Jeremiah Romeyn. Since his admission to the bar four years earlier, however, he had suffered a series of setbacks. For a time he practiced law on Broadway in New York for the firm of Clark and Rapals, but he had left there under a cloud, having been accused of embezzlement. Even more recently—since viewing Brown's casket—he had been fired from the newspaper, so that presently he was unemployed and needed money. Like his father, a former army major turned tavern keeper, Horatio was a staunch Democrat. He was also a supporter of the Fugitive Slave Law.[3]

The basis for the treachery occurred as Charles was trying to learn to read and write at the school and Crosby was helping him to compose some letters. During one of their reading and writing sessions, Horatio Averill (or possibly one of his siblings) intercepted or overheard the contents of one of Charles's private letters intended for his family. Thus he discovered that the newcomer's true identity was that of Charles Nalle, a fugitive slave, who was owned by Blucher Hansbrough, of Cole's Hill in Culpeper, Virginia. Averill sent a message to Hansbrough, sharing some of this intelligence and advising him that if he wanted to retrieve his runaway slave, he should retain Horatio F. Averill as his counsel, for Averill knew the lay of the land in that area and could arrange a successful apprehension.[4]

Whether at that time Charles sensed something was wrong, or whether any of the letters in question already had referred to what he was about to do, is unclear, but in early spring of 1860, shortly after the roads had become passable, Charles left quiet Sand Lake and moved to neighboring Troy, about fifteen miles away. By then he had been a fugitive for about seventeen months and may have come to expect that Hansbrough's desire to track him down had waned.[5]

Troy at that time was one of the richest cities in the United States. Known as the "city of iron" for Henry Burden's massive ironworks with its work force of mostly Irish laborers, Troy also hosted a large textile industry and garment trade with mills and assembly plants, printing presses, coach-making factories, and other assorted businesses.[6] Although most residents were white and foreign-born, blacks numbered 611 in a total population of 39,235—which was still very white compared to Culpeper but an improvement from what Charles had encountered in Sand Lake.[7] He must have been happy to be back among more people of color, especially because the city offered much more economic opportunity, cultural activities, and chances for mobility.

Parts of the black community there were downright exciting, a black oasis. Some black Trojans were active in the Underground Railroad, the abolitionist movement, and the cause of Negro rights, gaining a reputation as a vital and cohesive group. Over the years Troy had hosted several important Negro meetings such as the pathbreaking National Convention of Colored People and Their Friends that had gathered in town in 1847.[8] In September 1855, a state convention of white and black New Yorkers had convened there to organize opposition to the state's $250 property qualification that barred so many Negroes from voting. Frederick Douglass and Jermain W. Loguen were among those attending. The proceedings were chaired by Troy's most prominent and highly respected Negro, William Rich.

Rich, who was about fifty-eight years old, was originally from Worcester and had grown up as a household servant to a former Massachusetts governor. In his twenties he had served as an outrider on General Lafayette's coach when the marquis toured New England. Then he had come to Troy and started a high-class barber salon with baths at Troy House, a fashionable five-story hotel located on First Street at the corner of River Street. For many years the shop served as the headquarters of the Underground Railroad in Troy. Rich was its superintendent and money manager, but recently had let some others take more of a leadership role. Although still a bachelor, he continued to lead the way in organizing public education for blacks, having helped to pioneer the school for youngsters and adults in the basement of the Liberty Street Church. He also ran the most fashionable catering business north of New York.[9] But he was best known as the city's leading black political leader.[10]

Peter F. Baltimore, aged thirty, was one of Rich's closest friends and partners in his tonsorial resort. Baltimore's father Samuel had fought in the American Revolution as a slave, then later run away from bondage after his master reneged on his promise to free him. Peter had learned the barber's trade from his brother William and grown up to become an omnivorous reader. In his teens he had studied under the incomparable Reverend Henry Highland Garnet, who encouraged him to develop his remarkable ability with language, including ancient Greek and Latin. Impeccably mannered, Baltimore came off as refined and sophisticated. He was a master conversationalist and considered so well versed in English literature that visiting intellectuals, black and white, flocked to his literary salon to spend hours in his chair. Some of his black abolitionist friends included Frederick Douglass, Robert Purvis, and Charles Reasons.[11] The shop's constant comings and goings of clientele helped to mask its operation as the headquarters and hub of Troy's Underground Railroad.

Another associate of Henry, Rich, and Baltimore in the Vigilance Committee was John H. Hooper, aged forty-nine, a fugitive slave from Maryland's Eastern Shore, who had grown up in bondage with Frederick Douglass.[12] Hooper lived with his wife, Mary, aged forty-six, and other relatives in a two-story brick house at 153 Second Street, two blocks from the Liberty Street Church. John worked as a laborer and Mary was a washerwoman. He had been in Troy since 1844 and for much of that time had assisted the Underground Railroad.[13] Harriet Tubman was one of his cousins.

Tubman also had other relatives in Troy. She had especially deep connections to the Bowleys. William J. Bowley had been in the city since 1840. John Bowley was married to her niece, Kessiah, whom they had rescued, and the two had lived for a time with Tubman's brother Ben in Chatham, Canada West, back when Benjamin Drew interviewed Harriet.[14] In 1850 John Bowley had been a free Negro shipyard worker in Cambridge, Maryland, when he rescued his wife and children from a slave auction and got them away in a small boat to Baltimore, after which Tubman guided them to Philadelphia in her first rescue mission.[15] Some of Tubman's other close contacts in the Troy area included Anthony and Lucy Hooper, William and Margaret Jones, and Stephen Myers.[16] In May 1856 one of Tubman's rescues had brought her into Still's office in Philadelphia at about the same time as Lewis and Peter Burrell.[17] She often passed through Troy and Albany on her way back and forth between the South and her home in Auburn or Canada. Members of the underground knew her as "Moses."

Troy's Vigilance Committee handled fewer fugitives than Albany's, but its members openly thanked the public "for the assistance so promptly rendered, in affording shelter, food and means, whereby they were able to make glad the hearts of the afflicted." For the year closing September 15, 1857, the committee reported having helped fifty-five persons who had passed through, at a cost of $125 for their passage.[18] Years later, another former supporter wrote: "Fugitives from slavery always traveled from Troy to Canada with perfect safety—whether by steamboat and Lake Champlain—by [the two-leveled railroad] suspension bridge [at Rouse's Point]. When they reached Troy they only needed money to pay their fare for the rest of their voyage."[19]

Thanks to the Underground Railroad, Charles found excellent new lodging in Troy with William Henry, a fifty-six-year-old mulatto from North Carolina who was a top member of the Vigilance Committee and a successful Negro businessman. Boarding was common in the North and often carried with it many other advantages. Some hosts helped their boarders find employment, church connections, and community. They offered protection and often helped fugitives ease some of their loneliness and fears. Boarders received shelter, food, and sometimes clothing.[20] It seemed that Charles could not have landed in a better situation.

William Henry kept his popular grocery store at the corner of Franklin and Division streets, only a block or so away from the Liberty Street Presbyterian Church that served as the nerve center, school, and spiritual base for Troy's black community. Henry had been at that location for several years and his involvement in the Underground Railroad was public knowledge. Living with him in the cramped space above the store were his wife Ann, forty-five, who was originally from Pennsylvania, and their children, William, aged thirteen, and Ann, who was ten years old. Like Willis Madden back in Virginia, Henry too was a major player in his local community, and his store was a favorite meeting place and purveyor of all kinds of news for blacks and whites alike.[21]

One of Troy's claims to fame was that it had been the home stomping ground of Reverend Henry Highland Garnet, a former Maryland slave whom many considered the nation's greatest Negro orator and the most militant black man in America. From 1839 to 1848 he had headed the Liberty Street Presbyterian Church for blacks, a tiny framed white house that offered in its basement the city's first school for Negro children and adults.[22] Garnet had given his most famous speech at the National Convention of Colored Citizens in Buffalo in 1843, urging America's slaves to act boldly, even forcibly, to gain their own freedom. "Your condition does not absolve you from your moral obligation," he told them. "You had far better all die—*die immediately*, than live as slaves. . . . Let your motto be resistance! *resistance!* RESISTANCE!"[23] His appearance was made all the more powerful by the fact that he was a fugitive slave with a peg leg. He was somebody who practiced what he preached and his life was a living proof of black power. Although the Buffalo convention ultimately voted down Garnet's position by a margin of one vote, his militant message had an electrifying effect on Northern blacks for many years to come. Some of Garnet's positions alarmed many whites. One night as he was assisting a group of congregants in his Liberty Street Church, a white mob burst in and dragged him out into the street. They beat him and stole his crutch, spit on him, and left him moaning in the gutter. He had to crawl more than two blocks to get home.[24] A few years later, Garnet attracted more notoriety when he issued a second edition of *David Walker's Appeal to the Colored Citizens of the World*, which slaveholders considered the most incendiary Negro incitement for servile rebellion ever written, and appended his own "Address to the Slaves of the United States." As a result he received many death threats.[25]

While in Troy, Garnet had stayed active in the Underground Railroad, serving as a member of the executive committee of the Eastern New York Anti-Slavery Society.[26] Later it was Garnet and Loguen who had first recommended John Brown to their colleague Frederick Douglass.[27] John Brown had taken some of his inspiration from Garnet, coming away from a meeting with him with a strong belief that Northern blacks would decide to fight for freedom when the time came. When Brown was hanged, Garnet had hailed him as a martyr.[28] Black people around Troy still honored Garnet as their greatest champion.[29]

Garnet's white mentor in Troy, the Reverend Nathan S. S. Beman, was also nationally known for his antislavery activities, and his influence throughout the region was also very great. Beman long had served as pastor of the First Presbyterian Church and president of Troy's university, garnering strong popular approval from throughout the Northern states as a pillar of Christian ethics.[30] But Southerners ridiculed him based on his tempestuous estrangement from his second wife, Caroline Bird Yancey of Georgia, and his past sale of three of her slaves while he was in Georgia.[31]

Starting in the late 1830s, Beman had championed the American Anti-Slavery Society and often hosted many of the leading abolitionist speakers and meetings who visited Troy. Along the way he stood up to several mobs, showing that he wasn't somebody to run away from a fight. He condemned slavery as "an immense evil," and called the nation's capital "the central mart of the traffic in human flesh." Beman took his abolitionist crusade to congregations, classrooms, public podiums, and the general assemblies of the Presbyterian Church.[32] Among Troy's blacks he was best known for starting their Liberty Street Church and recruiting a young former slave of great intellectual and spiritual promise, Garnet, to study theology under his guidance and later become its first pastor. Beman was also friendly with William Rich and Peter Baltimore. He boarded downtown at Troy House, just above their hair salon that served as headquarters of the Underground Railroad.

Nobody hated Beman more than his wife's eldest biological son, and his stepson, William Lowndes Yancey. After attending nearby Williams College, Yancey relocated to Alabama where he became a leading champion of slavery. Hot-tempered and outspoken, he gained a reputation as one of the South's fieriest orators against the North, and he often advocated the reinstatement of the African slave trade, expansion of slavery in the territories, states' rights, and secession of the South from the Union.[33] Over time, the rift between Yancey and Beman publicly grew more acrimonious over slavery.

In November 1858, around the time of Charles Nalle's arrival from Virginia, and in response to the Supreme Court's *Dred Scott* decision, Beman rose to the pulpit for his annual Thanksgiving message. He couldn't contain his anger over what America had become. "Democracy and slavery—what a brotherhood!" he exclaimed. Glaring down from his elevated pulpit, the old man threw up his hands in disgust. "This must be a spurious democracy," he said. "What is the bud worth when the kernel is gone, and nothing but the shell is left. Away then with this last and most loathsome phrase of political hypocrisy! It would put Benedict Arnold to the blush—it would lead Judas Iscariot to cast down thirty pieces of silver and go hang himself!"[34]

Charles's good fortune reached new heights when one of Troy's wealthiest and most powerful citizens, Uri Gilbert, invited him to come to his place of business to interview for a possible coachman's position for his wife. (Mrs. Gilbert was still recovering from serious injuries sustained in a carriage accident.) Friends directed the former Virginia slave to the industrialist's immense factory located just across the river from Troy, on tiny Green Island in West Troy. The entrance to the Gilbert Car Manufacturing Company swarmed with carriages and wagons of every description. Gilbert's manufactory was a colossus that appeared more like a small city: smokestacks six or seven stories tall stood over its huge expanse; enormous windowed brick buildings, taller than most city apartment houses, stretched afar on each side, their long red rooftops lined with chimneys that poured smoke far into the sky. Rail lines connected it to the river, the canal, and the ocean, allowing Gilbert to ship his goods as far away as Cuba, South America, and Australia. His exquisitely appointed railcars were considered some of the finest in the world, and one of his company's most ingenious approaches was to make its parts in uniform size so they could easily be replaced when they became damaged or broken.

Gilbert himself was a gentleman about fifty years old, extremely sharp and vigorous. He wore a well-tailored suit that showed off his fine physique and a neatly trimmed gray beard that made him look like a New England sea captain. His father, an Episcopalian minister, was descended from some of Connecticut's early settlers, but his mother had been raised in slavery-dominated Savannah, Georgia. At age fifteen he had become apprenticed to Troy's Orsamus Eaton, fifteen years his senior, a brilliant mechanical engineer who already was becoming known as one of America's finest carriage makers and scientists, the father of American geology.[35] Eaton had established his carriage factory in Troy and he picked Gilbert as his protégé. As Gilbert grew in wealth and prominence, he devoted more of his time to other commercial interests and civic affairs: the Rensselaer Polytechnic Institute, the United States Bank, Emma Willard's Troy Female Seminary, the Whig Party, and, more recently, the Republican Party. He was a pillar of the community—not someone to trifle with.

The interview began abruptly when Gilbert looked up from the letter of recommendation that Charles had brought. The industrialist surveyed him closely, then asked, without any expression, a most penetrating question, "Are you a Negro?"

Charles was so taken aback by it, he didn't know how or on what level to respond. It was, after all, the central and defining characteristic of his life, even if it was not always obvious in his appearance. Finally he pulled himself together and managed to reply, "Well, sir, I suppose so."

Gilbert nodded and smiled. He explained that his wife needed a careful driver, for their last coachman had allowed her to be caught in a terrible accident. Charles expressed regret and assured him he was a very experienced driver. They also established that Charles was a family man with a wife and children in Columbia, Pennsylvania, who hoped to be able to reunite with them soon.

"Do you partake in alcoholic spirits?" Gilbert asked him.

Charles assured him he did not. This too apparently satisfied Gilbert, for he nodded approvingly and asked where Charles resided. The servant replied that he lived with William Henry and Gilbert responded that that was only a few blocks away from his house. They agreed that Charles would work as a coachman and groom for Mrs. Gilbert, six days a week, and at a good salary.[36] For Charles this represented a dream come true, and he could not have been happier when he left to tell his friends.

Trojans proudly referred to their city as the "birthplace of Uncle Sam," after a local meatpacker who had furnished supplies to the War Department in the War of 1812.[37] Uncle Sam already had become a national symbol for the United States government. A city with such a cozy relationship to federal power may not have seemed the best place for a fugitive slave to hide. Yet Charles's new life was going better than he could have imagined was possible. He had found a decent place to live, in an exciting city full of interesting and supportive people, he had landed lucrative employment doing something he liked, and now he would be exposed to all sorts of bright opportunities. All this meant that he would soon be able to reunite with Kitty and the children, thereby attaining the prize he had escaped for in the first place.

Five months after Brown's hanging, Harpers Ferry continued to fan the flames between the abolitionist movement and the slave power, thereby putting more pressure on the federal government to crack down on the Underground Railroad and other radical abolitionists.

On April 3, 1860, federal marshals forced their way into the Concord, Massachusetts, home of Franklin B. Sanborn, the young transcendentalist schoolmaster who had been identified as one of the Secret Six that had aided John Brown, and they attempted to arrest him on behalf of the U.S. Senate. Sanborn's sister and neighbors helped him ward them off until the police came, while Sanborn's lawyer hurried over to the judge's nearby house to obtain a writ of personal replevin.[1] Afterward, Sanborn convinced a state judge that marshals lacked legal authority to arrest him, and he was freed.[2] For once it seemed that abolitionists and the Underground Railroad had prevailed over the slavocracy, and abolitionists celebrated.

Back in Virginia, however, anger over the latest Northern assaults on slavery was becoming more heated. So when Blucher Hansbrough received a letter, postmarked from New York, about his missing slave Charles, he must have felt a call of sectional duty. It informed him that a local lawyer he did not know, named Horatio F. Averill, of Sand Lake, New York, had been suggested as someone who could help him to reclaim his lost property. Once he had received the news, Hansbrough started taking the necessary steps to get back his runaway slave. Knowing he had to move fast, he wrote back to Averill by telegram, offering to retain him as counsel in the case.

First thing on April 20, Hansbrough also hired a slave catcher to go and get him. Slave catchers were professional trackers and manhunters who knew how to run down their prey. They usually charged a set fee of several dollars per day, plus a few cents for every mile they traveled, plus expenses. Some charged extra for the whipping they administered back home, unless the master did the whipping himself. Many agents worked for a company, but others operated on their own.[3] In this case, with two slaves who were apparently living in upstate New York, the job appeared relatively simple, but one never knew. Hansbrough's choice, Henry J. "Jack" Wale, was an experienced slave catcher. He had done business with Wale before, most recently to escort Charles's brother to the Richmond slave market, and they had known each other all their lives. Wale had also known Charles "ever since he was a little boy."[4] Jack was favored among whites for his firmness and cunning, although his work manner could be crude and vulgar. Negroes hated him for his brutality and cruelty. Willis Madden was one of those who especially despised him. The previous spring, Madden had learned that his youngest daughter, Maria, was pregnant by Wale, and Willis tried to convince her to go away to live with relatives in the Shenandoah Valley, but she wouldn't leave. Instead, she stayed involved with Wale and kept in the area. On January 26, 1860, Maria gave birth to a son, whom she named Thomas Obed Madden. Wale was a slave trader, which was the vilest thing anyone could be as far as Willis and most blacks were concerned. He had also left the poor girl bearing a child that Wale would neither acknowledge nor support, which mortified Willis.[5] But it didn't seem to bother Wale or Hansbrough. When it came to handling a rebellious slave, Blucher knew he could count on good old Jack to be as rough as the situation required. To assist him in grabbing Jim Banks as well, Wale would bring along another experienced bounty hunter, William L. Parr, another rough fellow, who kept a dry goods store in nearby Richardsville. If anybody could get the job done, they would.

Hansbrough and his hirelings knew that under the provisions of the Fugitive Slave Act of 1850, any master who was owed service or labor was legally entitled to pursue and reclaim his fugitive, either by procuring a proper warrant or by seizing and arresting such fugitive without process, and then taking him before the proper court, judge, or commissioner, whose duty was to hear and determine the case of such claimants in a summary manner. All that was required was that "satisfactory proof" be made, by deposition or affidavit, and legally certified, to prove the identity of the alleged fugitive slave, that he did in fact owe service or labor to the person or persons claiming him or her, and that said person had escaped. In reclaiming his slave, a master or his agent or attorney could use "such reasonable force and restraint as may be necessary, under the circumstances of the case, to take and remove such fugitive person back to the State or Territory whence he or she may have escaped as aforesaid." And the law strictly prohibited anyone from molesting the slave catcher or trying to prevent the fugitive slave's return to his owner.[6] Hence, Wale and Parr expected to have the law on their side—not to mention the power of the federal government, with all of the power and authority that slavery represented.

Although it was then a Saturday, Hansbrough managed to get his lawyer and notary public, Fayette M. Latham, to prepare the necessary paperwork, attesting that he had a clue to the whereabouts of the two runaway slaves, Charles Nalle and Jim Banks.[7] Such documentation would be necessary in the event the slave catchers sought to enlist the U.S. commissioner and federal marshal to enforce the Fugitive Slave Law. In his sworn statement, Hansbrough said he had owned Charles Nalle for about eighteen years. Before that, his father had owned Charles until giving himself the title as a gift. The slave had continued in his possession until the 15th day of October 1858, when he'd escaped, and he hadn't seen him since, although he had certainly searched. Now he had cause to believe his servant was illegally living in New York state. To aid in the identification, Blucher specified, "the slave Charles, is about 32 [sic] years of age, is a mulatto, is about 5 feet 8 or 9 inches high as well as I can now state, without having ever measured him; has a bushy head of black hair, with black eyes and a long and prominent nose; and has a scar or seam on the first joint of the middle or large finger of his left hand, produced by the cutting of his finger with a hatchet."[8]

Hansbrough also made oath before William Stout, a local justice of the peace in Culpeper and his neighbor of many years who lived about a mile from Cole's Hill. Stout certified that he too had known the slave Charles, sometimes known as Charles Nalle, for about eight years. He added that Charles was the son of a slave woman named Lucy, who was also the property of Blucher Hansbrough. Stout as well described the runaway slave in question as about thirty to thirty-five years of age, a mulatto about five feet nine or ten inches high, with long bushy black hair.[9] As further proof, Hansbrough obtained an additional affidavit from Alfred L. Ashby, another close friend who also was a justice of the peace living about two miles away from Cole's Hill. Ashby attested he had known a slave named Charles, sometimes called Charles Nalle, for fifteen years or more. His description was the same as Stout's.[10] On advice of counsel, Hansbrough obtained an embossed certificate from Fayette Mauzy, the Culpeper clerk, and signed by Edward A. Freeman, the presiding justice of the peace for the court of Culpeper, containing other historical background.

Wale made an affidavit stating that he knew Hansbrough, Stout, Ashby, and Charles, and was prepared to reclaim him as a fugitive slave.[11]

Hansbrough gave the stack of documents to Wale and telegraphed ahead to alert his Northern contacts of their plans. Then he began to contemplate exactly what he'd do to Charles when he was brought back.

As soon as Wale and Parr had gathered all the necessary documents for convincing the federal authorities, they finalized their travel plans, packed their guns and other hardware, and boarded the train at Brandy Station, bound for New York City and beyond.

Miles Beach was only twenty-seven years old, but he was considered one of Troy's most prominent up-and-coming lawyers and officeholders, cast in the same mold as his distinguished father and law partner, William A. Beach.[12] As loyal stalwarts of the Democratic Party that was then in power at the city and federal level, the team enjoyed some of the finer fruits of patronage. Besides getting himself elected as Eighth Ward alderman representing one of the city's most fashionable downtown districts, young Beach had been appointed by the chief justice of the United States Supreme Court to serve in one of the region's few federal judicial posts.[13] Mainly titular and prestigious in nature, the position of United States commissioner required few official duties other than administration of a seldom-invoked federal law, thereby enabling Beach to devote most of his time to his private practice and political activities, the latter of which were already commanding much of his attention because of the Democratic Party convention down in Charleston and the fast-approaching presidential election. Although neither father nor son had made the trip South this time, they were closely following every new partisan development, particularly the struggle that was raging over the party's slavery platform.

However, when young Beach arrived at his Washington Place residence Wednesday evening, he discovered that issues of slavery's expansion, states' rights, and sectional divisions had suddenly come home in a much more personal way. For besides his wife and children, and his father, he came face to face in the parlor with a rough-looking stranger who was waiting to see him—a bowing visitor from Virginia, whom the elder Beach introduced as Mr. Henry J. Wale, an agent for his law client, Mr. Blucher W. Hansbrough of Culpeper County, Virginia. Mr. Wale, he said, had come on legal business on behalf of Mr. Hansbrough, who was the owner of a fugitive slave who had been traced to Troy. Wale himself made clear in his Southern drawl that he was imposing upon the younger Mr. Beach at his private residence this evening to avoid attracting any undue attention, since he was appearing before "Your Honor" related to his capacity as U.S. commissioner. He explained that he had been sent to reclaim two fugitive slaves from Culpeper who were known to be in the vicinity. Jim was working as a shoemaker over in West Troy and the other, Charles, was residing above a nearby "colored grocery store" and was employed as a coachman for one Uri Gilbert, the wealthy manufacturer and Republican who lived just a few doors up the street. That very night, Wale said, he and his associate, Mr. Parr, had tracked their quarry to William Henry's place on Division Street, where they'd observed them through a window. But Wale and the others agreed it would be best to act according to law. Raising a fist-ful of official-looking papers, the Virginian said he'd brought all the required proofs to ensure the commissioner would issue the necessary process for the fugitive's arrest under the Fugitive Slave Law.

With his father acting as counsel for the plaintiff, Miles Beach assured his visitor that as long as he held the office of U.S. commissioner, he would fully perform his duties to the best of his ability. But he added that in doing so, he should require from him the most ample preliminary proofs called for by the law under which he was governed to act. Accordingly, Commissioner Beach instructed Wale that on the morning following he would be in his office—also his father's office—at the usual hour, nine o'clock, and his petitioner might if he pleased wait upon him there.

The following morning Wale did indeed appear at the law office of Commissioner Beach and the elder Mr. Beach, the latter of whom had been retained by Blucher Hansbrough. The documentation process proved so tedious, with so much attention to the particularity and accuracy in the preliminary proofs, that it was not until the afternoon that the commissioner announced he was satisfied by the evidence that his duty was plain.[14] He thereupon issued and sent out for delivery to the deputy U.S. marshal a warrant in the name of the president of the United States commanding him to arrest Charles Nalle, a "a colored person charged with being a fugitive from labor," and bring him before the U.S. commissioner.[15]

His courier didn't have far to go to deliver this warrant. The marshal's office was located in the post office, only one building away on the other side of First Street. Like the post of the U.S. commissioner, the office of deputy U.S. marshal in Troy was currently filled by a part-time patronage employee, a fellow Democrat, John L. Holmes. Holmes worked as a clerk at the post office and lived a few blocks away. The offices of U.S. marshals and deputy marshals were among the oldest posts of the federal government, having been created by the first Congress as part of the same legislation that established the federal judicial system. The marshals were given extensive authority to support the federal courts within their judicial districts and to carry out all lawful orders issued by judges, Congress, or the president. Marshals and their deputies served the subpoenas, summonses, writs, warrants, and other process issued by the federal courts, made all the federal arrests, and handled all the federal prisoners. They also disbursed the money. Marshals paid the fees and expenses of the court clerks, U.S. attorneys, jurors, and witnesses. They rented the courtrooms and jail space and hired the bailiffs, criers, and janitors They made sure the prisoners were present, the jurors were available, and the witnesses were on time. As the primary local representatives for the federal government within their districts, they took the national census every decade, and were now preparing to do so again in a couple of months. Indeed, anything that the federal government needed to do but lacked the means to carry out usually fell on their shoulders. They were also the ones designated to capture fugitive slaves.[16] Therefore, they could sometimes be extremely busy. Troy was located in the huge Northern District of New York that covered most of the state outside New York City and its immediate environs, stretching all the way north and west to Canada. But although the district contained the primary routes of the Underground Railroad and was always teeming with runaway slaves who were either passing through on their way to the border or residing somewhere in the region, enforcement of the Fugitive Slave Law was not something that Deputy Marshal Holmes was accustomed to doing or relished. At best, it was one of the more unpleasant duties he was expected to carry out.

Troy's fashionable private residential square known as Washington Park was laid out in 1840 on the model of London's Bloomsbury and Manhattan's Gramercy Park, and served as home to many of the city's wealthiest citizens—captains of industry, lawyers, physicians, and successful businessmen.[17] The compact but lovely park with its manicured lawns and gardens was enclosed by a stately wrought-iron fence, and lined on each side with a perfectly neat granite curb and cobblestone street, spacious sidewalks, ornate lampposts, and healthy, budding trees. On the south side of the park, ten substantial row houses with massive stoops and a common pediment stood in a line known as Washington Place, one of which, Number Two, served as the residence of William A. Beach, his son Miles Beach, and their wives and children.

The park's most elegant home stood at the center of the western side of the square on Second Street. In this magnificently proportioned three-story Renaissance-Revival Italianate-style brownstone mansion of more than thirty rooms lived industrialist Uri Gilbert and his family.[18] Besides the coach manufacturer and his wife, Frances, there were six children, Mr. Gilbert's eighty-four-year-old mother, and six uniformed maidservants of whom five had been born in Ireland.[19] William and Miles Beach and Deputy Marshal Holmes knew Gilbert well, although they didn't share his politics. They were relieved to learn he would out of town on business.

The next morning, Friday, April 27, 1860, had started dreary and cold, but by ten o'clock the sky had cleared and the sun was shining, promising a fine spring day. The local papers carried stories about developments at the Democratic National Convention in Charleston, where the New York delegation had caved in under pressure to allow the party to adopt a slave code in its platform.[20]

Charles Nalle had been sent on an errand to get some bread at George Holeur's fashionable bakery at 2 Hake's Block, at Fulton and Fifth streets, several blocks away.[21] He was sitting in the driver's seat of Mrs. Gilbert's fine personal coach, parked outside the bakery, holding the reins, when he was suddenly set upon from behind in two directions by two aggressive white men. As soon as he recognized one of them, he started to struggle furiously, for he realized it was Jack Wale from Stevensburg, the vile slave hunter whom Hansbrough must have hired. But before Charles could resist, Wale slapped handcuffs on his wrists and already was taking pleasure in telling him that these were the same set of handcuffs he had used to pinion the hands of Charles's youngest brother when he sold him south from the Richmond market after Charles had run off.[22] Almost simultaneously, the other man, who was wearing the bright yellow star of a deputy U.S. marshal, announced, "Charles Nalle, I hereby arrest you in the name of the United States of America!" With that, Wale and Marshal Holmes yanked him down from his perch and onto the sidewalk. Before Charles knew what was happening, he felt himself being dragged over the pavement. Bystanders along the way gawked and stepped out of the way.[23]

After a five-minute walk, the trio ended up at First and State streets, where his captors took him inside a three-story orange-and-white brick building with multiple arches, called the Mutual Bank Building, which dated from the 1830s or so. The ground floor housed the Bank of Troy, the city's biggest financial institution, where William A. Beach was one of its longtime directors. Beach and his son Miles had a law office with Levi Smith on the second floor. So did the customs collector and inspector, Francis L. Hagadorn; the editor of the *Troy Daily Budget* newspaper; and Rensselaer County judge Gilbert Robertson. The third floor was occupied by Apollo Lodge No. 49 of the Free and Accepted Masons, whose members included many of the city's leading white citizens.

Within a minute the three had trudged up the first set of stairs to the second-floor hallway and entered a law office, just as a clock was heard striking half-past noon. A clerk directed them inside a second room with large windows close to the floor that faced First Street and State Street. From one of them a viewer could glimpse fashionable Troy House across First and look down over the mostly empty sidewalks and streets. There already were several men waiting for them in the room. Charles recognized one of them as Thomas Parr, Wale's sidekick from Culpeper. Another, he was shocked to see, was his betrayer, none other than Horatio Averill from Sand Lake. The oldest gentleman, addressed as "Mr. Beach," appeared to be serving on behalf of Blucher Hansbrough. A younger man who looked like Beach's son was sitting behind a mahogany desk piled high with legal papers, in front of an American flag on the side; he was obviously the judge, for the others addressed him as "Your Honor" and "Commissioner." Besides Wale and the marshal, whom Charles had already met, there were a few others milling about.

Somebody said most of the paperwork was already completed. The rest was only a formality. All that was necessary was for them to go through a little examination, swear the owner's agents, Wale and Parr, and Averill, and then declare the Negro a fugitive slave, and order his return.[24] The commissioner quickly shuffled some papers and began his proceedings.[25] Averill helped to establish that the prisoner had spent much of the previous year in Sand Lake, where it had been learned through intercepted letters that his true identity was Charles Nalle, an escaped slave from Culpeper County, Virginia. Then Wale raised his right hand and read an affidavit saying he had reason to apprehend that "the said Charles Nalle will be rescued by force from his possession before he can be taken beyond the limits of the State of New York," and he prayed that "the officer arresting said Nalle may retain him in his custody and return him to the State of Virginia, whence he fled."[26]

Charles stood by, handcuffed and mute, still in a state of shock as he began to contemplate what was happening. He may not have understood the full import of Wale's statement, although he could see that it appeared to be regarded as another legal formality. Then the commissioner began dictating a lengthy certificate of rendition that was copied down by his clerk, recounting in detail everything that had been done under the law. In conclusion, Commissioner Beach decreed, "And I do therefore hereby authorize the said Henry J. Wale to take and remove the said Charles Nalle back to the said State of Virginia, whence he escaped as aforesaid, and to use such reasonable force and restraint as may be necessary under the circumstances for that purpose."[27] With that, the lawyers all shook hands and thanked and congratulated each other, thereby telling Charles that his fate was sealed.

Meanwhile, one of Gilbert's sons, thinking it strange that Charles had not returned from his errand, went next door from Holeur's to the house on Division Street where the servant boarded to see if anyone there knew what had happened.[1] Charles's landlord and chief protector, William Henry, sensing that something was wrong, promptly left his grocery store and headed out to investigate.[2] The grocer quickly saw the empty carriage and other signs that led him to suspect what was wrong. After checking the jail and finding no trace of Nalle, and getting reports from bystanders who reported seeing a prisoner being led uptown in handcuffs, Henry promptly headed over to the vicinity of the U.S. commissioner's office.[3] As soon as he learned that Nalle had indeed been taken upstairs, Henry rushed over to the Underground Railroad office at Troy House, just across the street from the federal office, and hurriedly entered via the rear alley to find his friend James P. Harden, a colored barber, cutting hair. With William Rich out of town and Peter Baltimore not yet arrived at the shop, Harden had been left in charge of the Underground Railroad office.[4] As Henry tried to catch his breath, he informed Harden what had transpired, and the barber immediately dropped everything he was doing, locked up the shop, scurried across the street, made his way upstairs, and forced his way into Beach's office just as the clerk was sorting the papers.[5] Henry, meanwhile, ran a couple of blocks away to inform the man who served as the chief local lawyer for the Underground Railroad, Martin I. Townsend.

Townsend maintained a law office with his brother Rufus and Irving Browne, at 229 River Street, near newspaper row.[6] He was the only attorney in town who had successfully defended a fugitive slave, Antonio Lewis—but that had been

in 1842, under the old law—and he was known as a great friend of the Negro.[7]
Now at the height of his powers, Townsend was a highly respected member of
the bar who had prosecuted and defended capital cases, sued scoundrels and
defended scoundrels, and he was political in the right direction—a Democrat
until 1848, he had later switched from Barnburner to Free-Soiler and then to
Republican. Fifty years old, and descended from Puritans, he had grown up in
Hancock, Massachusetts, graduated from Williams College, and was always
known to be true to his antislavery beliefs.[8]

As soon as Townsend heard Henry's breathless report, he rushed over to the
U.S. commissioner's office, his silver mane trailing in the wind. By the time he
arrived at Beach's door, however, the decision already had been rendered. But,
as one black newspaper would later put it, "Mr. T., not being quite satisfied
with the terseness of the thing, left" the room and headed out of the building
and through the throng.[9]

As Townsend well knew, there was little legal recourse available to him under the abominable Fugitive Slave Law. After they had abolished slavery, some
"free" states, including Connecticut, Rhode Island, Massachusetts, Michigan,
Maine, New Hampshire, Vermont, New Jersey, Pennsylvania, Ohio, Indiana,
Iowa, and Wisconsin, had enacted "personal liberty laws" intended to encum-
ber enforcement of the measure, ostensibly to prevent the kidnappings of free
blacks, but in effect to try to preserve basic constitutional guarantees such as
the right to trial by jury and habeas corpus. But New York didn't have a personal liberty law on its books. Abolitionists had urged the state to follow the
example of Massachusetts and consider legislation to prohibit slave hunting,
and their campaign touted it as a needed check on Southern oppression.[10] The
issue had come up in Albany's last two legislative sessions and gained some
support. In 1859, a bill to enact a personal liberty law had passed the Assembly
but failed in the Senate after some legislators opposed it as an act of defiance
against the rule of federal law.[11] After John Brown's raid, some opponents attacked the approach as fomented in "hot-beds of abolitionism and treason,
by a class of fanatics who endorse the deeds of treason, murder, and bloodshed, lately perpetrated in the quiet and peaceful villages of our sister State,
and setting at defiance the power and authority of our federal government."[12]
The Republicans had continued to fight, but as of a few weeks ago, the bills
had stalled.[13] Nevertheless, Townsend wanted to adopt a similar approach by
asserting that a fugitive slave was entitled to a writ of habeas corpus and trial
by jury—something that was denied under the federal Fugitive Slave Law and
not especially created under any state personal liberty statute—but which he
still would claim under the New York State Constitution. In the meantime he

would seek to rake his adversaries over as many legal coals as he could, challenging everything in sight. By putting every principle to the test, maybe he would be able to loosen their grip on the runaway. There was nothing to lose by trying. Within a few minutes he was hurrying to get before Judge George Gould, of the New York Supreme Court, to seek a writ of habeas corpus.[14]

If such maneuvering accomplished nothing else, at least it might enable them to stall for time until something else could be fashioned. That was what lawyers had done in several other confrontations over the years, in Boston, New York, Syracuse, and other cities, and he aimed to use it in Troy as well. Assuming that he was able to slow down the slave's extradition back to Virginia, the question then would arise of just where the federal authorities might expect to keep their prisoner until everything was sorted out.

Townsend knew a fugitive slave would have to be confined in a secure place. Some localities wouldn't permit the federal government to use their city jail or county penitentiary to hold a suspected runaway. As a result, the federal government had been forced to create its own holding pens. Lacking its own federal prison system and in areas where it didn't have a separate federal courthouse, the government sometimes relied instead on customhouses to do the job. During the past few years Congress had authorized construction of numerous customhouses throughout the country, many of them comprehensive facilities complete with their own courtrooms and holding cells. When the government lacked its own separate customhouse in an area that collected significant custom duties, it rented suitable quarters to store the money and confiscated goods that the custom inspector had collected.[15] Albany was slated to get its own standalone multipurpose customhouse within a year or so, but Troy's customhouse still consisted of leased space at the Mutual Bank Building.

Troy's strategic location on the Hudson by the Erie Canal contributed to its importance in the federal pantheon. Its collectors levied duties on incoming goods, requiring them to monitor the passage of vessels, cargoes, and passengers along the Hudson. Collectors also confiscated illegal goods and cargoes, deposited the property in the customhouse, and auctioned it off from time to time if the charges had not been paid. At 5 State Street, the customhouse largely consisted of a small room on the second floor. But deep in the basement of the Mutual Bank Building, two floors below Beach's office, there was also a vault for storing confiscated property, including, if necessary, runaway slaves. Thus the building had its own potential jail—in this instance, the federal government's slave pen—set in the bowels of the basement in Troy, New York.[16] If it were necessary to hold Charles for a protracted period of time, that was where he would likely be confined. For the time being, however, the authorities' primary goal was to get him away and aboard the next available southbound train, so as it now stood they kept him handcuffed in the commissioner's suite.

By then it was after two o'clock. Captain Hawkins (another black man who belonged to the Vigilance Committee) and others had sent word to have it noised abroad that there was a fugitive slave in Beach's office, on the corner of State and First streets. This commotion both helped to raise a crowd and also established enough of an impediment to make sure that the prisoner wasn't easily taken away.[17] Pretty soon, several knots of ten or twelve persons had begun to gather on the sidewalk near the Mutual Building's entrance, which was just across First Street from the Underground nerve center.[18] Some spectators pointed up at the second story where a handcuffed man could be glimpsed moving about near an open window.[19]

William Henry climbed aboard a farmer's wagon parked at the curbstone and bellowed, "There is a fugitive slave in that office—pretty soon you will see him come forth! He is going to be taken down South, and you will have a chance to see him. He is to be taken to the depot, to go to Virginia in the first train. Keep watch of those stairs, and you will have a sight."[20] Henry asked his fellow citizens if they were willing to stand quietly by, and do nothing. In the background, a growing chorus of animated black women answered each statement with a shout, keeping up a constant chant.[21] New recruits were appearing from every direction.

The crowd grew and so did the excitement. As word of what was happening spread to other parts of the city, it seemed that every black person in the vicinity had hastened to join the throng. There were also several whites making their appearance: ink-stained printers in leather aprons who had scampered over from newspaper row, mutton-chopped merchants wearing stovepipe hats and business suits, ladies with long dresses and parasols, and farmers on their way to or from the market.[22] The clusters of people in the streets were halting wagons and horses from getting by.[23]

One of those who had heard the commotion and responded without hesitation was a short but powerfully built black woman wearing a bonnet and simple clothes.[24] Most persons about the street at that time did not know her by sight or reputation, but if they had, it too would have caused excitement. Many colored people had only heard of "Moses" or "Moll Pitcher." Yet Harden the barber addressed her as "Mrs. Tubman."

Harriet Tubman lived about two hundred miles west in Auburn, but she had been passing through town on her way to a series of antislavery meetings in Boston and had stopped in to visit her cousins. Since fleeing slavery eleven years earlier, she had made a growing name for herself in Underground Rail-road circles, based on several daring trips she'd made back to Maryland, the scene of her own bondage, to personally rescue slaves and guide them to free-dom. As a result of a serious head injury she had suffered as a young woman, she often experienced drowsy spells and sometimes fell asleep at inopportune times, but this was not one of them. Although she was only thirty-seven years old, she could make herself look much older, and sometimes deliberately cre-ated the impression she was a feeble old woman as a way of lulling her prey. But she was incredibly strong, vital, and resourceful.

As Tubman surveyed the scene, she noticed that a wagon apparently had been parked near the exit to carry off the man, but the crowd had become so thick and excited that the officers didn't dare yet to bring him down.[25] She also scanned the rooftops, windows, and alleyway before making her assess-ment. Somebody had set off a fire alarm that added to the uproar, bringing horse-drawn teams of shiny new fire carriages approaching with their bells clanging—a spectacle that created even more agitation and confusion in the crowded street.[26] Shrinking herself into the posture of an ancient grandmother, she then nudged and cajoled her way upstairs to the hallway doorway outside the U.S. commissioner's office, where she blocked the exit with her body. A few of the African American people who knew what she was up to stood on the opposite side of State Street and watched the hallway window for signs of her sunbonnet. So long as they could see it, they were assured the fugitive was still inside.[27]

Every now and then some bystanders would start to panic, crying out, "They've taken him out another way, depend upon that!" or other such warnings.

But the sentries watching her would reply, "No, there stands 'Moses' yet, and as long as she is there, he is safe."[28]

By then the city police had arrived in force. Mayor Isaac McConihe Jr. was out of town at the time, attending the Democratic Convention, but the acting mayor, Recorder John Moran, had issued an urgent call to the department for help.[29] As a result, Chief Timothy Quin had sent messengers to wake everyone up or find them at their jobs, mobilizing his entire department in an effort to keep the peace.[30]

Previous arrests of fugitive slaves in Boston, Syracuse, and other cities had triggered riots that in some instances had resulted in the loss of life and the prisoners' escape—something that Troy's law enforcers were duty-bound to prevent.[31]

Meanwhile, Peter Baltimore, the prominent barber and champion of Negro rights, had heard the ruckus while en route from his home on Eighth Street to his shop on First, and the sound of the fire bells from that vicinity had caused him to quicken his pace. Noting the throng in the streets, he asked some friends what was going on and was told that a fugitive slave—Uri Gilbert's coachman—had been arrested by the United States officers and was about to be taken back to bondage. He immediately realized it was Charles Nalle, one of his passengers from Virginia. Knowing the layout of the area, Baltimore hurried up First Street to River Street and ducked into the alley, entering the Mutual Building through the alley stairs. Just as he arrived on the second floor, he encountered Townsend coming out of the lawyer's office, on his way to Judge Gould's.

"Peter, you are just the man I want to see," Townsend told him.

"Why?" Baltimore asked.

"If we can raise $1,000, we can buy that man," he said.

Baltimore quickly responded, "I will give $200."

And Townsend added, "I will give $200."

"If we can get him out in the crowd, we can raise the money in five minutes."

The crowd outside the Mutual Building appeared unusually diverse. There were whites as well as blacks, women as well as men, girls and boys; now some of the editors from River Street had taken up prominent spots among the barbers from Troy House and neighborhood shopkeepers who had come over with some of their customers; and there were bank tellers, common laborers, lawyers, shopkeepers, boatmen, maids, college students, street toughs, housepainters, hotel clerks, scrub ladies, and farmers who happened to be passing by. Because of the time of day, many factory workers were still being kept away, so the raucous Irish ironworkers and mill workers were not so numerous. Some members of the crowd had begun to shout sentiments in favor of the slave, while others called for law and order. Most were simply curious bystanders who hadn't yet made up their mind about what to think about what was happening.

After a while, three or four white men became conspicuous in the crowd in urging and planning for a rescue, such as had occurred in Boston and Syracuse. But others lobbied strenuously against it, prompting some heated arguments to break out. One agitator, David Brockway, a lawyer from Greenbush, who had loudly denounced the arrest, had his coat torn for expressing these sentiments, for which one of his antagonists, an irate Democrat named Vandenburgh, then had his coat ripped from top to bottom, causing gasps all around. A few young roughnecks had taken to laughing and shoving, but most onlookers stood for maintaining the law, however much it ran against their feelings to see a man carried back to slavery.[32]

By now the crowd numbered nearly a thousand persons. The people and the blocked wagons, fire carriages, and standing horses stretched up State Street from First Street to the alley, and kept surging back and forth.[33] From time to time, somebody in the crowd shouted up to people in the commissioner's office with offers to buy the poor slave from his master. Spontaneous calls and bids erupted from one end of the crowd to another, including pledges from Baltimore and others, running all the way to twelve hundred dollars. But once that number had been subscribed, a voice (probably Wale's) yelled down from the office to raise the price, then to fifteen hundred dollars, thereby frustrating and angering some in the crowd. A gentleman yelled out from an adjoining window, "Two hundred dollars for his rescue, but not one cent to his master!" Upon hearing this, part of the crowd roared their satisfaction and some men angrily shook their upraised fists in defiance.[34]

Meanwhile, inside the Mutual Building, several representatives were admitted into the room where Nalle was being held. At one point there were as many as half a dozen of them in the law office, all of them trying to argue on his behalf or offering other observations to the marshal and anyone else who would listen. Wale and Averill and the others stood by apprehensively. Outside, an impatient throng jammed the stairway and hall seeking to gain admission.[35] As this was going on, at about half past 3 p.m., Nalle, who was sitting handcuffed alongside one of the swing windows opening upon State Street, managed to push open the sash with his elbow without being noticed by the police in the room and, leaping up, he prepared to jump backwards out of the window to the sidewalk below. Before anyone could stop him, his body was three-quarters out the window. Some bystanders started shouting, "Drop him!"

"Catch him!"

"Stop him!"

"Hurrah!"

All at once there was a wild hullabaloo, and every eye was turned up to see the legs and part of the body of the prisoner protruding from the second-story window as he was struggling to escape. Some onlookers became alarmed when they saw his bare calves, which were so white, and his face, looking more like a Caucasian than any Negro they had ever seen. This vision contributed to some of the wildest excitement in the crowd, as somebody shouted, "He's white! Let him down!"

"Come, old boy!"

"Catch him!"

"That's it!"[36]

But the attempt proved fruitless when someone inside the office, Walter P. Tillman, a coal dealer who lived at Troy House, suddenly grabbed Nalle by his chain and pulled him back inside again, amid the shouts of a hundred pair of lungs.[37]

By now, the crowd had become a mob. Blacks and whites, men and women, workingmen and pillars of the community, interspersed with defenders of law and order and common ruffians, were all excited by this spectacle that was being played out before their eyes. Through it all, Tubman remained in the hallway by the window, like a Trojan horse. Comrades below awaited her signal. Eventually the police assumed more control and took over the stairway, but she held her ground. Some of them barricaded the commissioner's office. Officers kept coming outside to try to clear the stairs, to allow them to take their captive down. The men were driven down, but Tubman remained anchored to the spot, keeping her head bent down and her arms folded, as if deep in prayer. Somebody kept saying she was related to the prisoner and here to offer her blessing.

"Come, old woman, you must get out of this," one of the officers told her. "I must have the way cleared; if you can't get down alone, some one will help you." But Tubman, still putting on a greater appearance of decrepitude, twitched away from him and refused to budge.[38]

Just before 4 P.M., Martin Townsend returned to the scene with Rensselaer County deputy sheriff Nathaniel Upham, who was clutching an important piece of paper. The two men made their way through the throng and headed upstairs, past the guards and Tubman, and were let inside the besieged room.[39] Commissioner Beach and his father were startled to see the scribbled handwriting of State Supreme Court Judge George Gould, which they deciphered to be a writ of habeas corpus, requiring Upham to bring Nalle to Gould's chambers, two blocks away at 39 Congress Street, as soon as possible.[40] The father and son shook their heads, saying there was no choice but to send him down with the police. Wale protested, but it was of no use. A grim-faced Chief Quin quickly deployed some of his men along the stairway to prevent the crowd from rushing in and grabbing the fugitive. At length an officer appeared and announced to the crowd that if they would open a lane to the wagon, the police would promise to bring the man down the front way.[41] Officers and bullyboys scrambled into position. By now the crowd seemed to become much bigger. Tensions were mounting.

Just before the escorts headed out they sent several persons running down the stairs with a decoy to distract those outside and they did draw off some, but others had been posted to stand guard and they weren't deceived. The black defenders waited for the signal from the old colored lady.

Just then, out the door onto State Street came Chief Quin in his blue uniform with Nalle, bareheaded and in his short sleeves, following close behind in handcuffs.[42] Accompanying him were two of his heftiest men, Charles H. Cleveland, a night watchman who lived at 96 First, and Levi Squire, a high constable who lived at Harrison Place, along with Marshal Holmes, Deputy Sheriff Upham, and several others, many of them looking scared.[43] There was no telling what a mob might do.

Townsend, Baltimore, Harden the barber, Tillman, and some others followed them down the stairs. As soon as the officers and their prisoner emerged from the door, Tubman, who now was standing at the bottom of the stairs, suddenly sprang to life and shouted, "Here they come!" causing many in the crowd to make a terrific rush at the party.[44] As Harden and Baltimore followed, they could see her immediately fight her way to his side, throw her arms around him and hold onto his clothes, refusing to let go.[45] She kept her iron grip even as the police tried to shove and pull her away. Baltimore would later recall, "Her action seemed to inspire the crowd, and it seemed a miracle that she appeared just at that time."[46]

The moment the prisoner emerged from the doorway, the crowd made one grand charge, and those nearest the prisoner seized him violently, with the intention of pulling him away from the officers. The police and their supporters fought back, tugging and pushing, thrashing and punching, getting struck as they went. Wale and Averill decided it was time to leave and they slipped away through the crowd. The distance from the Mutual Building to Judge Gould's chambers on Congress Street was less than two blocks, but it had become a battlefield. According to one eyewitness, "The city policemen very soon separated from the other officers, and left fighting promiscuously in the midst of a crowd of perhaps two thousand persons, who were swaying to and fro like billows, shouting, laughing, and swearing, according to their several inclinations." Despite his best efforts to stay close, Harden became separated from Tubman and watched helplessly over the bobbing heads until he finally encountered one of his friends, Thompson Gale, who took off his coat and said, "Jim, I'll help you. Give me your foot." Harden stuck his foot into Gale's interlaced fingers and Gale heaved him over the top of the crowd and he fell against Nalle and the officers.[47] Marshal Holmes and Deputy Upham were struck several times, pulled, pushed, and shoved, and they struggled to keep their balance. But Charles was the one who was getting it from all sides—still handcuffed and unable to protect himself, he feared he was being torn to pieces.[48] Upham clung to Charles, but he was eventually pummeled, torn from his prisoner, knocked down, and trampled. While some of the crowd still focused on him, Marshal Holmes continued to hold on, with great difficulty, as far as Congress Street.[49]

Exactly what went on within the mob is impossible to say, but the frantic pulling, hauling, mauling, and shouting by the rescuers was matched by a stern resistance from the conservators of the law. At Congress Street the rescuers overtook Marshal Holmes and they had a great fight. "The more law-abiding citizens, among whom were a number of colored men, were for allowing Charles to be taken before Judge Gould," one eyewitness would recount. "Others maintained that the only result would be to have him remanded back to the Commissioner's custody, and that delay might prove fatal to him. The most conspicuous person opposed to the legal course, was the venerable colored woman, who exclaimed, 'Give us liberty or give us death!' and who by vehement gesticulations kept urging the rescuers on."[50]

One officer drew his revolver and pointed it at the head of one of the rescuers, threatening to fire, but a colored man knocked his arm up, and another held a knife at the officer's throat until the pistol fell away. The combat seemed to reach its height in front of Judge Gould's office, where fists were flying.[51] Custody of the prisoner kept switching from one side to the other, as if he were a ball.

Through it all, Tubman kept thrashing like a demon, even as she was losing all her gearing except for a dilapidated outskirt.[52] She seized an officer and pulled him down, grabbed another and tore him away from Nalle, all the while keeping hold of the slave, as she cried to her friends, "Drag us out! Drag him to the river! Drown him! But don't let them have him!"[53]

No longer merely a subject of polite debate, the battle over slavery had become a bone of fierce contention. Charles's terrified face was battered, his manacled wrists streaming with blood.[54] The crowd was like a lynch mob in reverse—instead of unleashing their fury to string him up, the ringleaders of this mass chaos vented all of their pent-up rage to turn the Negro loose and rescue him from doom. Tubman held him tightly around his arm and wouldn't let go, regardless of what was done to him or her. In the melee, policemen's clubs rained down on her head and grip, but she never for a moment released her hold. She wouldn't let go when more of her outer clothes were lost and both of her shoes ripped off her feet. Eventually she simply wore out several of the policemen and their supporters around her. It was becoming impossible for them to continue their custody of him.

The crowd got Charles down Congress Street to the dock. Here another stand was made. Holmes and Upham had abandoned the prisoner, their hands now mummified by blows from clubs, chisels, and the like. But Chief Quin still clung to him like a bulldog. The last stand was made in front of F. A. Filo's store below Congress Street, where some of the mob made a concerted feint that distracted the officers and enabled two of their biggest men to seize Charles and run him off.[55] One of the rescuers held the prisoner's arms from behind, others grasped hold of the first, forming a long single line as if it were some sort of athletic contest, and this column, running at full speed and swaying from side to side, pushed him rapidly down to the river.[56] Alongside them, a band of helpers "cleared the tracks" to prevent any more seizures from being made.[57]

His friends rushed him down Dock Street to the lower ferry, only to discover it had just left the slip. Without hesitating they proceeded to the beach where there was a skiff lying ready to start. The crowd urged the colored man at the oars to move as fast as he could. The boatman panicked and jumped out, leaving Charles alone and gasping in the craft, until suddenly a fellow named Billy Loreman hopped in, took the oars, and pushed off from the beach. By now their pursuers were drawing close again. Marshal Holmes made one frantic lunge in an effort to grab the boat, but he fell short, and despite threats from some of the police that they would open fire, they held back. A few pursuers splashed into the frigid water in an effort to stop his flight, but they too failed. Loreman rowed as fast as he could, amid the hoarse shouts of hundreds who lined the banks of the river.[58] The mob had won at last, and Charles Nalle's liberation was accomplished.

The distance across the Hudson River looked to be merely about two hundred yards, but it might have seemed that Charles was crossing the Jordan. To his back, his assailants and saviors continued to mark his progress with muffled curses and cheers, while in the front he looked west into the four o'clock sun and saw the approaching outline of West Troy, with its belching smokestacks and warehouses, while to the south the center of town beckoned, where maybe he could reach the canal and Jim Banks's place and hopefully friends who would help him get away from his pursuers. To succeed he knew he'd have to move fast. But he had already endured a terrible beating. His face and his handcuffed wrists were streaming blood and his shirt was torn.

The ferryman headed straight to the dock, but before they had landed, a colored sympathizer waded into the chilly water and pulled Nalle from the skiff, set him on the ground and told him to run as quick as he could.[1] But the fugitive was in such a weakened state from his ordeal that he could barely clamber up the slippery slope, staggering toward the main road that ran along the river. Hank York, a stable hand from Whitbeck's, who had followed the melee from the West Troy side, helped wash his wounds and provide some comfort, and Nalle asked him and the other Samaritans to stick by him.

Somebody from the other side had telegraphed ahead, however, alerting Mayor William K. Oswald, who was at his job as superintendent of the gasworks for West Troy Gas Light Company.[2] Ever a controversial figure, Oswald immediately notified Constable Joseph N. Becker that a fleeing fugitive in manacles was headed up from dock, and Becker and another constable, Abraham S. Brown, dutifully responded in a rig before Nalle and his allies had made it up the grassy hill.[3] When some of his protectors resisted, Brown struck one of them and they seized Nalle, tossed him into the rig, and bolted away. They headed a few blocks south to the Corporation Hall Building, a solid, three-story brick structure on Broad at the corner of Canal near the ferry dock. Together they went upstairs to the third-floor office of Justice Daniel C. Stewart to await the arrival of the federal marshal.[4] Given that the *West Troy Advocate* was located in the same building, the incident already was sure to receive special coverage.[5] York and the others continued to pursue them, yelling, "Help! Help! Help!" on hopes of arousing the community.[6]

This was no longer Troy, but a village of Albany County, and competition between the two could be fierce, particularly as persons on each side of the river often looked down on their neighbors and felt superior to them. As a precaution against any further problems, several more lawmen joined the constables. Among them was postmaster Patrick Grattan and Albany County deputy sheriff Andrew J. Morrison and their crews, all of them armed and determined to prevent another rescue.[7] They bolted the door, loaded their weapons, and eyed the bloodied prisoner they had inherited from across the river, expecting that they would soon be joined by further reinforcements who would take him off their hands.

By then, only about ten minutes had elapsed since the rescue in Troy, but in that time Charles's rescuers had watched helplessly as their hard-won victory was snatched away. Tubman and some of the others refused to allow this atrocity to continue, and hundreds of them flocked to the steam-ferry that had now landed on the Troy side, and they took it by storm. The vessel was unable to accommodate them all at once, so the rest commandeered every other vessel they could find, from rowboats to skiffs and leaky old tubs, until they had formed a sizable armada carrying several hundred warriors.[8] Both ferries, the *Jennie Lind* and the *Brommie Dyer*, were among those conscripted. Blacks and women probably made up about a third of the force, many of them shouting and hallooing as they crossed the waters.[9]

As soon as they docked, Tubman started asking bystanders on the West Troy side where the police had taken the slave, and a group of excited schoolchildren hurried over and pointed toward a large brick office building, saying, "He's up in that house, third story." York and others also helped to direct some of the reinforcements toward the judge's office building.

By the time Tubman and her band reached the Corporation Hall building at Broad and Canal, a crowd of West Trojans had surrounded it to prevent Charles from being taken out from either exit, and some very determined fellows already were making preparations to storm the castle.[10] It housed the offices of the *West*

Troy Advocate newspaper, the West Troy Gas Light Company, and other businesses, along with the law office of Justice Daniel C. Stewart where Nalle was being held—on the second floor, not the third. Part of the mob tried to enter the building, but found it barricaded, so they burst through.[11]

A score or more of them immediately stampeded up the stairs, shouting and cursing. Two intrepid journalists from the *Troy Daily Times*, in their intense desire to cover the battle, bounded to the front. Somebody hurled a stone against the door--then another—and suddenly two gunshots rang out, releasing a sound of explosions that was greatly amplified in the closed quarters. Constable Becker had commenced his firing from the head of the stairs, blasting at the crowd with little effect, except to drill a hole in Harden's hat.[12] Harden also discovered he had two more bullet holes in his coat, but miraculously he wasn't wounded.[13] The shooting caused the attackers to retreat for a moment until they could regroup.

"They've got pistols!" somebody yelled.

"Who cares?" shouted another. "They can only kill a dozen of us—come on!"[14] Harden's retreat had continued only as far as the middle of the road below the besieged window, where he made an apron with his coat, which he and a white man used to fill with stones. Then he and several others re-entered the foyer and began hurling them upstairs. Harden's first throw into the office struck a man so hard it sent him reeling to keep his balance. His second pitch hit the judge on the head, prompting the lawmen to pull the wounded jurist to safety and shut the door.[15] With that came the sound of more stones peppering the door, followed by more pistol shots.[16] Gunsmoke filled the stairway.

As Tubman entered the building, more men already were attempting to make their way up the stairs. Harden crawled on his hands and knees, feeling the floor for more stones to throw. Officers fired down, leaving at least two of the men knocked down and lying on the stairs, groaning. Some of the shots had wounded badly in the thigh Richard S. Redy, who worked for T. C. Wright in West Troy near the Arsenal, and shaved off a side whisker from a farmer named William Barnhart, taking with it a small slice of his cheek.[17] The sweet smell of gunpowder wafted into the street.

Now enraged, the mob returned with whatever missiles they could seize. A paving stone struck an officer on the head, knocking him down.[18] Some of the mob grabbed an empty dry-goods box from the foot of the stairs and carried it forward as a shield. Others armed themselves with brickbats, clubs, and anything else they could find.[19] Somebody used the box as a battering ram to smash at the door.[20] Harden heard voices inside the room and, groping about the floor for another projectile, he came upon a hatchet on the floor, which he then directed near the doorknob, successfully breaking the lock. One of the newspapermen—W. E. Kisselburgh, who lived near Townsend and Hooper— jimmied open the door despite being fired at twice. As it opened, Harden hurled the hatchet inside the room and stuck a large mirror, causing a loud crash. Into the doorway stepped a giant colored man named Martin, who used his might to knock the door wide open.[21] But as soon as he entered, Deputy Sheriff Morrison picked up the hatchet and smashed him on the forehead with the blunt side. The blow stunned him, but to Morrison's horror, the giant collapsed into the doorway in such a position that his body prevented the door from being closed.[22] This enabled others, including Tubman, to pour into the room.

From his vantage point on the floor, Harden heard a desperate voice cry out, "Throw that damn nigger out of here, or we'll all be killed."[23] Instantly, Nalle's body came flying out the doorway and landed on top of Harden, followed immediately by Tubman, who fell onto them both.

"It's me, Harden," the barber told Nalle. "Come on, you're safe."[24] With that, the three of them got up and tumbled down the stairs.[25] To prevent more shooting, some of the mob grabbed the policemen's revolver barrels or knocked them reeling.[26]

Out the door and down the street they ran. Somebody had sent runners sprinting ahead to clear the way and others posted behind to protect their rear flank.[27] By now, Nalle's scratched and battered face was streaming blood and his mouth was frothing, and the heavy shackles upon his arms had scraped part of the skin from his wrists.[28] Harden spotted Peter Baltimore, Hank Latour, Andrew Parker, and other friends running escort. Near the post office they stopped a farmer in his wagon and urged him to give them a ride. The man took one look and declined the invitation, but somebody seized the reins as Harden, Baltimore, and others deposited Nalle inside. Several of them hopped aboard, so many, in fact, that it suddenly collapsed from all the weight.[29]

Although Charles was bleeding and hobbled from his wounds, and was almost too exhausted to move, with his clothes ripped nearly from his body, he got back on his feet and resumed running, running for his life.[30] Tubman, meanwhile, apparently decided it was time to make her exit, and she faded into one of the side streets and vanished again before she could be captured.

The runners continued sprinting along Broadway for another half-mile when they approached on their right a towering flagpole, several stories high, that had a large American flag flapping in the wind. They soon passed alongside a long low wrought-iron fence that stretched alongside the curb. It was, of all things, the federal arsenal. The Watervliet Arsenal was the oldest in the United States and considerably larger than the one in Harpers Ferry that had recently been the target of John Brown's shocking surprise attack. This institution's commander, Major Alfred Mordecai, had taken extraordinary steps to resist any assault. He had erected a massive cast-iron storage building designed to contain any munitions explosions and withstand heavy bombardment. His great expertise was in ordnance, artillery, and field gun carriages—a useful specialty for someone located only a mile or so away from Uri Gilbert's carriage and car manufactory, the university, the Burden Iron Works, the railroad, the Hudson River, and the Erie Canal. But Mordecai, now fifty-six years old and at the twilight of his military career, had been mulling over whether or when he might return to warmer clime. Charles and the others would not have relished the fact that he was also a Southerner, a proud native of North Carolina, with four sons who would soon be serving the military in their native state. But Mordecai was also the only Orthodox Jewish officer in the U.S. Army, something that already was occupying his mind, for the Sabbath was approaching in just a few hours, and that may have accounted for his absence at the time.[31] Luckily for Nalle, the arsenal's sentries must not have seen them, for the entourage was somehow able to proceed past the institution's front gate unmolested.[32]

The crowd continued west toward the Shaker Road until they approached the rear of the arsenal wall. At Temperance Hill, the resourceful Hank York overtook them in a rig pulled by a fleet horse he had procured from Whitbeck's stable.[33] He was joined by Peter Baltimore and Andrew Parker, another hairdresser from Troy.[34] Some of them were armed. Helping Charles into the rig, they headed west toward Schenectady. Becker and Brown tried to pursue them, but the mob intervened and roughed them up.

As the escape party drove up the Shaker Road, York jumped out of the rig, tied his suspenders about his waist, and ran behind the wagon to prevent it from breaking down. They had hoped to stop at the Shaker Hotel to give the semiconscious Nalle a drink of water, but the place was too crowded, so they continued moving northwest for about four miles from the rescue, until they reached Whitbeck's, where York had been raised. Although Mr. Whitbeck was too afraid to assist them, they were able to locate a sledge and a chisel, which they used to break apart his blood-caked shackles, although a handcuff was left on each wrist. As Nalle gulped some water, out came Mrs. Whitbeck with a package of cakes and dainties for him, and away they went.[35]

Switching to another road, they cut east to Vischer's Ferry, by the Erie Canal dry dock, and waited for the ferry that would take them across the Mohawk River. While pinned against the water, they spotted an approaching band of riders on horseback racing down from a hill and feared the worst—until they recognized them as friends coming to help. After crossing on the ferry, they took up a collection for Nalle and gave him the money. After heading about a mile toward Schenectady, they met up with a friend named Fisher, who contributed another three dollars to the cause.[36]

Charles was at large again, but he wasn't free. About 11:30 o'clock that night they arrived in the Mohawk River town of Schenectady, where York led them to his cousin's house. The cousin went out and gathered some friends, who helped to cut off the handcuffs, and they gave him food and washed him. Although he was extremely weak, he gradually began to recover. Once he had regained some energy, at about 4 o'clock, they escorted him over State Street to the towpath for the Erie Canal. After they had introduced him to the canal boat captain and told him of Nalle's situation, the captain was all too glad to assist him, and he put the fugitive aboard his boat alone, leaving his friends on shore offering their fond good-byes. From there, they thought, the canal might take him west to Canada and freedom.

Nalle arrived at Amsterdam, about twenty miles away, at daylight, but remained in the bushes until dark, when he located more friends who cared for him, and apparently decided to remain in the area instead of proceeding on to Canada. The following night he went ten miles back into the countryside, where he found friends and temporary employment so he could support himself. He remained a fugitive, feeling more hunted than ever, for nearly a month.[37]

In order to legally liberate the slave they had freed by force, citizens of Troy and West Troy got together and offered to buy him for $650. Hansbrough, seeing no ready alternative, accepted, and the purchase was completed, thus enabling Charles to emerge from his hiding.[38] Nobody recorded how Charles felt about having his freedom purchased, as had been done for Frederick Douglass, Anthony Burns, and numerous other fugitive slaves. It was a controversial practice as far as some abolitionists were concerned, for some thought it seemed to implicitly acknowledge that one man possessed the right to own another.[39] Indeed, some radical abolitionists contended that aiding slaves to liberty was injurious to the antislavery cause, for it failed to directly confront the immorality of slavery.[40] On the other hand, for Charles and his family, emancipation represented the dream of a lifetime, a dream that had taken untold generations to obtain. At the time, it must have seemed like a good idea.

On Friday afternoon, May 25, 1860, Charles Nalle returned to Troy a free man. A friendly newspaperman who interviewed him that evening reported, "Nalle was considerably fatigued with his journey yesterday, and was not inclined to be over communicative in regard to the facts of his escape." He wouldn't reveal anything about the Underground Railroad. He didn't want to see others prosecuted or hurt on his behalf.[41] More likely than not, he felt great ambivalence about what had transpired. It remained to be seen whether he or any of his supporters would be prosecuted, and he still remained worried about his brothers and mother and others back in the South, as well as his wife and children.

After he returned, Uri Gilbert welcomed him into his household and gave him back his old employment. Later, the Underground Railroad arranged for Charles to live in a house at 146 Third Street with his family.[42] A few weeks later, Kitty and the children arrived and they enjoyed a joyous reunion for the first time in more than four years. Much had changed. It would require many adjustments. But for the first time in their lives, they were able to live together under one roof, like other families. Lewis and Winna Burrell joined them. Charles and Kitty's goal of keeping the family together was fulfilled.

It seemed for a while that the U.S. government was aiming to prosecute some of the rescuers. On May 2, two federal officials from Troy traveled to Washington to present a detailed report to the Department of State. Court officers issued subpoenas to four policemen and one newspaper reporter who had witnessed the rescue in West Troy. The press reported that Deputy Marshal John L. Holmes had received summonses for at least seven other witnesses to testify before the federal grand jury in Rochester that would be investigating the episode.[43] Inside sources told the *Argus* newspaper that prosecutors wanted to convict a dozen of the city's "Black Republicans" (the Democrats' derisive term for abolitionists and Republicans, whom they wished to depict as being pro-black), including William Henry, Martin I. Townsend, John T. Perry (another Troy attorney), E. F. Wait (a teller at the Mutual Bank), Charles P. Hartt (a cashier at Farmer's Bank), John W. Armitage (a sewing machine manufacturer), W. E. Kisselburgh (the printer who had crashed in Justice Stewart's door), John D. Billings (a stove manufacturer), George Demers (assistant editor of the *Troy Daily Times*), Anthony Lawton of Troy (a tailor), Richard Sharpe, and at least one other unnamed person (possibly Tubman).[44]

On July 18, John M. Van Buskirk became the first person arrested in connection with the rescue, based on allegations that he had incited the mob by offering to pay $200 for the prisoner's forcible freeing, but his case was postponed at the prosecution's request.[45] A week later, John T. Perry was taken into custody, charged with resisting authority. It was also rumored that two others, Thompson Gale and J. W. Armitage, had also been arrested.[46] In August, a grand jury at Auburn was scheduled to begin hearing testimony, and one newspaper reported that additional arrests might occur at the upcoming Republican State Convention scheduled to begin in Syracuse on August 22.[47] But nothing more seems to have come of the prosecutions, because other political events were taking center stage. The national battle over slavery would see to that.

15 AFTERMATH

Right after the exciting events of April 27, 1860, as she was still recovering from her injuries sustained in the rescue, the black woman the slaves called "Moses" had continued on her way to Boston as planned to attend a series of meetings on abolitionism and women's rights.[1] In the wake of her latest exploits in Troy, the movement spread the word about how her "intrepidity" in the face of danger had saved the day. "She acted like a heroine," said the *Weekly Anglo-African*.[2] Another story in the *Anti-Slavery Standard* observed: "In this rescue, a colored woman was prominent, very active and persevering, until success crowned their efforts—a woman known among the colored people extensively as 'Moses,' because she has led so many of their number out of worse than Egyptian bondage into the goodly land of freedom."[3] The abolitionist press increasingly depicted her as a hero of the cause.

For Tubman personally, the Troy rescue had occurred at a crucial time in her own struggle. Coming on the heels of John Brown's momentous raid, it may have helped her redeem herself to herself. Two years earlier, her friend Reverend Jermain Loguen had taken her to meet Brown for the first time in St. Catharines. During the introduction, Loguen had said, "Among slaves she is better known than the Bible, for she circulates more freely."[4] Brown seemed so impressed that he paid her his highest compliments and counted her among his most trusted allies.[5] Later, at Wendell Phillips's home, Brown had introduced Tubman to the orator with the words: "I bring you one of the bravest and best persons on this continent."[6] Based on their meetings, Brown had expected she would join him in his holy war as the fight against slavery reached another stage. But things had not gone according to plan—for whatever reason, she hadn't gone along with him as expected. And she had felt guilty about that.

Now, amid spring's rebirth, Tubman arrived in the noble village of Concord that had figured so proudly in the opening fight of the first American Revolution, eighty-five years earlier. She appeared alone at the door of Frank Sanborn's home, a square, wood-frame place that looked like a farmhouse—the same house that John Brown had visited, and the place federal agents had raided and been repulsed just a few weeks earlier. Sanborn welcomed her warmly into his lair. Like him, she too had been targeted after the Harpers Ferry raid, for some of the incriminating documents left behind by Brown had mentioned Tubman as well as Sanborn.[7] In fact, a U.S. marshal from Virginia had been looking for her in Auburn on behalf of the Senate investigating committee when he'd stumbled across Osborne Perry Anderson, one of Brown's former raiders, who had miraculously escaped from Harpers Ferry during the confusion. But before the lawman could arrest him, Anderson, a free black from Pennsylvania, had escaped again—this time to Canada.[8] Tubman was fortunate that she too had evaded capture.

Sanborn showed his guest to a room that contained a gleaming marble bust of the great martyr himself that Edward Brackett had made from his sketches at the jail.[9] "The sight of it, which was new to her, threw her into a sort of ecstasy of sorrow and admiration," Sanborn would later write, "and she went on in her own rhapsodical way to pronounce his apotheosis." Tubman told him it wasn't John Brown who had died at Charleston. "It was Christ—it was the Saviour of our people."[10]

United by their common beliefs, Tubman and Sanborn shared some of their private memories of Brown, reflecting on how the old man and two of his sons and the others had sacrificed their lives trying to free the slaves. As the somber black woman hovered near the white marble head, she told her host about a recurring dream that had haunted her in recent times. As Sanborn would later tell it, "She thought she was in a 'wilderness sort of place, all full of rocks and bushes,' when she saw a serpent raise its head among the rocks, and as it did so, it became the head of an old man with a long white beard, gazing at her 'wishful like, just as if he were going to speak to me,' and then two other heads rose up beside him, younger than he—and as she stood looking at them, and wondering what they could want with her, a great crowd of men rushed in and struck down the younger heads, and then the head of the old man, still looking to her 'so wishful'." This nightmare about Brown had plagued her for months.[11]

Brown's fate, and her own failure to save him from it, had often been on Tubman's mind. At the time of his hanging, she had sought comfort with another friend, Ednah Cheney, but she couldn't be consoled.[12] "I've been studying and studying upon it," she had told Cheney, "and its clar to me, it wasn't John Brown that died on the gallows. When I think how he gave up his life for our people, and how he never flinched, but was so brave to the end; its clar to me it wasn't mortal man, it was God in him. When I think of all the groans and tears and prayers I've heard on the plantations, and remember that God is a prayer-hearing God, I feel that his time is drawing near . . . God was always near. . . . He gave me my strength, and he set the North Star in the heavens; he meant for me to be free."[13]

In the wake of the news about the thrilling Troy rescue, Sanborn and Cheney took Tubman into many of their friends' parlors around Boston, where she told many amazing stories about her adventures. She also spoke at some public meetings, usually identified only as "Moses."[14] At one of these gatherings, a Drawing Room Convention held on Independence Day at Boston's classical Melodeon Hall, she appeared with leading suffragists to talk about abolitionism and women's rights, and electrified the crowd with accounts of some of her slave rescues and narrow escapes, including what had happened in Troy and how she had rescued her aged parents from slavery in eastern Maryland and aided them to freedom in Canada.[15] An item in *The Liberator* later reported: "A colored woman of the name of Moses, who is herself a fugitive, has eight times returned to the slave states for the purpose of rescuing others from bondage, and who has met with extraordinary success in her efforts, was then introduced. She told the story of her adventures in a modest, but quaint and amusing style which won much applause."[16]

These rescues and her role in them also incited Southerners to express their displeasure. A proslavery writer from Philadelphia, John Bell Robinson, would later publish a long and disgusted commentary about the black woman fugitive slave who had appeared on a Boston stage before a "congregation of traitors."[17] Other Southerners found in the Troy incident still more confirmation that the time for reconciliation had ended.

The rescue received attention on the national political stage. It had occurred during the contentious Democratic National Convention held at Charleston at which many Southern Democrats had arrived on April 23 determined to have their party adopt in its platform a new federal slave code for the territories. Without one, they were afraid most territories would enter the Union as free states, thereby tilting the balance of power away from slavery and threatening to result in a constitutional amendment that would abolish slavery everywhere. Many Northerners entered the arena in fear for their safety. Their leading standard-bearer, Senator Stephen Douglas of Illinois, favored popular sovereignty and opposed endorsing the slavery platform, thereby undermining his support in the South. The vocal Southern opposition was headed by William Lowndes Yancey, the fire-eating stepson of Troy's Reverend Beman, and a few others.

A few hours after the Nalle rescue, Yancey angrily addressed the convention and advocated that the South secede from the Union in response to the North's continued outrages. His two-hour tirade received strong applause, not only from Southerners but also from proslavery northerners such as New York City's former mayor, Fernando Wood, who had so much anticipated the intense rancor over the party's slavery platform that he had taken boxing lessons before the convention in order to prepare himself for the infighting.

Yancey and his associates, however, failed to convince the majority of delegates to back the federal slave code platform. In response, the entire delegations from Alabama, Florida, Mississippi, and Texas, and most of the members from Georgia, South Carolina, and Virginia, as well as some delegates from Arkansas and Delaware, dramatically stormed out of the convention, thereby preventing Douglas from being able to achieve the necessary two-thirds requirement to win his nomination. After fifty-seven futile ballots, the remaining delegates finally voted to adjourn for six weeks, until such time as they might resume on June 18 in the friendlier atmosphere of Baltimore. The Southern fire-eaters, on the other hand, agreed to meet in Richmond on June 11, but later descended on Baltimore amid considerable jostling and confusion. Douglas was ultimately nominated on June 23. But the Southerners remained disgruntled and subsequently nominated their own slate.

The Republicans, meanwhile, held their national convention in Chicago on May 16–18, exhibiting surprising unity. The Republican platform opposed the expansion of slavery into the western territories without condemning it in the South, thereby incurring more Southern wrath. After front-runner Senator William Henry Seward failed to win the nomination on the first ballot, the momentum shifted to native son Abraham Lincoln, who eventually won on the third ballot.[18]

A few days before the national election, Yancey gave a big speech in Manhattan in which he said, "Your fathers and my fathers built this government on two ideas: the first is that the white race is the citizen, and the master race, and the white man is the equal of every other white man. The second idea is the Negro is the inferior race."[19]

On November 6, Lincoln won the election with a plurality of votes. Four days later, South Carolina voted to call for a convention to decide whether to secede. On December 20, its delegates unanimously approved a resolution to secede from the Union, becoming the first of eleven states to do so. Now the split over slavery was entering another phase.

16 THE WAR HITS HOME IN CULPEPER, 1861–65

Less than a year after the Troy rescue, and four months after South Carolina's secession, the real deadly fighting began. Soon, normally quiet little Culpeper found itself in the path of hurtling armies. Its environs became the scene of several bloody battles, among them Kelly's Ford, Brandy Station, and Cedar Mountain. The area would change hands countless times before the fighting ended, serving as a bivouac of commanders from Robert E. Lee, J. E. B. Stuart, Thomas "Stonewall" Jackson, and Richard S. Ewell, to George G. Meade, John Pope, and Ulysses S. Grant, along with tens of thousands of troops and suppliers. Beset by the war's shifting fortunes, Culpeper's populace endured constant pillaging by invaders and deserters, and experienced bitter suffering, humiliation, and hardship for three long years.[1] Many of these events occurred in the very hamlet of Stevensburg where Hansbrough and his slaves had lived—the precise spot from which Charles Nalle had fled a few years before. Some of the local families and sites that were affected by the Civil War in those parts were connected to the Nalles, the Thoms, the Maddens, and the Hansbroughs, both blacks and whites—the people who earlier had shaped the life of Charles Nalle, his mother and siblings, wife and children, and all of the others in their extended family. The chickens had come home to roost.

After serving as a prime recruiting ground, training station, and hospital for the victorious Confederate army in the early stages of the war, Culpeper in May of 1862 suffered its first partial Union occupation, lasting thirty-one hours. Two months later, another intrusion occurred after advance troops of the Army of the Potomac defeated Confederate cavalry on Culpeper's main street. George Alfred Townsend, the great correspondent for the *New York Herald*, described what it was like as the conquerors entered the town. "The shutters were closed in the shop windows, the dwellings seemed tenantless, no citizens were abroad," he wrote. "[O]nly a few cavalry-men clustered about an ancient pump to water their nags, and some military idlers were sitting upon the long porch of a public house, called the Virginia Hotel. I tied my horse to a tree, the bole of which had been gnawed bare, and found the landlord to be an old gentleman named [William] Paine. . . . A sabre conflict had taken place in the streets; and these events, happening in rapid succession, combined with the insolence of some Federal outriders, had so agitated the host that his memory was quite gone, and he could not perform even the slightest function. There is a panacea for all these things . . . I produced my flask, and gently insinuated it to the old gentleman's lips. He possessed instinct sufficient to uncork and apply it, and the results were directly apparent, in a partial recovery of memory. . . . I discovered . . . that the people of the village were almost starving; that beef had been fifty cents a pound during the whole winter, flour twenty-five dollars per barrel, coffee one dollar and a quarter per pound, and corn one dollar per bushel. The [Confederate] army had swept the country like famine, and the citizens had pinched, pining faces, with little to eat today, and nothing for tomorrow." Townsend recounted being in the hotel office, crowded with bluecoats, when some Southern women burst into the room, exclaiming, "'Pop, Yankees thieving in the garden!' or 'Pop, drive those Yankees out of the parlor!'" "Every afternoon when the pavement was unusually patronized by young officers," Townsend jotted, "these women would sally out, promenade in crinoline, silk stockings, and saucy hoods, and the crowd would fall respectfully back to let them pass. . . . Now and then a woman made her appearance at a front window, stealthily peeping into the street, or a neighboring farmer ventured into town upon a lean consumptive mule. The very dogs were skinny and savage for want of sustenance, and when a long, cadaverous hog emerged from nowhere one day, and tottered up the main street he was chased, killed, and quartered so rapidly." Regiments of Union troops marched past the Culpeper Court House, their bobbing bayonets stretching as far as the eye could see, enlivened by dozens of martial bands, "throbbing all at the same moment with wild music . . . 'St. Patrick's Day,' intermingled with the weird refrain of 'Bonnie Dundee,' and snatches of German sword-songs were drowned by the thrilling chorus of the 'Star Spangled Banner.' . . . Suddenly, as if by rehearsal all hats would go up, all bayonets toss and glisten, and huzzas would deafen the winds, while the horses reared upon their haunches and the sabers rose and fell. Then, column by column, the masses passed eastward, while the prisoners in the courthouse cupola looked down, and the citizens peeped in fear through crevices of windows."[2]

Federals took over Val Verde, the estate of Thomas Botts Nalle, one of Martinette's first cousins and a Yankee sympathizer. Townsend, the reporter, described the scene as Union troops burst onto the farm. "To realize the horror of the night," he wrote, "imagine a common clay road, in a quiet, rolling country, packed with bleeding people -the fences down, horsemen riding through the fields, wagons blocking the way, reinforcements in dark columns hurrying up, the shouting of the well to the ill, and the feeble replies—in a word, recall that elder time when 'the earth was filled with violence.'"[3] Fields of fresh cornstalks were trampled down in a giant rustling rush, some of the officers swinging their sabers like scythes that cut down the stalks like so many helpless foe. Frenzied soldiers occupied Nalle's fine brick house, dragged a kitchen table out to a locust grove, and began using it as an operating platform, leaving one shaken victim to write: "Blood, carnage, and death among the sweet shrubbery and roses."[4] Another surgeon transformed the parlor into a second butcher's shop.[5] Later, the Confederates came back with a fury. Nalle's son, William, was trapped for a while between the lines of the opposing armies; another time he returned to his grandmother's house to discover everything destroyed; even the slave quarters had been ransacked, and the cruel Yankees had forced one old slave to strip naked and dance in the snow.[6] A few days later, the boy came upon three dead Yankee soldiers and one badly wounded bluecoat in the woods near his grandmother's home. The injured one was brought to a nearby house for treatment, but a party of Confederates later rode over to finish him off.[7] Nearby, at Charles Doggett's little farm, next to Cole's Hill, a Yankee spy was found to be posing as a Confederate courier and carrying fraudulent dispatches, for which he was hanged on the spot and his body left dangling as a warning to others.

William Yager was a young teenaged slave who lived at Forest Grove, which also was located nearby. One Sunday morning he went out with some other boys after the Confederates had slaughtered some Yankees in the fields. They came across a Yankee lying in a washout. "He wuz alayin' there," Yager later recalled, "the sun broilin' down in his face, his arms jus' agoin' it. But he couldn't talk none. His throat seemed like he wuz wounded. An' I come on him alayin' there. I always wuz a right brave boy. An' so I went an' unbuckled his canteen off'n him an' went over the hill little ways an' got some water an' come back an' turned the canteen up an' put the neck right to his mouth." Young William must have tilted the canteen too much when he poured because the soldier gagged and choked. The slave became scared and left, assuming the soldier must have died.[8]

In another incident nearby, Willis Madden opened his tavern door one snowy night to find three scraggly-looking rebel soldiers seeking shelter in his warm home. According to an account left by one of the visitors, Madden said he would have "nothing to do with no stragglers," and turned them away. But the trio persisted and one of them decided to have some fun at his expense. After banging on the door again, the spokesman identified his companions as "the great General Lee himself; the other as the French ambassador just arrived from Washington," and himself as "a staff officer of the general's who is quite mad at being kept waiting outside so long after riding all this way on purpose to see you." The prankster added, "In fact, if you let him stay any longer in the cold, I'm afraid he'll shell your house as soon as his artillery comes up." Seeing no alternative, Madden let them in and cared for their horses, offering his visitors a "repast suited to the distinguished rank of his guests." The one making the account later laughed over the trick they had played on the "stupid old nigger," since their actual rank did not approach that of what they had claimed.⁹ A few days later, the tormentor fell dead with a piece of shrapnel lodged in his brain. Madden had been forced to endure many insults and injuries during the twenty-eight or so years he had run his farm and tavern, but somehow he had always managed to please everybody, even though he was a free Negro in a slavery society. By war's end, however, his home became a feeding trough and playground for one group after another of rough Union soldiers, many of whom looted his belongings and denuded his entire timber lot for their own amusement and comfort. They ate his chickens, gobbled his corn, stole his livestock, knocked down his fences and outbuildings, and otherwise ruined his property, leaving him financially broke and spiritually depressed.¹⁰

Before the war had started, Blucher Hansbrough had been sinking under the weight of mounting debts and nagging court judgments. On June 9, 1863, Charles's former home experienced a worse calamity when Cole's Hill became the scene of heavy fighting during the Battle of Brandy Station, the greatest cavalry battle of the war. Dozens of Southerners fell dead, wounded or captured in Hansbrough's trampled wheat fields and woods, leaving heaps of fallen horses and riders scattered over the countryside and vultures circling overhead. Other skirmishes occurred nearby, around Madden's tavern, Berry Hill, Carrico Mill, and other familiar family haunts. From November 26, 1863, to May 4, 1864, Hansbrough's Ridge served as the encampment of ten thousand omnivorous soldiers of the Second Corps of the Army of the Potomac—a prolonged curse upon the land—and Cole's Hill itself served as the Second Corps headquarters, turning the household into a giant pantry for the crude invaders. As a result, all of the crops and woods were stripped, the sparkling streams were befouled, and all of the local game was killed, leaving a muddy expanse of devastation, oozing latrines, and discarded tin cans.[11]

Although tiny Stevensburg occupied such an important strategic place for the federal invaders and the Yankee troops often completely took over the bigger homes to serve as officers' quarters, Blucher enjoyed friendly relations with some of them, particularly a young and flamboyant general, George Armstrong Custer, who had brought along his new bride, Elizabeth (Libby) Bacon Custer, and he was apparently allowed to remain with his family at Cole's Hill. Hansbrough made available his fine carriage to the couple so they could carry on their romance and enable her to ride up to Mount Pony to look down across the Rapidan and see, as she would later put it, "Wild rebels on the other side of the river." Custer later named one of his favorite dogs, a Scotch staghound, Blucher after his genial Southern acquaintance.[12]

Walt Whitman accompanied the federal army in Culpeper at that time. "Authorities have chased each other here like clouds in a stormy sky," he wrote. "Before the first Bull Run this was the rendezvous and camp of instruction of the secession troops. I am stopping at the house of a lady who has witness'd all the eventful changes of the War, along this route of contending armies. She is a widow, with a family of young children, and lives here with her sister in a large handsome house. A number of army officers board with them."[13]

When federal troops first approached the Reverend Thornton Stringfellow's Belair estate, the stern-faced minister greeted them with copies of some of his proslavery pamphlets, but by October 5, 1863, he noted glumly in his diary that all his slaves had fled—kidnapped by the Yankees, he insisted.[14]

Time and again, the Yankee incursions resulted in many of the slaves fleeing or being carried off, regarded by the U.S. Army as "contrabands." Once separated from their masters, many of the former slaves worked as camp servants for the Northern officers or as laborers for the troops who used them to provide wood and build their fortifications, or they simply suffered the plight of refugees. Most of the uprooted packed their meager belongings together onto rickety carts and set off with loved ones and friends on the arduous trek north, toward the Promised Land. Many were never heard from again. Charles Nalle knew many of those who were killed or displaced.

At Berry Hill, where Charles's wife had lived, every remaining Negro except one, he being too old to walk, fled the once-glorious Thom estate with the Yankees during their last retreat. The soldiers took with them "every living thing, biped and quadruped, . . . the furniture, which was all new and handsome, much broken and injured."[15] They grabbed all of Lucy Thom's fancy clothes and valuables, leaving her to watch helplessly as they carried her melodeon to the slave quarters, it being a favorite Yankee gesture to encourage the slaves to play some music for their Northern liberators before they set off on the road to freedom.[16]

Elsewhere some of the Yankees encouraged the remaining local slaves to help themselves to their masters' gardens and belongings and told them they were free to leave, free to do as they wished. At one place near Raccoon Ford, a black coachman entered his master's bedroom, put on some of the white gentleman's best clothes, complete with watch and chain, and sauntered out of the house telling anyone who would listen that his master "might for the future drive his own coach."[17] Some observers later reported seeing bold female slaves smack their mistresses in the face before they departed.[18]

Union General Alexander Hays commandeered the old Fitzhugh house at Carrico Mill, just down the road from Cole's Hill, and made himself perfectly at home, "with a good fire, and fancy furniture and a comfortable bed." The old man and two ladies who had remained at their house seemed to him the "most sensible people" he had met in Virginia, for they "do not talk 'secesh,' although they are full of it."[19]

At Rose Hill, the ancestral home of Martinette Nalle Hansbrough's father, Martin Nalle, Lieutenant General H. Judson Kilpatrick overcame his boredom by riding his steed into his headquarters' open door, cantering down the center hall, and exiting by the rear door. Then he rode back in and retraced his route to exit from the front, to the shock of the Nalles and the disdain of some of Kilpatrick's men.[20] The clunk of hooves on the floorboards and the jangle of spurs and scabbard would echo for some time to come.

At last, when Grant and Meade finally made their exit from Culpeper, Meade and his staff paused on their horses atop Hansbrough's Ridge and looked down at the troops crossing the Rapidan. "As far as you could see, in every direction," one staff officer recorded, "corps, divisions, brigades, trains, batteries, and squadrons, were moving on in a waving sea of blue; headquarters and regimental flags were fluttering, the morning sun kissing them all, and shimmering gaily from gun barrels."[21] Down below, on Hansbrough's tattered farm, the war front and the home front were one; the battle over slavery had struck home in ways that hardly could have been imagined by Charles Nalle or any of his contemporaries just a few years before. After years of being in the middle and torn by contesting forces, as Charles had been up north, Culpeper's slaves were now cut loose and unshackled. The centuries-old system of slavery, with all of its visible oppressions and deep, dark secrets, had finally been wrecked.

During most of the Civil War, Charles and his family continued to live in Troy, away from the carnage and upheaval of their ancestral land. Winna Ann and Lewis Burrell moved there to be with them.[1] In 1863 Charles took new work as a porter for a local druggist, A. B. Knowlson, sometimes accompanied by his six-year-old son, John.[2]

That summer, however, the Nalles and other black residents of Troy experienced a riot of a different kind than the one that had liberated Charles. It occurred after the simultaneous occurrence of three events set off a violent reaction among many white workers. First, the posting of casualties from the Battle of Gettysburg struck many local families hard. Then came the start of the government's intensely unpopular program of military conscription, the draft, that allowed men of means to evade service by hiring a substitute or paying Uncle Sam $300, which amounted to a year's wages for the average laborer. Irish immigrants were especially enraged because the unfair law reminded them of actions by the British Crown they hated. Many Irishmen also blamed Negroes as the cause of the bloody war and they worried that the blacks would take their jobs when they were off to fight. The third contributing cause came in the form of news about the riots against the draft that had just been put down in New York City, at a cost of hundreds of lives and tremendous loss of property.

At nine in the morning on July 15, four hundred angry Irish workers gathered at Henry Burden's Nail Factory in south Troy and began agitating over all three of the outrages. Many threw down their aprons and started marching north toward the federal offices downtown. Other mechanics and laborers joined the procession. Church bells sounded a warning, merchants bolted their doors. A column of marchers confronted the orange-brick Mutual Bank building that formerly had housed the U.S. commissioner's office and which now contained the office of the detested provost marshal—the official responsible for carrying out the draft. Their mood turned ugly. But before the mob started an attack, one of the besieged officials inside sent out a frantic message announcing that the provost marshal had decided to suspend the draft in this district. This victory moved some of the rioters to stop and cheer.

But others proceeded down to the corner of First and River streets to vent their rage against the headquarters of the city's staunchest pro-draft and anti-slavery supporter, the *Troy Times*. Several prominent citizens who tried to intervene were shoved aside. The mob smashed down the doors and burst into the newspaper offices, strewing paper and dumping the printers' lead trays and ink pots as they went. Hooligans also began targeting Negroes. A few blocks away, a mob engulfed the Liberty Street Presbyterian Church, threatening to burn it to the ground, but two brave Catholic priests stood in their path and refused to move. One of them was knocked down, but the other—Peter Havermans—held his ground and shoved them back until the ruffians finally left.

Roughnecks stormed the jail and seized control. Others broke into the Second Street house of Martin I. Townsend, the lawyer who had defended Charles Nalle three years earlier, and carted off or destroyed everything they could find. "Kill the niggers! Kill the niggers! Kill the niggers!" some of them chanted. With Troy's mayor urging them to run for their lives, many of the city's people of color fled in terror, some of them heading for safety in Sand Lake, Greenbush, or Albany. To restore order the mayor called up four military companies, one of which aimed a loaded six-pound howitzer at the crowd to get them to disperse. The commander of the Watervliet Arsenal also brought in four hundred local volunteers to aid his sixty-five troops. But it was not until seven hundred more troops arrived to bolster the city's defenses that the provost marshal finally started drafting Trojans.[3]

In 1865, shortly before the war had ended, Charles and Kitty took their eight children to live in Washington, D.C., in order to be closer to their other relatives. Charles found employment as one of the city's first (unsalaried) colored postal carriers and his wife worked as a seamstress.[4] Over the next several years, three of their daughters ended up in New Orleans and one, Agnes (Alice) married state senator George Ruby of Texas, a freeborn mulatto from Maine who had served as James Redpath's assistant in Haiti.[5] Uri Gilbert was elected mayor of Troy and Horatio Averill, the man who had betrayed Charles, later returned to the area and rehabilitated his image so well that he had his village named after him. Minot Crosby became a school principal in Connecticut and John Nalle started his educational career in the District of Columbia schools.

Charles Nalle died of heart disease in Washington, D.C., on July 13, 1875, and he was buried in Rock Creek cemetery.[6] One obituary in Troy reported he had "caused more stir in this city than any other man has before or since."[7] Another said he was "highly respected, and although his life was one of turmoil and persecution up to the time when he received his freedom, he has since enjoyed the blessings of peace and of the emancipation which was given to his race. He has numerous friends in this city who are among his sincerest mourners."[8]

Tubman died in 1913 and a few months later her hometown of Auburn erected a bronze tablet that said, albeit with colloquial spellings typical of the day: "ON MY UNDERGROUND RAILROAD I NEBBER RUN MY TRAIN OFF DE TRACK AND I NEBBER LOST A PASSENGER."[9]

It wasn't until almost twenty years later that Charles Nalle's elderly son, John, finally learned about the rescue and Tubman's involvement in it, leaving him to wonder why his father hadn't told him about such an extraordinary series of events. Although John Nalle tried to discover answers to that question, it's not clear that he ever gained a complete understanding. Part of the reason, he would write, may have been ascribed to his father's "innate modesty (so he would not appear as a hero)," or perhaps it was due to Charles's "hatred of the damnable institution and those who fostered the institution."[10] Nevertheless, it appears that the son never completely grasped his father's motivation.

So many years later, it's all the more difficult for an outsider to try to solve the mystery, yet we should at least try to consider some of the possibilities. Certainly the episode must have evoked painful memories for Charles about traumas he wished to keep buried or repressed. Like other former slaves, he had much suffering to try to forget, and in some people's minds having been a slave carried its own stigma, regardless of who and what was really responsible for the enslavement. Charles too likely endured some measure of "survivor's guilt" for having survived and escaped his bondage, since he knew that others had not run away or made it out. Indeed, his own mother and his brothers had declined to flee with him, and as a consequence some of them had been punished and put through horrible and humiliating things; his own wife as well had been imprisoned and degraded and almost lost her life as a result of *his* escape—some of his loved ones had suffered on his account, and he may have felt responsible. Running away and being a fugitive had made him a criminal before the law, and that too may have seemed hard to bear, particularly for someone such as himself who appeared to respect law and moral authority. Then there had been the unseemliness of his betrayal back in Sand Lake, and the distastefulness of it, the shock of being put under arrest by Jack Wale the disreputable slave catcher and a federal marshal, then adjudicated by an officer of the United States government. How might he have felt about the fierce division it had spawned among persons who believed in abiding by the law, or who hated him because he was a slave and a man of color, versus others who saw him as a pawn or an object of contention, or those who risked all to defend him? A lynch mob was one thing, but he had been subjected to two contesting forces and almost torn limb from limb—not only once, but twice; he was lucky he hadn't been killed—it was almost like a man who was being hanged but the rope broke, and on two consecutive tries. Then he had finally been bought and sold once more, underscoring his status as chattel. Not to mention the fact that his master was his own half-brother, a man he had faithfully served and supported over many trying years. Was it any wonder he would not wish to divulge such matters to his son?

The horrors of slavery, like memories of war and the Holocaust, weighed heavily on its survivors and their descendants, from one generation to the next. And the society and governments and other institutions that had kept them enslaved would also bear their guilt.

Those who aided Charles Nalle to escape had something to feel good about. In Troy, many residents continued to regard his liberation and their participation in it as the greatest thing that had ever happened in that city. Yet freeing Charles had not proved easy or quick—not simple for anyone, especially for himself. Even after such a difficult and protracted ordeal, the struggle for freedom and equality would continue going on for some time to come.

In 1993, I took my first research trip down to Culpeper, hoping to find some trace of Charles Nalle, the slave. Culpeper is a charming town of about 10,000 residents that recently was voted "one of the ten best small towns in America." Before my initial arrival archaeologists had come upon more than two thousand dinosaur tracks dating back 208 million years, and other imprints of its not-so-distant past were also remarkably intact, prompting me to realize the place still contained a lot of history under one's feet.[1] When Captain John Smith had mapped the place in 1608, he encountered carvings in the rock of a local 791-foot-high summit that the Indians (probably the Ontponeas) had left as proof of their dominion there, before they were eradicated.[2] More than a century later in 1749 a big-boned surveyor named George Washington, who was then only seventeen years old and working his first job, had taken his measure of the newly created Culpeper County, drafting meticulous plats that included room for its first colonial courthouse, jail, and gallows.[3] Twenty-five years after that, Culpeper's Minutemen had marched off to fight in the American Revolution under a flag that showed a coiled rattlesnake that was about to strike, alongside slaveholder Patrick Henry's words, "LIBERTY OR DEATH!"[4] By the mid-nineteenth century, Culpeper County was known far and wide as a bastion of slavery, with a population that in 1860 numbered 12,063 persons of whom 4,959 were whites, 429 were free Negroes, and 6,675 were slaves.[5] Then, when the War Between the States broke out in 1861, Culpeper and its environs served as a loyal recruiting ground for the Confederate army until troops of both sides ravaged the area in years of battle and occupation.[6] Ending slavery there, I was soon to learn, had taken a terrible toll.

As I began my quest, the wonderful Culpeper County and Town Library offered several excellent local histories, detailed historical maps, archaeological descriptions of some of the old plantations, census records, newspapers, genealogies, and oral histories by some of the former slaves who had inhabited the area. Some of Stevensburg's surviving antebellum structures, landmarks, and battle sites were still recognizable from faded photographs and drawings. The bucolic landscape seemed to have barely changed since the days when saber-wielding cavalry charged over the rolling golden fields, and surveying such scenery I could almost imagine slaves harvesting the property's wheat crop and tending the master's grand coach. Everyone I met was exceedingly well mannered, courteous, and refined, although at the start I sensed an invisible barrier between us, a line between North and South that still existed after more than a century and a half. There remained certain issues that one didn't discuss in polite society, and unfortunately for me, these were the issues I was seeking to explore.

Soon I began to find that trying to piece together evidence about a slave's life is extremely difficult. Slaves weren't allowed to keep diaries, write letters, give testimony, or utter pronouncements. For them there were no birth certificates, no death records, no license applications, headstones or cemetery records, or military records and most other forms of official documentation—like ethnic cleansing. The record keepers enumerated them in bills of sale, as they did with land, livestock, or other chattel.

Hence, finding the first bill of sale involving Charles Nalle amounted to a momentous occasion for me and my wife: there for the first time lay an official primary source clue about Charles Nalle's enslavement and the Hansbroughs' enslaving. There it was, the first legal proof of his bondage, evidence committed to paper in the very same courthouse where it had been recorded and officially sanctioned 156 years earlier. By working our way from that starting point, through the dense legal and mercantile environment of deeds, wills, and judgments, as revealed through business transactions involving "grantors" and "grantees," "legatees" and "indenturers," witnesses, clerks, and justices of the peace, we gradually assembled more tiny fragments about Nalle and his mother and siblings. All the while we also dug for clues about Nalle's wife, Kitty, and their children, who were owned by Colonel John Thom of nearby Berry Hill, as well as legal records about some of the other characters in the story.

At the well-appointed Virginia Historical Society in Richmond, nestled among Confederate statues, and at the University of Virginia Library in resplendent Charlottesville, we found Colonel Thom's will and manumission papers, as well as notes about runaway slaves and other Thom, Hansbrough, and

Nalle family records that provided more crucial information about the forced breakup of Charles and Kitty's family and other aspects of their lives.[7]

But records about Kitty (and Lucy, Fanny Simms, Winna Ann, Lucinda Wormley, and other slave women in the story) turned out to be even scarcer than information about Charles. Nothing else in my investigative quest would prove so sadly elusive or tantalizingly suggestive.[8] Slave women suffered a double oppression, both as women and as African Americans, and as a result they remain largely invisible and overlooked in history.[9] Kitty's life seemed almost blanked out, except for occasional evidence of *her* deeds—not the kind of deeds that one might find recorded by lawyers and scribes for storage in a county clerk's log, but real-life powerful deeds, the kind of actions that spoke louder than any words on a page. Through it all, one could catch glimpses of a woman who was smart, courageous, resourceful, loyal, compassionate, physically strong, determined, gracious, dignified, ingenious, hard-working, enterprising, tough, and committed to her family. For most of her life, she would live outside the company of her husband and raise their children largely on her own, yet Kitty and Charles appear to have been extremely devoted to each other, leaving behind a story that speaks to the power of love between a man and a woman who were determined to remain together despite all the obstacles placed in their way. I only wish there was more information about her.

Fortunately, more information was available about one of the other great black women in the story, Harriet Tubman, although in her case the enveloping mythology sometimes made it difficult to get through to her as a real person.

One of my first Stevensburg interviews involved T. O. Madden Jr., who like Charles Nalle was a very light-colored African American from a long-established family that lived very close to Cole's Hill and was part of the same tiny enclave. At the time of our initial meeting, T. O. was ninety-one years old, but full of vitality, wit, and mischief, and he had been written up in *Smithsonian* and recently come out with his wonderful family memoir and history, *We Were Always Free: The Maddens of Culpeper County, Virginia: A 200-Year Family History* (1992), showing how he and his free-black forebears had accomplished so much with dignity, despite all of the burdens that racism had placed on them over their two-century stay in Virginia. His book was filled with important details about the very countryside and characters I was investigating, and this too helped me a great deal. His great-grandfather, Willis Madden, had been a contemporary, neighbor, and close friend of Charles Nalle, and T. O. spoke about Charles's master, Blucher Hansbrough, as if he were still alive, regaling me with tales about his rakish behavior that had been passed down in the Madden family's oral accounts. Opening an ancient hidebound trunk,

T. O. graciously allowed me to examine some of his precious family records and gently corrected me regarding some of my early errors and misconceptions, such as the pronunciations of many key names. As we sat in the cozy, low-ceilinged dining room of his ancestral antebellum farmhouse, at the spot that Colonel Thom and Blucher ("BLOOKER") Hansbrough and Charles Nalle ("NOLE") had frequented when it was a popular tavern and meeting place, the old man recited a mysterious old rhyme from the vicinity that he said had summed up local life in those days. "Chinquapin Neck, land of peth," he said, "one half lived and the other half starved to death!" When I told him I wished to learn more about a former slave who had lived next door to his farm, he chuckled and warned, "You'll really be poking into some buzzard's nests." Later I would come to realize that my aged host was not only related to someone who had likely aided my subject to escape, but he also was a direct descendant of Jack Wale, the white slave catcher who had arrested Charles Nalle in Troy in 1860, making him a living link to some of the people and places I was studying.[10] (Years later, I would also hear reports that T. O. shared blood with Blucher Hansbrough.)

Hoping to learn as much as possible about life in that vicinity before the Civil War, I consulted American slave narratives, the gut-wrenching personal accounts left by former slaves, many of them former fugitives. Among those that had been published in the era of Nalle's slavery and liberation were several classic books and stirring lectures attributed to Frederick Douglass, William Wells Brown, Solomon Northrup, William and Ellen Craft, Harriet A. Jacobs, and Moses Roper, and several others that had found their way into print years later, which proved very useful and moving—testimony that laid bare slavery from inside the belly of the beast, and stories that told of daring escapes and painful adjustments. This shelf of searing works provided much insight about the lives of those in bondage and fed my historical imagination about what Charles may have thought and felt under comparable circumstances. But I wanted to find out more about his inner life.

Charles Nalle was forced to remain illiterate until late in his life and therefore he was unable to write his own story. Unlike Douglass, he hadn't left behind a published slave narrative, speeches, or letters. No contemporary writer had served as his amanuensis or aided him to produce a detailed account of his life or written a fictionalized slave narrative based on his experiences. This made it more difficult to document his version of the events I was exploring. Lacking such an autobiographical account, I searched for any pertinent interviews with other slaves and former slaves from his time and region. The most informative ones I found were contained in the works of two pioneering abolitionists, *The Refugee: A North-Side View of Slavery* (1856), by Benjamin Drew, and the journalistic dispatches of James Redpath that were collected in *The Roving Editor* (1859), sources that are described in detail in this book.

Moreover, from 1936 to 1938, trained writers operating under the aegis of the federal Works Progress Administration had interviewed more than 2,300 former slaves from across the South, including more than three hundred elderly Negroes who were documented by the Virginia Writers' Project. About half the Virginia records were lost or destroyed, but the rest were recovered and excerpted in various works. The best annotated collection of them I found was edited by Charles L. Perdue Jr., Thomas E. Barden, and Robert K. Phillips as *Weevils in the Wheat: Interviews with Virginia Ex-Slaves* (1976). These unadorned firsthand accounts by former Virginia slaves, recounting their experiences on plantations and in cities and small farms throughout Virginia before and during the Civil War, in my view remain probably the most useful source for understanding the lives of those in bondage. Each narrative offers a fragmentary personal glimpse into a lost world, remembered after seven or more decades, yet some of their details remained as vivid and rich as if they had just happened. To be sure, like any source, the interviews had their limitations—for example, they suffered from occasional transcriptional errors and value-laden editing and contained some factual errors that arose from the compilers mistakenly attributing some accounts to the wrong interviewees; also, more than seven decades had passed before the subjects were finally interviewed. Nevertheless they provided an invaluable record of what slavery was like from the slave's perspective. When studied together, with the aid of an excellent index and systematic consultation, I found the assembled voices revealed consistent themes about slave labor, resistance and flight, family life, relations with masters, food and material culture, and religious belief. For this book, I tried to be careful to stick to those oral histories that involved some of the specific places, persons, and time periods I was studying. In the end, I selected a number of these comments as quotations and used many others to help me inform the reader about the subject at hand by means of comparable observations.

Eyewitness newspaper accounts about the rescue were most helpful, not only because they were so numerous and detailed, but also because they showed such a remarkable degree of consensus about the important facts. Altogether I found more than a dozen published stories in a variety of journals spanning the political spectrum. One of my most useful sources was a *Troy Daily Arena* newspaper article from May of 1860 in which a sympathetic white journalist printed a brief but factually detailed account based on his interview with

Charles Nalle while the fugitive was still hiding out after his rescue and waiting
for go-betweens to arrange his legal liberation. In it, Nalle recounted some of
his formative personal history and explained his multiple reasons for running
away.[11] (The interviewer, Charles L. MacArthur (1824–98), was the abolitionist Republican editor of the *Troy Daily Arena* and the person later credited
with starting the subscription to purchase Nalle's freedom.) Very few fugitive
slaves left even a secondhand account of their escape, so I felt fortunate to
have found it. Not surprisingly, though, given the legal implications, Nalle
and his interviewer didn't explain how he had fled or reveal his whereabouts
prior to his capture. Nothing was said about his exciting rescue because many
of the participants were still facing possible prosecution. Vengeance was still
at work. And Nalle still hadn't broken completely free of his master.

When I began my investigation, the subject of the Underground Railroad
loomed large and blurry, shrouded in myth and old wives' tales. Some of the
reasons for this were quite understandable. Fearing possible prosecution or
other reprisals, most participants hadn't wanted to leave behind any incriminating evidence about themselves or their accomplices. This meant the operations of the secret networks that aided fugitive slaves were just as veiled
and hidden as the inner workings of slavery itself. It was, after all, a criminal
conspiracy, and even after the Civil War many of its former participants rightly
feared it might become necessary again someday. The writing about it has
necessarily remained very political as well as racially sensitive, even to this
day. Much of the common mythology surrounding this touchy subject has
cast the enterprise in romantic terms, full of melodramatic fixtures such as
hidden tunnels, military-style code names, code-bearing spirituals, and quilts
that secretly convey clandestine instructions. Yet since the time I started my
project, it became evident that the Underground Railroad was undergoing a
newfound renaissance or reawakening of interest, some of it geared toward
gaining a more realistic understanding of what it was, how it operated, and
what it meant in the larger context of American history.

The greatest source of authentic, firsthand documentary information about
the Underground Railway was and continues to be the records compiled by
William Still (1821–1902). Although never a slave himself, Still was born into
a family of fugitives and spent sixteen years of his life assisting runaways in
Philadelphia, which was one of the most important offices for ushering slaves
to safety. Fortunately for history, he kept meticulous records regarding his
activities, and later used them as the basis for a comprehensive, richly detailed,
day-to-day account chronicling his contact with 649 fugitives who passed
through his office—a substantial resource made all the more precious by the

fact that Still conducted intensive interviews with his subjects and shortly thereafter committed his impressions to paper as a means of memorializing the encounters and maintaining his files. Upon examining his incomparable compendium, *The Underground Railroad* (1872), I came across his brief but incisive account about the arrival of Charles Nalle and two other fugitives in the Philadelphia Vigilance Committee office, immediately after their escape from Georgetown. It was a revealing record that other scholars may have overlooked because Still used the phonetic spelling "Charles Nole" (probably as Nalle himself had pronounced it with his Virginia accent), and other historians simply had not recognized him as the same figure who was later rescued at Troy. Without Still's notation, I never would have learned the names of Nalle's two companions, or the fact that they had escaped to Philadelphia from Georgetown. Indeed, his represents the only record containing those facts that I could find. Still's report also gave me some other good clues about their flight as well as a deeper understanding of Nalle's psychological state.[12] His contribution too proved crucial.

The task of trying to identify those who assisted Charles to escape proved especially challenging. Even as late as 1858–60, aiding a runaway slave to flee was considered a serious offense, punishable by lengthy imprisonment and fines, and in some places of the South or border states by lynching, beating, or tar and feathers. Federal law made the Underground Railroad a criminal organization and its participants targets of U.S. law enforcement, although in reality, transgressors were very rarely prosecuted and even more seldom convicted. Yet as I eventually discovered, the worst penalties were incurred by the fugitive's fellow slaves—by his or her family or friends. Often it didn't matter whether they had actually aided someone to escape. What counted was that the escape had occurred and slaves had to suffer the consequences. Slaveholders used punishment like a sledgehammer that they wielded based on a finding of collective guilt, and the pain it caused must have proved a powerful deterrent as well as a heavy price to bear. The impact could be felt for years.

Fugitives and those who had assisted them weren't the only ones feeling the need to cover their tracks. My task was not made easier by the fact that the federal government had destroyed nearly all of the records regarding its administration of the Fugitive Slave Law in the Northern District of New York, from evidence about the activities of the U.S. commissioner, marshal, and customhouse to the operations of the court for the period in question. The official paper trail has largely been erased.

In trying to learn as much as I could about the operations of the Underground Railroad from Washington, D.C., and Philadelphia during the period in question, I began, like many scholars, by studying Larry Gara's slim but enormously influential study *The Liberty Line: The Legend of the Underground Railroad* (1961). Gara's work was famous for having debunked myths about a clandestine network with hidden tunnels, mysterious signals, secret codes, and romantic heroes that legend had depicted in businesslike railroad nomenclature. He had showed that, contrary to some popular beliefs, the Underground Railroad hadn't consisted of a single, unified apparatus operated mostly by white Quakers. He also pointed out that blacks were much more deeply involved in assisting runaway slaves than commonly thought. Rejecting much of the prevalent mythology as "melodrama" and "folklore," Gara opted in favor of a more "realistic," pragmatic, and complex picture. He tried to place the fugitives themselves at the center of their struggle for freedom, which was appropriate. But the deeper I dug, the more it seemed to me that his approach was extremely general, purporting to cover the whole "legend" from start to finish, from all over the country to Canada, in only a couple hundred pages. In addition, as Stanley Harrold has correctly noted, Gara mistakenly suggested that "there were few, if any, coordinated escapes along predetermined routes," and he further erroneously dismissed the notion that any white abolitionists had helped to organize any escapes from the South.[13]

Gara's views have remained very influential, however. Recently, a seemingly comprehensive quantitative study of fugitive slaves, *Runaway Slaves: Rebels on the Plantation*, by John Hope Franklin and Loren Schweninger (1999), which relied on runaway notices and judicial and legislative records to examine hundreds of slave escapes, barely mentioned the Underground Railroad, abolitionists, or slave rescues at all; instead treated such networks and actions as largely inconsequential for many runaways; and mainly characterized the phenomenon of flight as a form of individual resistance by the slaves who generally absconded alone and with little if any outside support by whites or anyone else. It also tended to lump fugitives from different regions and time periods into the same one-size-fits-all box.[14] It too did not seem to jibe with what I was seeing based on my study.

After Still's indispensable documentation, the first work to elevate the Underground Railroad into a subject of serious historical scholarship was Wilbur H. Siebert's *The Underground Railroad from Slavery to Freedom* (1898), which utilized interviews, surveys, and other sources to document 3,211 individuals (nearly all of them white men) whom the author claimed had been part of a nationwide effort to assist slaves to escape. Although Siebert's history covered a wider time period and geographical area than Still's, it too had its limitations, ultimately leaving the impression that even the larger group he identified as agents and other operators must have actually accounted for only a fraction of the total number. Since that time, the field of study has also benefited from popular overviews by Charles L. Blockson and Fergus M. Bordewich, as well as from painstaking scholarship by Stanley Harrold and a few others. As a result, more of the dramatis personae and modus operandi of the Underground Railroad have assumed greater clarity and more significant standing in American history. The field still has a long way to go before it can claim its rightful place or enjoy general consensus, but the phenomenon lately has enjoyed a resurgence in interest among scholars, activists, and tourism boosters, even if many of the players have taken widely different views of what the phenomenon actually entailed.[15] Writing more than forty years after Gara, Bordewich observed that "[f]or generations, Americans thought of the Underground Railroad as a mostly monochromatic narrative of high-minded white people condescending to help terrified and helpless blacks." While acknowledging that Gara helped restore African Americans to their "rightful place at the center of the story," Bordewich also argued, I think correctly, that the Underground Railroad is "no more 'black history' than it is 'white history': it is *American* history; and it swept into its orbit courageous Americans of every hue." He has rightly called it "one of the most ambitious political undertakings in American history."[16]

Another prominent writer on the subject, David W. Blight, has characterized the Underground Railroad more as a "process" than a well-organized machine, although ultimately conceding: "This traffic in escaped slaves exerted pressure on slavery itself, caused significant political tensions between the North and the South, and prompted a small but important group of abolitionists to resist the law by aiding fugitives to freedom."[17]

Gara asserted that the "high publicity" given to a few rescues or attempted rescues of persons arrested as alleged slaves under the Fugitive Slave Law "helped popularize the idea that a conspiratorial underground organization networked the North," even though "most of them were actually the result of impromptu action rather than any long-range planning." Arguing that the records of the rescues "give no evidence that they were connected with a general conspiracy," he dismissed all such incidents as "betray[ing] a lack of the organization, discipline, and planning which would characterize a successful underground."[18]

Bordewich, on the other hand, has rightly argued that "by the 1850s, the underground had developed into a diverse, flexible, and interlocking system with thousands of activists reaching from the upper South to Canada." He has painted a picture of an enterprise that had no formal organization, constitution, officers, bylaws, or written operating agreements, yet which existed with a common strategic goal and purpose—to aid fugitives to escape. He has said it "incorporated a broader infrastructure of itinerant preachers, teamsters, and peddlers who carried messages for the underground into the South, slaves who themselves never fled but provided information regarding escape routes to those who did, sailors and ships' stewards who concealed runaways on their vessels, lawyers who were willing to defend fugitives and those who were accused of harboring them, businessmen who provided needed funds, as well as an even wider pool of family members, friends, and fellow parishioners who although they might never engage personally in illegal activity, protected those who did and made it possible for them to continue their work."[19]

As the Nalle story indicates, the "underground" had its own intelligence system, spies and counterspies, regional headquarters, supply system, network of safe houses, and its own propaganda apparatus that utilized many different media and channels to communicate its ideas and secretly pass information. Not all runaways utilized this apparatus to make good their escape or support their flight. Yet at least by the late 1850s, the infrastructure and the movement existed to help them, just as their adversaries had devised their own system of lobbyists, legislators, lawyers, judges, police, informers, patrollers, bounty hunters, insurance agents, propagandists, slave pens, and jails to serve their cause.

Organized resistance to slavery and the Fugitive Slave Law took several forms, of which the Underground Railroad was only one. Individuals and communities mobilized to raise money to support abolitionist causes, transport or secrete fugitives, employ escaped slaves, operate vigilance committees, provide food and clothing to runaways and their families, defend slaves and their protectors in court, establish schools and social welfare programs for blacks, circulate petitions and newspapers, participate in mass meetings, and engage in more radical civil disobedience and other direct action designed to free slaves by force. My own study has led me to detect a strong improvisational ability on the part of blacks to resist the white slave catchers.

The only comprehensive study of enforcement of the 1850 Fugitive Slave Law, Stanley W. Campbell's *The Slave Catchers*, lists only twenty-two slaves including Charles Nalle as having been rescued from federal custody.[20] A few of these cases have been the subject of a case study.[21] However, most studies of the Underground Railroad haven't included much detailed consideration of slave rescues, and vice versa, perhaps leaving the impression that those involved in carrying out such activities were different and distinct, or that the latter events, as Gara claimed, were largely spontaneous and lacking in planning, timing, and coordination. This book suggests the two as being more highly linked and interconnected than many historians have heretofore assumed. The timing of both his capture and his rescue appear to have been very politically significant.

My investigation has led me to conclude that, contrary to what Gara suggested, by the 1850s the Underground Railroad was an integral part of the struggle against slavery, and its activities displayed a significant and increased degree of planning and coordination both in a number of rescue attempts and in the development of sophisticated networks and routes to move fugitive slaves. Both sides—the slave catchers and the rescuers—became remarkably well organized, resourceful, and coordinated in their slave seizures or rescue attempts. A number of these high-profile incidents appear to have been strategically staged political events, and when they suddenly occurred, both sides snapped into action with surprising alacrity, showing that they were both determined and ingenious as well as extraordinarily opportunistic both sides attempted to seize the opportunity of the moment, in some instances after they had made elaborate preparations to capitalize on such a situation. Thus the Underground Railroad, slave rescues, abolitionist efforts in Kansas, and John Brown's raid all were part of a larger civil rights movement that most historians have failed to examine in depth, but which Bordewich and others have aptly placed at the head of a long tradition. It may still be an open question whether the abolitionist movement ultimately succeeded in undermining and eroding the institution of slavery and precipitating the Civil War, just as historians may always quibble over the motives and agenda of some of its leaders. But it would be wrong to dismiss the abolitionists as an ineffectual minority, just as it is mistaken to underestimate the significance of rescues such as the one that occurred in Troy, just as it is unfair to label abolitionists as "fanatics" without characterizing the slaveholders and slavery's defenders. In Nalle's case, I managed to find some important clues about his escape, his companions, escape route, and those who aided his flight and provided shelter and other support while he was a fugitive slave, which led me to conclude that dozens, possibly hundreds of persons, contributed to his liberation—just as a whole system of government, law, and custom had kept him enslaved.

As I was putting together this book, excellent new biographies of Tubman (by Kate Clifford Larson, Jean M. Humez, and Catherine Clinton) as well as David S. Reynolds's astute analysis, *John Brown, Abolitionist*, were adding to the growing understanding of those two important abolitionist characters.[22] Larson's painstakingly researched and solid portrayal of Tubman penetrated the guise surrounding one of history's mythic figures to reveal a hero of enormous strength and complexity, and Humez's scholarly exegesis of Tubman's legacy compared the great hero's presentation of herself with descriptions others constructed. Likewise, Reynolds's welcome biography and some of the other newer works about Brown have reinstated his power as a champion for social justice—as opposed to a Hollywood "madman" stereotype. Both of these towering individuals (Brown and Tubman) figure prominently in Nalle's story. Tubman, of course, was one of his saviors (along with dozens of others) and literally held his fate in her hands. But Brown also cast a large shadow over his life and the lives of other participants, especially Tubman. I've tried to place Nalle and his rescue in relation to what we know about Tubman and Brown and their likely impact on his life. In the process, I've also sought to offer some new insights into each of these icons.

While Charles's story embodies the deeply imbricated issues of race and kinship as they existed in antebellum America, these conceptions and conventions are now viewed very differently than they were in 1860. Indeed, the prevailing views about them seem to have changed just during the span I was doing this book. And that too has made this project particularly challenging. W. E. B. DuBois wrote, "The colored slave woman became the medium through which two great races were united," and so-called miscegenation or race-mixing looms in the background as an important but ambiguous and ever-changing part of this story.[23] The sources and implications of this racial intermixture have long been hotly contested, but today the issue is not as violently charged as it was in antebellum days, even in Virginia. At the time most of the incidents in this book occurred, accusations about "amalgamation" could result in a duel or a lynching, and commentary on the subject took on the most scandalous hue. Instances of interracial sexual intercourse were hidden from view and notions about them were ascribed to powerful lust. Society persisted in casting interracial sexual unions in strictly moralistic terms. A hundred years later, some of the more progressive analysts characterized its impact as engendering emotional confusion and tortured self-contempt, leaving it to a Marxist historian, Eugene D. Genovese, to dissent: "The tragedy of miscegenation lay, not in its collapse into lust and sexual exploitation, but in the terrible pressure to deny the delight, affection, and love that so often grew from tawdry beginnings."[24] Yet the subject of racial intermixture remained—and still is—extremely sensitive.

In August of 2004, I attended a family reunion in Manassas, Virginia, that attracted about three hundred persons of every race and hue, mostly African Americans, many of whom who openly identified themselves as blood relatives of the white slaveholder Blucher Hansbrough—something that never would have been conceivable a century ago. Two years later, I participated in an even larger reunion that was held in Culpeper itself. To my surprise, it received extensive friendly coverage from the Culpeper's hometown newspaper, the *Star-Exponent*, including detailed stories about Charles Nalle, Blucher Hansbrough, and other characters in this book, some of it based on my research. The airing showed just how much some things have changed in recent years.[25] That never would have happened a generation ago, when such discussion was taboo. It indicates how historiography itself keeps changing.

Just as my writing of the book was entering its final phase, Senator Barack Obama gave his electrifying speech, "A More Perfect Union," about the complexities of America's racial discourse. In it he said:

> I am the son of a black man from Kenya and a white woman from Kansas. I was raised with the help of a white grandfather who survived a Depression to serve in Patton's Army during World War II and a white grandmother who worked on a bomber assembly line at Fort Leavenworth while he was overseas. I've gone to some of the best schools in America and lived in one of the world's poorest nations. I am married to a black American who carries within her the blood of slaves and slave owners—an inheritance we pass on to our two precious daughters. I have brothers, sisters, nieces, nephews, uncles and cousins, of every race and every hue, scattered across three continents, and for as long as I live, I will never forget that in no other country on Earth is my story even possible.
>
> It's a story that hasn't made me the most conventional candidate. But it is a story that has seared into my genetic makeup the idea that this nation is more than the sum of its parts—that out of many, we are truly one.[26]

During my work on this project, I came into contact with several direct or collateral descendants of Charles Nalle, Willis Madden, Harriet Tubman, Peter Baltimore, and other characters in the story. Some of these living links helped me to realize that historical memory stretches beyond the generations that directly experienced the events. My social encounters with them, as well as visits to many of the fields and river crossings and street corners that figured in the story—the physical sites—haunted me with a sense of living history.

Pierre Nora has suggested that "history" represents an incomplete reconstruction of something that happened but which is no longer present, whereas memory constructs "remains in permanent evolution" and is always open to reinterpretation and deliberate or unintentional forgetting.[27] According to Nora, history is a history of the present, a backward projection that is constituted in discourses and environments of the present. Although most historians claim that historiography offers a singular, authoritative, objective narrative, in reality history is polyphonous, consisting of heterogeneous and multiple voices that are engaged in both contest and dialogue over time and remembrance.

Some professional academic historians I encountered through this project tended to marginalize (as "soft" and unverifiable history) the "folk" practices of genealogy, oral family history, local history, and individual interpretive accounts in the mistaken belief that they aren't valid or worthwhile. Conversely, I found folk historians who were prisoners of their own frames of reference and sometimes unwilling to search beyond their own, constructed realms of memory for empirical clues about the past.

Popular branches and practices of history—genealogy, family reunions, and DNA—are changing the face of racial discourse in America and serve as powerful enfranchising tools for marginalized historical subjects. Once the province of socially elite white families and historical societies, but now one of the most popular areas of historiography, genealogical research has lately expanded to include African Americans who are searching to document their ancestors' roots and DNA specialists who are providing powerful new tools for determining molecular genealogy, including ethnic background and places of origin.[28] Suddenly the potential of DNA testing hangs over genealogy like a sword of Damocles, enabling those who wield it to empirically identify and reinterpret their lineage and background.

As a result of recent developments, aspects that were taboo or unarticulated in Nalle's time and that served as another tool of oppression are now breaking open and exposing the social chimera of race itself. Today, some of the Hansbrough descendants are doing just that: they are staking their claim to what are often multiple historical and racial identities.

Ultimately I concluded that neither history nor memory held all the answers. But used together with visits to the historical sites—those contested and evocative "memory places"—the combination of sources came together in my own historical imagination to supply a richer understanding about the persons, events, and issues I was trying to reconstruct. Thinking about the plaque at the rescue site led me to realize the important role that commemoration has played: without the memorial tablet, the incident never would have been noticed or regarded as real by subsequent generations. Like the event of the rescue itself, the Troy plaque has acted as a mirror of the conscience of the community, and it has supplied a crucial part of the legacy that took shape that day.

When I started my investigation, Charles Nalle seemed nearly invisible, not because of what he had done or not done, but because history refused to include him. As far as the government's records and history books were concerned, it was practically as if he never had existed. He wasn't considered a full-fledged person. History had not granted him any birth certificate, marriage certificate, court testimony, record of his service as a postal carrier, death certificate, burial record, or inscribed tombstone. Even to his only son, the most momentous events of his life remained unsaid, making him seem in some ways all the more a cipher. The valiant persons of conscience who physically protested and resisted his slavery had also been largely ignored by history.

It is not enough to have liberated Charles. We also must liberate history and memory. Traces of the hidden past lie all around us and inside of us. Delve closely and you can find them.

APPENDIX

Were Robert E. Lee's future surgeon general and a future president of the United States involved in helping Kitty and Charles Nalle in October 1858?

As noted in Chapter 12, Kitty Nalle's medical problem in October 1858 involved treatment by a "Dr. Herndon," thus raising another mystery.

The Hansbroughs and the Herndons were interrelated. Blucher Hansbrough had a first cousin, Lucy Eleanor Hansbrough Herndon, with whom he stayed in contact. (It was her brother William who had attended the Fauquier cockfight with Blucher that was described earlier.) Lucy Hansbrough was married to Dr. Brodie Strachan Herndon of Fredericksburg and Washington (formerly of Culpeper)—a gentleman of high social stature who was one of the leading physicians in the South (he soon would become even more famous as surgeon general of the Confederate army for General Robert E. Lee).

In 1858 Dr. Brodie S. Herndon was fifty-eight years old.[1] He knew Blucher and Charles well from their family visits. A decade earlier, under the date of October 14, 1847, he had written in his diary: "Blucher Hansbrough meets with a great loss in the burning of his barn and all of his wheat—is compelled to sell 6 of his slaves, Jacob amongst the number. . . . Oh, the awful evils of slavery!!"[2] However, his later diary entries don't shed any light on whether he treated Kitty in late 1858.

This Dr. Brodie S. Herndon had two sons, Brodie S. Herndon Jr. and Dabney Herndon, both of whom attended medical school in New York and received their medical degrees in New York in 1856, so each of them was a Dr. Herndon too.[3] Brodie Junior also would later become a Confederate medical officer in the Civil War and serve time in prison camps; and Dabney was known to be more liberal in his politics and friendly with some prominent abolitionists in New York City, making him the more likely choice as the "Dr. Herndon" who treated one of the former Thom slaves. It appears he was the one responsible for saving Kitty's life and getting her out of jail.[4]

Involvement in the matter by either Dr. Herndon would raise additional tantalizing questions. Another one of Blucher Hansbrough's Virginia cousins, Frances Elizabeth ("Kit") Hansbrough Herndon, was married to Commander William Lewis Herndon, one of the great naval figures of the era. A year before Charles's escape, Commander Herndon had gone down with his gold-laden ship, the *Central America*, setting off the Panic of 1857—the financial disaster that had sealed Blucher Hansbrough's economic downfall and hence contributed to Charles's need to run away. Upon the shipmaster's heroic death, the widow "Kit" Hansbrough Herndon moved to New York City, where she lived among the high society set at 34 West Twenty-first Street, attended by a slave, and summering at the exclusive Saratoga Springs resort near Troy. One of her several children who accompanied her to New York was her beautiful daughter, and Dr. Brodie Strachan Herndon Sr.'s favorite niece, Ellen ("Nell") Lewis Herndon, whom the dutiful doctor continued to watch over in his late brother's behalf.[5]

This complicated story becomes historically significant because Nell's relative, Dr. Dabney Herndon, a physician in New York, boarded at Bancroft House on Broadway with a tall and handsome young lawyer, Chester A. ("Chet") Arthur— who would later become president of the United States.[6]

It was Dabney Herndon who had introduced the dashing Mr. Arthur to members of his family, including Nell, and Dr. Brodie S. Herndon. Nell Herndon and Chet Arthur quickly fell in love and while on a holiday to Saratoga with Kit Herndon and others, the couple subsequently announced their engagement. Blucher Hansbrough would likely have been among those invited to attend the wedding.[7]

At the time of Charles's escape and Kitty's jailing in 1858, Chester Arthur was a twenty-nine-year-old, up-and-coming lawyer and Republican Party activist in New York City who was deeply involved in civil rights cases. He had first achieved public notice in 1855 for his successful representation of Miss Elizabeth Jennings, a respectable colored woman, who had been forcibly thrown off a Third Avenue horse car after she had paid her fare. Although only a recent law graduate, working in Brooklyn under Erastus D. Culver, Arthur sued on her behalf and won $225 in civil damages. The next day the car company issued an order to admit colored persons to ride on their cars, and the other car companies quickly followed their example, thereby opening New York City's public transportation to nonwhites, in what was duly hailed as a historic victory for Negroes, and something that civil rights leaders in other cities, including William Still and Stephen Myers, wished to emulate—indeed, Arthur helped to make Jennings the nineteenth-century predecessor of Rosa Parks.[8]

Chester Arthur had grown up in an Irish-Canadian-American household with close connections to Gerrit Smith. His father, a Baptist minister, was a cofounder of the Eastern New York Anti-Slavery Society. Young Arthur had roots in Rensselaer County near Troy, where he had briefly taught school and his father had served several churches in the area around Albany, Troy, and Sand Lake.

Through his activities on behalf of Lizzie Jennings and others, Chet Arthur also collaborated with leaders of a number of New York City's black churches, including the Reverend Henry Highland Garnet and the Reverend James N. Gloucester.[9] Arthur was such a committed abolitionist that in 1856, after Culver left their law firm to become a judge, the young lawyer had headed out to the Kansas Territory that was then embroiled in conflict over slavery, in order to learn what he could about the struggle. Returning to New York after four months to resume his law practice, he continued to handle law work for the New York Vigilance Committee—the Underground Railroad—from his law office located directly across the street from the American Anti-Slavery Society office on Nassau Street. Most notably, he served as counsel in the famous Jonathan Lemmon fugitive slave case involving eight Virginia slaves who had run away from their master in Manhattan in 1852—a protracted legal battle that would still be going on until early 1860.[10]

Might Chester Arthur, the future president of the United States, have assisted in Charles's escape or Kitty's release from jail? Unfortunately for history, Arthur's activities on behalf of the antislavery cause have been virtually ignored by historians, in part because at the end of his life, Arthur ordered most of his private papers burned.[11]

NOTES

Introduction

1. Garnet Douglass Baltimore (1859–1946) was the youngest son of Peter F. Baltimore, a legendary Troy barber and civic leader. Named after Henry Highland Garnet and Frederick Douglass, the youngest Baltimore was the first Negro graduate of Rensselaer Polytechnic Institute and a prominent civil engineer. As a young man he had worked for Uri Gilbert's Gilbert Car Works. "Garnet D. Baltimore: Civil Engineer—His Wonderful Success—Credit to the Race," *Cleveland Gazette*, January 25, 1890, 1.

2. "Son of Fugitive Slave Visitor to Troy Today: John C. Nalle's Coming Recalls Stirring Times in Troy before the Civil War," *Troy Times*, August 10, 1932, 1.

3. John Coleman Nalle's (1856–1934) educational career is recounted in G. Smith Wormley, "Educators of the First Half Century of Public Schools of the District of Columbia," *Journal of Negro History* 17, no. 2 (April 1932): 124–40; and E. Delorus Preston Jr., "William Syphax, a Pioneer in Negro Education in the District of Columbia," *Journal of Negro Education* 20, no. 4 (October 1935): 448–76. Recently retired from a long and distinguished career in public education, John Nalle had been conceived in bondage and born free, to a slave father and a recently manumitted mother, and his advancement in American society had been a testament to his parents' belief in the abiding power of education. As teenagers in Washington following the Civil War, he and his younger sister Mary had been selected to become two of the first four students in the first Preparatory High School for colored youth in the basement of the Fifteenth Street Presbyterian Church, putting them among the most elite group in the District's black public educational history to that point. Both of them would always excel in their studies. After completing his

secondary school classes, John had entered the Normal Department of Howard University, graduating in 1872, and later pursued further study in higher mathematics at Columbia University. Working first as a teacher until 1902, then as supervising principal until 1926, he had compiled a notable public school career that spanned fifty-three years. His younger sister, Mary Nalle, was also a prominent educator in Washington, D.C. Mary Nalle is cited in Wormley, "Educators of the First Half Century," 131. An older sister, Alice, was born in slavery and later described as "always distinguished as a young lady of considerable accomplishment." See "A Troy Colored Girl Marries a Texas Senator—Life's Romance," *Troy Press*, October 4, 1870. She later married George T. Ruby, a pathbreaking reformer who served as an assistant to abolitionist journalist James Redpath before he went on to become one of the first Negro state senators in Texas in the 1870s. See Randall B. Woods, "George T. Ruby: A Black Militant in the White Business Community," *Red River Valley Historical Review* 1 (1974): 269–80; James Smallwood, "G. T. Ruby: Galveston's Black Carpetbagger in Reconstruction Texas," *Houston Review* 5, no. 1 (1983): 24–33.

4. *Troy Times*, August 10, 1932; "Arrest of Nalle, Fugitive Slave, Created Furor: Son of Nalle, Fugitive Slave, Created Furor: Son of Principal Figure in Episode Sends Letter to the Troy Times," *Troy Times*, October 14, 1932.

5. Brief sketch of John C. Nalle, in "Biographical Directory of the Public Schools of the District of Columbia, compiled in the Office of the Statistician, Revised edition, 1953," unpublished document at Washingtoniana Division, Martin Luther King Jr. Library, District of Columbia. At his death, John C. Nalle was survived by his sister, Mrs. Kate Carter; a daughter, Mrs. Blanche N. McDuffie, principal of the Toner Health School; and two sons, Charles Coleman Nalle of Brooklyn and John Wendell Phillips Nalle of Ithaca, New York. *Washington Post*, July 24, 1934. His wife Rosa L. Jones Nalle and his other siblings predeceased him. *Washington Post*, May 11, 1926. A copy of his will and newspaper clippings about his death were found in the Charles Sumner School Archives in Washington, D.C.

6. Telephone interview with Ray Langston, deputy mayor and chairman of the Highland Beach Historical Commission and descendant of the late Judge Robert H. Terrell, who had been one of John C. Nalle's closest friends.

7. *Washington Post*, August 4, 1934. A public high school, John C. Nalle School, was later named in his honor. "Names of D.C. Schools Reflect Heritage of Black Leadership," *Washington Post*, February 21, 1980. President George W. Bush conducted a public event there in September 2001.

8. See Clayton Rand, *Sons of the South* (New York: Holt, 1961); Ralph B. Draughon, "The Young Manhood of William L. Yancey," *The Alabama Review* 29, no. 1 (January 1996): 28; and John W. DuBose, *The Life and Times of William Lowndes Yancey* (Birmingham, Ala.: Roberts & Son, 1892).

Chapter 1. Genesis

1. Frederick Douglass (1818–95) wrote after escaping from slavery in Maryland: "Of my father I know nothing. Slavery had no recognition of fathers, as none of families. That the mother was a slave was enough for its deadly purpose. By its law the child followed the condition of its mother. The father might be a freeman and the child a slave. The father might be a white man, glorying in the purity of his Anglo-Saxon blood, and the child ranked with the blackest slaves. Father he might be, and not be husband, and could sell his own child without incurring reproach, if in its veins coursed one drop of African blood." Frederick Douglass, *Life and Times of Frederick Douglass, Written by Himself: His Early Life as a Slave, His Escape from Bondage, and His Complete History* (1892; reprint, New York: Collier Books, 1962), 29. Harriet Ann Jacobs (1813–97), another former slave, from North Carolina, wrote in her narrative: "The secrets of slavery are concealed like those of the Inquisition. My master was, to my knowledge, the father of eleven slaves. But did the mothers dare to tell who was the father of their children? Did the other slaves dare to allude to it, except in whispers among themselves? No, indeed! They knew too well the terrible consequences"; also, "She had forgotten that it was a crime for a slave to tell who was the father of her child." Harriet A. Jacobs, *Incidents in the Life of a Slave Girl, Written by Herself*, edited by L. Maria Child (1861; reprint, Cambridge, Mass.: Harvard University Press, 1987), 35, 11, 13.

2. Unfortunately, no surviving images of Charles Nalle, Peter Hansbrough, Blucher Hansbrough, or Kitty Nalle have been found.

3. Allen to Allen, dated 20 September 1805. Deed Book AA, p. 48, Culpeper Court House.

4. Allen Wife to Dyer, 1820, Deed Book KK, pp. 272–73, Culpeper Court House.

5. Deborah Gray White, *Ar'n't I a Woman? Female Slaves in the Plantation South* (New York: W. W. Norton, 1999), 61.

6. Allen to Ward, 21 July 1823. Deed Book NN, p. 303, Culpeper Court House.

7. Bill of sale from George Thom to Peter Hansbrough, dated December 28, 1823, recorded by the clerk on May 3, 1824. Deed Book QQ, p. 470, Thom to Hansbrough, August 1824, Culpeper Court House.

8. John W. Hansbrough, *History and Genealogy of the Hansborough-Hansbrough Family with Data on the Hanbury, Garrard, Lash, Devous, Davis, Wathen, and Bell Families* (Austin, Tex.: J. W. Hansbrough, 1981), 107–8.

9. *Hansbrough v. Thom*, 3 Leigh 147, November 1831 [150]. "Hansbrough observed he had some women and children that rendered him but little service; that, on his way down he should call at Thom's house, and expected to let him have some of his Negroes. That, some time previous to this conversation . . . Hansbrough told the witness, he intended selling a parcel of his Negroes to

Thom [the husband of his granddaughter]; that Thom might pass them off to Armistead, for a debt he owed him"; Order to Hansbrough's overseer: "Mr. John Henderson will shew and deliver to Col. George Thom, the following Negroes, viz: Pompey (he has seen), Moses, Harry, Sarah and her three children with her, Patt. (about the house), Caroline and her two boys, Sally and her three children, Linda and her child. And oblige P. Hansbrough. 16th September 1822." From Helen D. Catterall, ed., *Judicial Cases Concerning American Slavery and the Negro*, vol. 1 (Washington, D.C.: W. F. Roberts, 1932), 168.

10. Harriet Jacobs, a former slave, recounted how her mistress demanded for her to look her in the face and say all that had gone on between her and her lecherous master. When Harriet did so, "[s]he felt that her marriage vows were desecrated, her dignity insulted; but she had no compassion for the poor victim of her husband's perfidy. She pitied herself as a martyr; but she was incapable of feeling for the condition of shame and misery in which her unfortunate, helpless slave was placed." Jacobs, *Incidents in the Life of a Slave Girl*, 33.

11. "Miscellaneous Documents, Colonial and State. From the Originals in the Virginia State Archives. Petition in Regard to a Slave, 1773," *Virginia Magazine of History and Biography* 28 (1910): 394–96.

12. Culpeper Deed Book, Culpeper Court House.

13. See Stephen B. Oates, *The Fires of Jubilee: Nat Turner's Fierce Rebellion* (New York: Harper & Row, 1975). Henry "Box" Brown (b. 1815/16), a fugitive slave who later published a narrative about his enslavement and escape, wrote that he had lived in Richmond at the time of the Turner rebellion, but he never knew precisely what had happened because his master wouldn't provide any satisfactory information. "He only said that some of the slaves had plotted to kill their owners. . . . Many slaves were whipped, hung, and cut down with the swords in the streets, and some that were found away from their quarters after dark were shot. The whole city was in the utmost excitement, and the whites seemed terrified beyond measure. . . ." Henry "Box" Brown, *The Narrative of Henry "Box" Brown, Written by Himself* (Manchester: Lee & Glynn, 1851), in *Black Men in Chains: Narratives by Escaped Slaves*, edited by Charles H. Nichols (New York: L. Hill, 1972), 189. An earlier law requiring manumitted slaves to leave the state had been passed in 1806.

14. Rose Hill is described in Eugene M. Scheel, The Historic-Site Survey and Archaeological Reconnaissance of Culpeper County, Virginia, unpublished report prepared for the County of Culpeper, November 1992–April 1994, p. CE-28.

15. Sally Nall Dolphin and Charles Fuller Nall, *Nall Families of America, including Nalle, Naul, Nalls* (West Coeur d'Alene, Idaho: privately published, 1978); Culpeper County Marriage Register (G.S. Film No. 7354).

16. Charles later described Blucher as "a sporting man who kept racehorses, went to all the cockfights in that region, and always kept a barrel of whiskey on draught in the house." *Troy Daily Arena*, May 26, 1860.

17. The episode is recorded in Hansbrough, *History and Genealogy of the Hans-borough-Hansbrough Family*, 241–45, based on a contemporary article by Dr. Alban Smith Payne, entitled "The Great Chicken Pick," that was originally published under the pseudonym of Nicholas Spicer.

18. After his death, it would be rumored that he had sired as many as one hundred children. Personal interview with T. O. Madden Jr., Stevensburg, October 1, 1994; personal interview with Anna Davis, Devon, Pennsylvania, July 10, 2004. One black mistress, Lucinda Wormley, born about 1829, appears to have had at least eight, and she would continue her intimate relationship with Blucher until well after the Civil War, later reportedly telling her children that she was proud he was their father, thus indicating that their bonds were much deeper and more complex than latter-day historians would have ever acknowledged. Hansbrough family genealogy prepared by Anna Davis of Devon, Pennsylvania, a descendant of Rose Hansbrough. I am indebted to Anna Davis for sharing her family photographs and extensive research.

19. Charles later told an interviewer he never saw his master strike one of his slaves. *Troy Daily Arena*, May 26, 1860.

20. Gabriel, leader of Virginia's ill-fated Gabriel Prosser slave rebellion of 1800, was also a coachman. See Douglas R. Egerton, *Gabriel's Rebellion: The Virginia Slave Conspiracies of 1800 and 1802* (Chapel Hill: University of North Carolina Press, 1993); and Arna Bontemps, *Black Thunder, Gabriel's Revolt: Virginia, 1800* (Boston: Beacon Press, 1968).

21. His skill later enabled him to be hired as personal coachman to Uri Gilbert, a wealthy Troy industrialist who was one of America's leading coach manufacturers.

22. In 1854 Scotland-born journalist James Redpath (1833–91) interviewed a freeborn mulatto confectioner in Richmond who estimated that not more than one-tenth of that city's slaves were "contented," and the free Negro added: "I do say that *those who have good masters are as little contented as those who have bad masters.* . . . Kind treatment is a good thing but it isn't liberty, sir; and *colored people don't want that kind of privileges; they want their rights*" (emphasis in original). James Redpath, *The Roving Editor, or, Talks with Slaves of the Southern States*, edited by John R. McKivigan (1859; reprint, University Park: Pennsylvania State University Press, 1996), 31. Professor McKivigan suggests that the unidentified confectioner was actually Thomas Atkinson, who later moved from Richmond to Philadelphia.

23. Delia Garic, a former slave in Virginia, in George Rawick, ed., *The American Slave: A Composite Autobiography*, 41 vols. (Westport, Conn.: Greenwood Press, 1972–79), ser. 1, vol. 6 (*Alabama*), 129–32.

24. Frederick Douglass, *My Bondage and My Freedom* (1855; reprint, New York: Dover, 1969), 320.

25. Earl E. Thorpe, *Eros and Freedom in Southern Life and Thought* (Durham, North Carolina: Harrington Publications, 1967), 8.

Chapter 2. Revelation

1. "Culpeper's Landmark: Cole's Hill Was Once Headquarters of General Grant, a Place with a History," *Washington Post*, December 3, 1899, 21.

2. The only part of the house that remains visible today is a line of bricks and stones in a twenty-foot depression of the earth within a small grove. Peter Hansbrough's grave is located nearby in another grove. Scheel, Historic-Site Survey and Archaeological Reconnaissance of Culpeper County, p. CE-30. Northern visitors to northern Virginia were often struck by the multiplicity of outbuildings that were arrayed on Southern estates. "They have a queer way of building on one thing after another," Theodore Lyman wrote, "the great point being to have a separate shed or out-house for every purpose. . . . You will find a carpenter's shop, tool room, coach-shed, pig-house, stable, kitchen, two or three barns, and half a dozen Negro huts, besides the main house." Quoted in John Michael Vlach, *Back of the Big House: The Architecture of Plantation Slavery* (Chapel Hill: University of North Carolina Press, 1993), 77. Vlach, the leading authority on the architecture of American slavery culture, has noted that although slave cabins in architectural terms were "humble, almost inconsequential structures, they were nevertheless a public index of a planter's wealth and a proof of his or her right to be treated with deference" (153). Given the status of the Hansbroughs and the relatively modest size and history of Cole's Hill, one can expect that the slave quarters, including the quarters for field hands, were modest and reasonably neat and well-kept, neither rundown nor grand.

3. According to one typical published account of the time, written by a British visitor who toured Southern plantations in 1857, house servants were treated better than field hands. The former, it was claimed, "is frequently born and bred in the family he belongs to; and even when this is not the case, the constant association of the slave and his master, and master's family, naturally leads to such an attachment as ensures good treatment. . . . Midway between house servants and plantation hands stand the farm servants of small proprietors. Of all slaves these are, probably, the best off. They are neither spoiled like pet domestics, nor abused like plantation cattle. They live much in the farmer's family, work with himself and his children, take an interest in his affairs, and, in return, become objects of his regard. Such is the condition of many slaves among the small farmers in the upland districts of Virginia, Kentucky, Tennessee, Georgia, and the Carolinas." James Stirling, *Letters from the Slave States* (New York: Kraus Reprint Co., 1969), 287–91. In Charles's case, his role as coachman also carried a higher status because of the importance of horses and carriages among Virginia's planter elite. Some horses were valued at greater amounts than some slaves and the horses' accommodations could be "better built, warmer, more commodious, and in every way more comfortable than the shanties occupied by the human cattle of the plantation," according to one observer. Quoted in Vlach, *Back of the Big House*, 111.

4. United States Census of 1850, Culpeper; see Scheel, Historic-Site Survey and Archaeological Reconnaissance of Culpeper County, pp. CE-33–CE-34.

5. Cole's Hill was described in a real estate advertisement that appeared in many newspapers, including the *Alexandria Gazette*, November 1, 1860.

6. Interview with former Virginia slave, Frank Bell, quoted in *Weevils in the Wheat: Interviews with Virginia Ex-Slaves*, edited by Charles L. Perdue Jr., Thomas E. Barden, and Robert K. Phillips (Charlottesville: University Press of Virginia, 1976), 26. "An overseer, is regarded in all those parts of slave-holding America, with which I ever became acquainted, very much in the same light in which people, in countries uncursed with slavery, look upon a hangman; and as this latter employment, however useful and necessary, has never succeeded in becoming respectable, so the business of an overseer is likely from its nature, always to continue contemptible and degraded." Richard Hildreth, *The White Slave, or, Memoirs of a Fugitive* [a novel] (Boston: Tappan & Whittemore, 1853), 24–25.

7. Interview with former Virginia slave Robert Ellett, quoted in Perdue et al., *Weevils in the Wheat*, 85.

8. Charles later told William Still he was "used very well," and made other comments indicating that Blucher Hansbrough was a "first-rate master." William Still, *The Underground Railroad: A Record of Facts, Authentic Narratives, Letters, etc.* (Philadelphia: Porter & Coates, 1872), 487.

9. "A *necessary consequence* of slavery is the absence of the marriage relation. No slave can commit bigamy, because the law knows no more of the marriage of slaves than of the marriage of brutes. A slave may, indeed, be formally married, but so far as legal rights and obligations are concerned, it is an idle ceremony. . . . *Of course*, these laws do not recognize the *parental* relation, as belonging to slaves. A slave has no more legal authority over his child than a cow has over her calf" (emphases in original; Jay's Inquiry, p. 132). Quoted in William Goodell, *The American Slave Code in Theory and Practice: Its Distinctive Features Shown by Its Statutes, Judicial Decisions, and Illustrative Facts* (New York: American and Foreign Anti-Slavery Society, 1853), 113.

10. Interview with former Virginia slave Matthew Jarrett, quoted in Virginia Writers' Project, *The Negro in Virginia* (New York: Hastings House, 1940), 80.

11. White, *Ar'n't I a Woman?* 147.

12. One slave explained: "There was two kinds of marriage, one was marrying at home and the other was called marrying abroad. . . . If a man married abroad it meant that he wouldn't see his wife [but] only about once a week." Ophelia S. Egypt, J. Masuoka, Charles S. Johnson, eds., *God Struck Me Dead: Religious Conversion Experiences and Autobiographies of Negro Ex-Slaves* (Nashville, Tenn.: Fisk University Press, 1945), 156–57.

13. Bessie Jones and Bess Lomax Hawes, *Step It Down: Games, Plays, Songs and*

Stories from the Afro-American Heritage (Athens: University of Georgia Press, 1987), 182.

14. Much of this account about the events of 1847 is based on an interview of Charles Nalle that appeared in the *Troy Daily Arena*, May 26, 1860.

15. *Troy Daily Arena*, May 26, 1860.

16. A confrontation at a fan mill also proved a turning point for Frederick Douglass, as he wrote in *Life and Times of Frederick Douglass*, one of the classics of American literature. He described the time he collapsed from heat exhaustion after fanning wheat and was flogged by Covey, the brutal overseer. That time he responded by striking back.

17. *Troy Daily Arena*, May 26, 1860.

18. "Blucher Hansbrough meets with a great loss in the burning of his barn and all of his wheat—is compelled to sell 6 of his slaves, Jacob amongst the number. Kitty goes down to the cars. Jacob seems to bear a stout heart. Kitty wept a good deal. (Lucy went down to the cars to see Mrs. Cooke and Mrs. Noland on their way through.) Lucy's eyes wet too at the parting of Jacob and Kitty. Oh, the awful evils of slavery!! The other boys seemed indifferent." Dr. Brodie S. Herndon of Fredericksburg, in his diary under the date of October 14, 1847. Brodie S. Herndon Papers, University of Virginia Library, Charlottesville, Virginia. Jacob is referenced in note 64.

19. In Richmond "it was a crime, punishable with imprisonment and stripes on a bare back for a Negro, whether free or bond, male or female, to take the inside of a sidewalk in passing a white man! Negroes are required to 'give the wall,' and, if necessary, to get off the sidewalk into the street." Redpath, *Roving Editor*, 100.

20. Frederic B. Bancroft, *Slave-Trading in the Old South* (Baltimore: J. H. Furst, 1931), chap. 5.

21. Fredrika Bremer, *The Homes of the New World: Impressions of America*, vol. 2, trans. by Mary Howitt (New York: Harper and Brothers, 1853): 533–35. Bremer was a Swedish woman who spent two years touring the United States.

22. Bancroft, *Slave-Trading in the Old South*, 102–3.

23. Frederick Law Olmstead, *A Journey in the Seaboard Slave States, with Remarks on Their Economy* (New York: Dix & Edwards, 1856), 57.

24. Olmstead, *Journey in the Seaboard Slave States*, 55–56.

25. Bancroft, *Slave-Trading in the Old South*, chap. 5.

26. Eyre Crowe, *With Thackery in America* (London: Cassell & Co., 1893), 130–36.

27. For a journalist's description of one of these Richmond auctions a few years later, see Redpath, *Roving Editor*, 214–18.

28. Charles later described Colonel Thom's role at the auction in an interview he gave to the *Troy Daily Arena*, May 26, 1860.

29. Bancroft, *Slave-Trading in the Old South*, 104.

30. I am indebted to the late author Shelby Foote for describing his knowledge of some of these slave inspection methods to me when we talked in Albany, New York, on March 20, 1997.

31. One of those sold appears to have been Jacob. On March 7, 1840, Peter Hansbrough sold to Blucher for $850 "my Negro man slave named Jacob about 36 years old and a black colt about 2 years old called Chuckaluck." Culpeper Deed Book, #4, Part 2, p. 336. See letter of Dr. Herndon noted above that reports that Jacob was among those to be sold.

32. Charles's account of the auction is found in *Troy Daily Arena*, May 26, 1860. A similar experience was recounted in Hildreth's novel, *The White Slave*. "At length came my turn. I was stripped half naked, the better to show my joints and muscles, and placed upon the table or platform, on which the subject of the sale was exposed to the examination of the purchasers. I was whirled about, my limbs were felt, and my capabilities discussed, in a slang much like that of a company of horse-jockeys. Various were the remarks that were made upon me. One fellow declared that I had 'a savage sullen look'; another swore that my eye was 'devilish malicious'; a third remarked that these light-colored fellows were all rascals;—to which the auctioneer replied, that he never knew a slave of any smartness who was not a rogue."

33. Charles recounted the revelatory impact of his experience in his interview that appeared in the *Troy Daily Arena* on May 26, 1860.

Chapter 3. Master and Slave Relations

1. *"My Dear Brother": A Confederate Chronicle*, compiled and edited by Catherine Thom Bartlett (Richmond, Va.: Dietz Press, 1952), 9–27. On February 3, 1840, Abby's sister Elizabeth wrote: "Abby passes nearly the whole of her time down the hill with her Mammy, who has the most unbounded influence over her. Indeed she often says she likes nobody but Papa and Fanny her Mammy, who it is thought, has the whole plantation under her control." Bartlett, *"My Dear Brother,"* 22–23. For a critical assessment of much of the mythology and common idyllic stereotypes regarding the "black Mammy," see White, *Ar'n't I a Woman?*, esp. 46–53.

2. Thom Family Papers, Virginia Historical Society, Richmond; Bartlett, *"My Dear Brother,"* 7–9, 130–31; David Pembroke Neff, "The Thom Family of Culpeper County" (Ph.D. diss., George Mason University, 2004). A fine contemporary description of a similar local plantation, Springfield, includes the following passage: "In our beds we had seringas, coral honeysuckle, sweet peas, violets, snowdrops and narcissus. On each terrace was a summerhouse of lattice with vines. The cherry orchard was in front of the house. The apple orchard was on the north." Anne Mercer Slaughter's account is quoted in Eugene M. Scheel, *Culpeper: A Virginia County's History through 1920* (Culpeper, Va.: Culpeper Historical Society, 1982), 169.

3. Margaret Jeffries, "Maddensville Tavern," Works Progress Administration of Virginia Historical Inventory, May 7, 1937.

4. T. O. Madden Jr., *We Were Always Free: The Maddens of Culpeper County, Virginia: A 200-Year Family History* (New York: Random House, 1992), chap. 5. I am deeply indebted to the late T. O. Madden Jr. for sharing with me some of his personal papers and memories as well as his extraordinary book of family history.

5. Redpath, *Roving Editor*, 239–40.

6. Scheel, *Culpeper*, 158.

7. Madden, *We Were Always Free*, 78.

8. Catterall, *Judicial Cases*, vol. 2, 358–59.

9. Madden, *We Were Always Free*, 2–3.

10. Ibid., 26–27.

11. Ibid., 35–39.

12. Her father, William Clark, a veteran of the American Revolution, appears to have been a descendant of Judith Clark, a white servant of Joshua Slade of York County, Virginia; Judith admitted in court in 1694 that she had committed the sin of fornication with a Negro. The child born of this "sin" was John Clark, the father of William. Paul Heinegg, *Free African-Americans of North Carolina and Virginia* (Baltimore: Genealogical Publishing, 1995).

13. Madden, *We Were Always Free*, 64–67, 95–96.

14. Scheel, *Culpeper*, 50, 107. Scheel is a top-flight cartographer and historian who writes articles for the *Washington Post*.

15. Arthur Dicken Thomas Jr., and Angus McDonald Green, eds., *Early Churches of Culpeper County, Virginia: Colonial and Ante-Bellum Congregations* (Culpeper, Va.: Culpeper Historical Society, 1987); Scheel, *Culpeper*, 107.

16. James G. Birney, *The American Churches: The Bulwark of American Slavery*, 3rd ed. (Concord, N.H.: Parker Pillsbury, 1855). Also see Eugene D. Genovese, *Roll, Jordan, Roll: The World the Slaves Made* (New York: Pantheon Books, 1974), 186–89.

17. Quoted in Thomas and Green, *Early Churches of Culpeper County*, 223.

18. Goodell, *American Slave Code in Theory and Practice*, 330–31.

19. Redpath, *Roving Editor*, 33.

20. Scheel, *Culpeper*, 107.

21. Interview with former Virginia slave Cornelius Garner, quoted in Perdue et al., *Weevils in the Wheat*, 102.

22. Interview with unnamed former Virginia slave, quoted in Perdue et al., *Weevils in the Wheat*, 322; interview with former Virginia slave Mrs. Alice Marshall, quoted in Perdue et al., *Weevils in the Wheat*, 202.

23. Interview with former Virginia slaves Mrs. Alice Marshall and Horace Tonsler, quoted in Perdue et al., *Weevils in the Wheat*, 201, 287.

24. Interview with former Virginia slaves Samuel Walter Chilton, Mrs. Julia

Frazier, and Mrs. Alice Marshall, quoted in Perdue et al., *Weevils in the Wheat*, 71, 97, 202.

25. John Walker Woodville, Diaries and Papers of John Walker Woodville, Culpeper Historical Society, at Culpeper Library, p. 106; Scheel, *Culpeper*, 116, 400 n. 25.

26. Scheel, *Culpeper*, 116.

27. Quoted in Thomas and Green, *Early Churches of Culpeper County*, 92; Madden, *We Were Always Free*, 45. Also see Genovese, *Roll, Jordan, Roll*, 188–89.

28. See Bertha Norman, "History of Stevensburg Baptist Church, 1833–1985," in Thomas and Green, *Early Churches of Culpeper County*, 233–46.

29. Stringfellow's best-known writings included several articles in the *Religious Herald* as well as books including *A Brief Examination of Scripture Testimony on the Institution of Slavery* (1850); *Scriptural and Statistical Views in Favor of Slavery* (1856); and *Slavery: Its Origin, Nature and History . . . Considered in the Light of Bible Teachings, Moral Justice, and Political Wisdom* (1860).

30. "In a point of worldly wealth, Elder S. is more highly favored than most Baptist preachers." *Religious Herald*, September 19, 1844. Summerduck had been Landon Carter's Fauquier plantation. See Scheel, *Culpeper*, 408 n. 8; Scheel, Historic-Site Survey and Archaeological Reconnaissance of Culpeper County, p. CE-39.

31. Thomas and Green, *Early Churches of Culpeper County*, 234–35. Harriet Jacobs, a former fugitive slave, wrote: "The slave is sure to know who is the most humane, or cruel master, within forty miles of him." Jacobs, *Incidents in the Life of a Slave Girl*, 15.

32. See Melville Herskovits, *The Myth of the Negro Past* (Boston: Beacon Press, 1941); Genovese, *Roll, Jordan, Roll*; Albert J. Raboteau, *Slave Religion: The "Invisible Institution" in the Antebellum South* (New York: Oxford University Press, 2004); interview with former Virginia slave Matilda Henrietta ("Sweet Ma") Perry, recorded by Roscoe Lewis, Folk Song, Library of Congress, quoted in Perdue et al., *Weevils in the Wheat*, 224.

33. One ex-slave defined pattyrollers as "a gang o' white men gittin' together goin' threw de country catchin' slaves, an' whippin' an' beatin' 'em up if dey had no 'remit'" (slave pass). Interview with former Virginia slave Charles Crawley, quoted in Perdue et al., *Weevils in the Wheat*, 79.

34. Goodell, *American Slave Code in Theory and Practice*, 331–32.

35. The Reverend Noah Davis (b. 1804) had been a slave in Fredericksburg and Stevensburg, the child of pious Baptist parents. His father, John Davis, belonged to a merchant who was associated with Colonel John Thom in a mill at Crooked Run. In his memoir, written after he had become an ordained minister, Noah Davis recalled: "My father could read a little, and make figures, but could scarcely write at all. His custom, on those Sabbaths when we remained at home, was to spend his time in instructing his children, or the neighboring servants, out

of a New Testament, sent him from Fredericksburg by one of his older sons. I fancy I can see him now, sitting under his bush arbor, reading that precious book to many attentive hearers around him." See Noah Davis, *A Narrative of the Life of Rev. Noah Davis, a Colored Man: Written by Himself at the Age Fifty-Four* (Baltimore: John F. Weishampel Jr., 1859).

36. Interview with former Virginia slave Charles Grandy, quoted in Perdue et al., *Weevils in the Wheat*, 119.

37. Interview with former Virginia slave Elizabeth Sparks, quoted in Perdue et al., *Weevils in the Wheat*, 276.

38. Scheel, *Culpeper*, 117.

39. Leo Marx, *The Machine in the Garden: Technology and the Pastoral Ideal in America* (New York: Oxford University Press, 1964), 194. For an excellent analysis of the changes going on in Virginia at this time, see William A. Link, *Roots of Secession: Slavery and Politics in Antebellum Virginia* (Chapel Hill: University of North Carolina Press, 2005).

40. Scheel, *Culpeper*, chap. 18.

41. Hinton Rowan Helper, *The Impending Crisis of the South: How to Meet It* (New York: Burdick Brothers, 1857), 22.

42. Redpath, *Roving Editor*, xvi–xvii, xxii, 91–92. Redpath's book was first published in November 1859 and dedicated to John Brown. See Charles Horner, *The Life of James Redpath and the Development of the Modern Lyceum* (New York: Barse & Hopkins, 1926).

43. *New York National Anti-Slavery Standard*, December 2, 1854. Redpath wrote this more than a year before he met John Brown in Kansas for the first time. *Roving Editor*, xxii.

44. David S. Reynolds, in his fine work, *John Brown, Abolitionist*, 257–58, is one of the few historians to incorporate Ross into the tapestry of abolitionism, John Brown, and the Underground Railroad. See Reynolds, *John Brown, Abolitionist* (New York: Alfred A. Knopf, 2005). The work on which he bases his account is Alexander Milton Ross, *Recollections and Experiences of an Abolitionist: From 1855 to 1865* (Toronto: Roswell & Hutchinson, 1875).

45. Valentine Mott, M.D. (1785–1865), one of the greatest figures in nineteenth-century American medicine, founded the university medical college in New York City where Ross studied. Some of his papers are located in Valentine Mott Correspondence, 1807–1864, Modern Manuscripts Collection, History of Medicine Division, National Library of Medicine, Bethesda, Maryland, MS C 281. A New York Quaker, he was married to Louise Dunmore Munns Valentine and related to numerous prominent abolitionists, including sisters Abigail Mott (1803–50), Lydia Mott (1807–75), and Lucretia Coffin Mott (1793–1880) of Philadelphia. See *Quaker Crosscurrents: Three Hundred Years of Friends in the New York Yearly Meetings*, edited by Hugh Barbour and Christopher Densmore et al. (Syracuse: Syracuse University Press, 1995).

46. See William O. Scroggs, *Filibusters and Financiers: The Story of William Walker and his Associates* (New York: Macmillan, 1916).

47. Alexander Milton Ross, *Memoir of a Reformer* (Toronto: Hunter, Rose, and Company, 1893), 2–14.

48. Fergus M. Bordewich, *Bound for Canaan: The Underground Railroad and the War for the Soul of America* (New York: Amistad, 2005), 357–61. See also Mrs. Kate E. R. Pickard, *The Kidnapped and the Ransomed* (Syracuse: William T. Hamilton, 1856).

49. See Stanley Harrold, *The Abolitionists and the South, 1831–1861* (Lexington: University Press of Kentucky, 1995), 17, 23.

Chapter 4. The Shakeup

1. The Virginia Historical Society has three collections of Thom family papers spanning the years 1670–1953. The Maryland Historical Society has some family papers and cased photographs, daguerreotypes, and ambrotypes of some of the Thoms in its Warner-Wright-Thom Collection circa 1845–58.

2. Upon the death of the master, his slaves "are liable to be 'distributed,' like other 'property,' among the 'heirs,' whoever and wherever they may be, 'for goods they are, and as goods they are esteemed,'—chattels personal, in the hands of their owners and possessors, THEIR EXECUTORS, ADMINISTRATORS AND ASSIGNS, to all intents, constructions, and purposes whatsoever."—Goodell, *American Slave Code in Theory and Practice*, 75.

3. John Catesby Thom Account Book, Thom Family Papers, Virginia Histori cal Society, Richmond.

4. In 1782 Virginia had repealed its fifty-nine-year-old prohibition against private manumission. Walter Waller Hening, comp., *A Collection of All the Laws of Virginia, from the First Session of the Legislature in the Year 1619*, vol. 6 (Richmond: J. & G. Cochran, 1819), 39–40. At that time, St. George Tucker estimated the number of free blacks in the state at about 2,000, but this had grown to 12,000 at the time of the 1790 federal census, and by 1810 it had risen to over 30,000. Ira Berlin, *Slaves Without Masters: The Free Negro in the Antebellum South* (New York: Pantheon, 1974), 48. Virginia tried to control the size of the free Negro population by passing legislation in 1793 to prohibit free Negroes from immigrating into the commonwealth, and also required all urban free Negroes to register with the town clerk, at their own expense. Samuel Shepherd, comp., *The Statutes at Large of Virginia, from October Session 1792 to December Session 1806, Inclusive, in Three Volumes*, vol. 1 (Richmond: Samuel Shepherd, 1836), 238–39. In a series of laws in 1806, 1815, and 1837, Virginia also required masters freeing newly manumitted blacks to remove them from the state and hold them liable to seizure for any unpaid debts. *Virginia Laws*, 1815, c. 24, 1836–37, chap. 70.

5. "If any slave hereafter emancipated shall remain within this commonwealth

more than twelve months after his or her right to freedom shall have accrued, he or she shall forfeit all such right, and may be apprehended and sold by the overseers of the poor of any county or corporation in which he or she shall be found, for the benefit of the poor of such county or corporation." Samuel Shepherd, ed., *Statutes at Large of Virginia* (1835; reprint, AMS Press, 1970), vol. 3, 252.

6. John Catesby Thom Account Book, Thom Family Papers, Virginia Historical Society, Richmond.

7. White, *Ar'n't I a Woman?* 154–55.

8. Still, *Underground Railroad*, 385.

9. The emancipation fund amounts and date of Kitty's departure appear in the Thom Family Papers, Virginia Historical Society, Richmond.

10. *The Case of William L. Chaplin: Being an Appeal to All Respecters of Law and Justice, against the Cruel and Oppressive Treatment to Which, under Color of Legal Proceedings, He Has Been Subjected, in the District of Columbia and the State of Maryland* (Boston: Chaplin Committee, 1851), 17.

11. *Records of the United States District Court for the District of Columbia Relating to Slaves, 1851–1863* (National Archives Microfilm Publication M433, 3 rolls), Record Group 21, NACP, Roll #3.

12. By a Member of the Washington Bar, *The Slave Code of the District of Columbia, Together with Notes and Judicial Decisions Explanatory of the Same* (Washington, D.C.: L. Towers & Co., 1862).

13. *Albany Evening Journal*, May 24, 1856.

14. Warren Wilkes, letter to the *Charleston Mercury*, quoted in Franklin B. Sanborn, *The Life and Letters of John Brown* (Boston: Roberts Brothers, 1885), 165.

15. See William Addison Phillips, *The Conquest of Kansas, by Missouri and Her Allies* (Boston: Phillips, Sampson & Co., 1856); Hannah Anderson Ropes, *Six Months in Kansas* (Boston: John P. Jewett, 1856).

16. A good account of Brown's upbringing is found in Evan Carton, *Patriotic Treason: John Brown and the Soul of America* (New York: Free Press, 2006).

17. Recollection of Jason Brown, quoted in Oswald Garrison Villard, *John Brown* (1910; reprint, New York: Harper & Row, 1969), 151 (emphasis in original).

18. The battle for Kansas is best described in Reynolds, *John Brown, Abolitionist*, chap. 7.

19. Quoted in Edward J. Renehan Jr., *The Secret Six: The True Tale of the Men Who Conspired with John Brown* (New York: Crown, 1995), 97. See James Redpath, *The Public Life of Capt. John Brown* (Boston: Thayer & Eldridge, 1860), 112–13.

20. David Hackett Fischer, *Liberty and Freedom: A Visual History of America's Founding Ideas* (New York: Oxford University Press, 2005), 296–97.

21. In 1840 the census showed 56.7 percent of Culpeper County's population were black; by 1860 the number had climbed to 58.9 percent. Scheel, *Culpeper*, 158.

22. American Anti-Slavery Society, *Anti-Slavery Tracts, Series 2, No. 1–14* (1860; reprint, Westport, Conn.: Negro Universities Press, 1970), 117.

23. Harvey Wish, *George Fitzhugh: Propagandist of the Old South* (Baton Rouge: Louisiana State University Press, 1943), 160–61.

24. *Dred Scott v. Sandford, 19 Howard (1857), 393;* see Don E. Fehrenbacher, *The Dred Scott Case; Its Significance in American Law and Politics* (New York: Oxford University Press, 2001); Walter Ehrlich, *They Have No Rights: Dred Scott's Struggle for Freedom* (Greenwich, Conn.: Greenwood Press, 1979).

25. See Arthur M. Schlesinger Sr., *Paths to the Present* (Boston: Houghton Mifflin, 1949); Arthur M. Schlesinger Jr., *The Cycles of American History* (Boston: Houghton Mifflin, 1987). Link, *Roots of Secession*, analyzes the complex interrelationship of Virginia slavery, slaves, and politics in this era.

26. Interview with former Virginia slave Frank Bell, quoted in Perdue et al., *Weevils in the Wheat*, 27.

27. Olmstead, *Journey in the Seaboard Slave States*, 83.

28. Interview with former Virginia slave Mrs. Virginia Hayes Shepherd, quoted in Perdue et al., *Weevils in the Wheat*, 255.

29. Still, *Underground Railroad*, 487–88. On March 1, 1857, Willis Madden leased slave Jeff Dent, who belonged to William Redd of Culpeper, to work on his farm. To do this he put up a bond, binding himself and his heirs to pay Redd and his heirs the sum of sixty dollars "for his hire on the 1st day of January 1858 and permit him to return to Redd on December 25, 1858, well clothed & shod and in mean time to furnish him with the usual summer clothing." Madden Family Papers, reprinted in Madden, *We Were Always Free*, 95–96.

30. *Troy Daily Arena*, May 26, 1860.

31. See James L. Huston, *The Financial Panic of 1857 and the Coming of the Civil War* (Baton Rouge: Louisiana State University Press, 1987).

32. *Troy Daily Arena*, May 26, 1860.

33. *Washington Star*, October 13, 1858.

34. John Hope Franklin and Loren Schweninger, *Runaway Slaves: Rebels on the Plantation* (New York: Oxford University Press, 1999), esp. chap. 9, "Profile of a Runaway."

Chapter 5. Making the Break

1. Speculation persists about the origins and reason for the term, which appears to have been common by the early 1840s, about the time that a real underground railway had opened for business in Newcastle, England. "Underground railroad, railway," in Oxford English Dictionary (Oxford University Press Online, 2005). The term was used in Harriet Beecher Stowe's best-selling book, *Uncle Tom's Cabin*, published in 1852. In this usage the term "Underground Railroad" refers to the secret system by which slaves were able to get from the South to the "free states" and Canada prior to the abolition of slavery in 1865.

2. Benjamin Drew, *A North-Side View of Slavery: The Refugee, or the Narratives of Fugitive Slaves in Canada*, edited by Tilden G. Epstein (Boston: John P. Jewett and Company, 1856; reprint, Reading, Mass.: Addison-Wesley, 1969), introduction.

3. Stanley W. Campbell, *The Slave Catchers: Enforcement of the Fugitive Slave Law, 1850–1860* (Chapel Hill: University of North Carolina Press, 1970).

4. Douglass, *My Bondage and My Freedom*.

5. Redpath, *Roving Editor*, 239–41.

6. Amherst College, Biographical Record, Centennial Edition, Class of 1850.

7. "Erskine goes to school at home to Mr. Crosby, and I am at a great loss about Mary Cameron." Bartlett, *"My Dear Brother,"* 40.

8. Scheel, Historic-Site Survey and Archaeological Reconnaissance of Culpeper County, pp. CE-13–CE-14.

9. From 1861 to 1870 Crosby served as principal of Edward Beecher's Hartford Female Seminary, which was considered, along with Emma Willard's school in Troy, New York, as one of the finest and most progressive educational institutions for women in the United States, and a strong abolitionist institution. See *The Town and City of Waterbury, from the Aboriginal Period to the Year Eighteen Hundred and Ninety-Five*, edited by Joseph Anderson (New Haven, Conn.: Price & Lee Co., 1896), 514.

10. Douglass, *My Bondage and My Freedom*, 281.

11. William and Ellen Craft, in *Great Slave Narratives, Selected and Introduced by Arna Bontemps* (Boston: Beacon Press, 1969): 288–89.

12. Douglass, *Life and Times of Frederick Douglass*, 193.

13. James W. C. Pennington, in *Great Slave Narratives*, 214, 215.

14. *Troy Daily Arena*, May 26, 1860.

15. James W. C. Pennington, in *Great Slave Narratives*, 216.

16. Ibid., 214–15.

17. Records of the United States District Court, District of Columbia, Slavery Records, Fugitive Slave Cases, Petition of John C. Cook, 1 March 1861, Record Group 21, Entry #31, Box 1, NA; quoted in Franklin and Schweninger, *Runaway Slaves*, 116.

18. Raymond A. Bauer and Alice H. Bauer, "Day to Day Resistance to Slavery," *Journal of Negro History* 27 (October 1942): 412–13.

19. William and Ellen Craft, in *Great Slave Narratives*, 308–10.

20. Brown, *Narrative of Henry "Box" Brown*. Brown's thrilling story is also told in William Still, *The Underground Railroad* (Philadelphia: Porter & Coates, 1872), 81–83. See also Jeffrey Ruggles, *The Unboxing of Henry Brown* (Richmond: Library of Virginia, 2003). Frederick Douglass was among those who later criticized the decision to publicize the stories, saying: "Had not Henry Box Brown and his friends attracted slaveholding attention to the manner of his escape, we might have had a thousand *Box Browns* per annum. The singularly original plan adopted by Wil-

liam and Ellen Crafts, perished with the first using, because every slaveholder in the land was apprised of it." Douglass, *My Bondage and My Freedom*, 323.

21. Interview with Charles Nalle, *Troy Daily Arena*, May 26, 1860.

22. Two years earlier, Clark had suffered the loss of one of his slaves, Lewis Burrell, who had run away. Lewis's wife, Winna, was a sister to Kitty Nalle and Jenny Gibbs. But she was still a slave of Pembroke Thom back in Culpeper, although her master sometimes took her with him when he traveled to Baltimore and other places. And Lewis, it turned out, was in Toronto, having been aided in his escape by the Underground Railroad.

23. The 1850 Census lists John J. Rickard (1801–85), forty-eight, a saddler, and several members of his household including Henry Banks, forty-one, a mulatto employed as a blacksmith. Rickard was an officer of the Stevensburg Baptist Church.

24. Still, *Underground Railroad*, 487–88.

25. *Troy Daily Arena*, May 26, 1860.

26. Douglass, *My Bondage and My Freedom*, 164.

27. Crosby's wife had given birth to a second child fourteen months earlier and the circumstances of their need to suddenly leave town may have caused young Minot Jr. to become ill. Two months later, the boy would be dead.

28. The term "citadel of slavery" was often used to describe Washington, D.C. See Frederick Douglass, "We Have Decided to Stay," speech delivered to the American Anti-Slavery Society, New York, May 9, 1848, in *National Anti-Slavery Standard*, May 18, 1848.

Chapter 6. The Escape

1. Charles Torrey, quoted in Stanley Harrold, *Subversives: Antislavery Community in Washington, D.C., 1828–1865* (Baton Rouge: Louisiana State University Press, 2003), 5.

2. The leading work on this subject is Harrold's *Subversives*, a magnificent feat of original research. See also Hilary Russell, *The Operation of the Underground Railroad in Washington, D.C., c. 1800–1860, Final Research Report* (Washington, D.C.: Historical Society of Washington, D.C., and the National Park Service, July 2001). See also Eugene Scheel, "Journey to Freedom Was Risky for Slaves and Guides," *Washington Post*, May 27, 2001, LZ203. Leonard Grimes (1815–74) was one of the earliest known conductors, or rescuers of slaves, who was based in Leesburg and Washington, D.C. A free Negro, he was an independent hackman with carriages and horses for hire. In October 1839 he was transporting a slave woman named Patty and her six children out of Loudon County to Washington when he was arrested at Leesburg. He ended up spending two years in the Virginia State Prison and was fined $100. After his release from prison, he moved to New Bedford and Boston where he became pastor of the Twelfth Baptist Church

(known as the "Fugitive's Church") and continued to work in the Underground Railroad. He was notably involved in assisting his parishioner Anthony Burns gain freedom during and after the thwarted slave rescue in Boston. See Kendra Hamilton, ed., *Essence of a People II: African Americans Who Made Their World Anew in Loudon County, Virginia, and Beyond* (Leesburg, Va.: Black History Committee of the Friends of the Thomas Balch Library, 2002), 21–25; Hilary Russell, "Underground Railroad Activists in Washington, D.C., *Washington History* 12, no. 2 (Fall/Winter 2001–2): 37–38; Harrold, *Subversives*, 52–53; William J. Simmons, *Men of Mark: Eminent, Progressive and Rising* (1887; reprint, Chicago: Johnson, 1970), 662–63. Regarding the Underground Railroad in Loudon County, see Lynn Wolstenholme, "Going Underground in Loudon County," *Loudon Times-Mirror*, February 22, 2005.

3. Joseph Lovejoy, *Memoir of Rev. Charles T. Torrey*, 2nd ed. (1848; reprint, New York: Negro Universities Press, 1969), 1–33. Some of the historical context for the religious movements of this period are examined in Douglas M. Strong, *Perfectionist Politics: Abolitionism and the Religious Tensions of American Democracy* (Syracuse, N.Y.: Syracuse University Press, 1999); John R. McKivigan, "The Sectional Division of the Methodist and Baptist Denominations as Measures of Northern Antislavery Sentiment," in *Religion and the Antebellum Debate over Slavery*, edited by John R. McKivigan and Mitchell Snay (Athens: University of Georgia Press, 1998), 343–63; and William R. Sutton, *Journeymen for Jesus: Evangelical Artisans Confront Capitalism in Jacksonian Baltimore* (University Park: Pennsylvania State University Press, 1997).

4. For information about Abel Brown (1810–44) see Catherine S. Brown, *Abel Brown, Abolitionist*, edited by Tom Calarco (Jefferson, N.C.: McFarland & Co., 2006), a well-annotated and illustrated version of the memoir published by Brown's widow in 1849.

5. Calarco, *Abel Brown, Abolitionist*, is also the best source about Edwin W. Goodwin. See also the *Tocsin for Liberty*, Albany, New York (October 15, 1841–December 1842). His most effective propaganda technique was to paint portraits of fugitive slaves and exhibit them at the group's recruiting table during county fairs. In an era before photography, his lifelike images caused a sensation, attracting droves of new recruits to the cause because they put a human face on slavery.

6. Thomas Smallwood, *A Narrative of Thomas Smallwood (Coloured Man): Giving an Account of His Birth—The Period He Was Held in Slavery—His Release—and Removal to Canada, etc., Together with an Account of the Underground Railroad, Written by Himself* (Toronto: James Stephens, 1851), 17–18; Harrold, *Subversives*, 73.

7. Lovejoy, *Memoir of Rev. Charles T. Torrey*.

8. Harrold, *Subversives*, chap. 3; see also William W. Patton, *Freedom's Martyr: A Discourse on the Death of the Rev. Charles T. Torrey* (Hartford, Conn.: William H. Burleigh, 1846); Eliza Wigham, *The Anti-Slavery Cause in America and Its Martyrs*

(1863; reprint, Westport, Conn.: Westport Universities Press, 1970), 61–64. See also *Case of William L. Chaplin.*

9. See Daniel Drayton, *For Four Years and Four Months a Prisoner (for Charity's Sake) in Washington Jail, Including a Narrative of the Voyage and Capture of the Schooner Pearl* (New York: Bela Marsh, 1855); Josephine F. Pacheco, *The Pearl: A Failed Slave Escape on the Potomac* (Chapel Hill: University of North Carolina Press, 2005); John H. Paynter, "Fugitives of the Pearl," *Journal of Negro History* 1, no. 3 (July 1916): 1–3; G. Franklin Edwards and Michael R. Winston, "Commentary: The Washington of Paul Jennings—White House Slave, Free Man, and Conspirator for Freedom," *White House History* 1 (n.d.): 52–63; Mary Kay Ricks, "Escape on the Pearl," *Washington Post Magazine* (August 12, 1998), H01.

10. G. B. Howe, *Genealogy of the Bigelow Family of America* (Worcester, Mass.: privately published, 1890), 62–63, 115, 201, 203–4; Harrold, *Subversives*, 96 n. 3.

11. Still, *Underground Railroad*, 178–79; Harrold, *Subversives*, 216.

12. Harrold, *Subversives*, 216.

13. Sandra Fitzpatrick and Maria R. Goodwin, *The Guide to Black Washington: Places and Events of Historical and Cultural Significance in the Nation's Capital*, 2nd ed. (New York: Hippocrene Books, 1998), 48–49. Bowen's residence is now the site of L'Enfant Plaza.

14. Still, *Underground Railroad*, 183–84.

15. Ibid., 183.

16. Harrold, *Subversives*, 220–21. Tappan was known as a skinflint whose criticisms of Underground Railroad operators sometimes took on racist tones, such as when he wrote of David Ruggles, the treasurer of the New York Vigilance Committee: "Like most every colored man I have ever known, he was untrustworthy about money matters. I do not accuse him or others as deficient in integrity, but no regular account appears to be kept of moneys received or paid." Lewis Tappan to Gerrit Smith, January 4, 1839, Gerrit Smith Miller MSS, Syracuse University Library.

17. Fitzpatrick and Goodwin, *Guide to Black Washington*, 48.

18. By 1850 the Chesapeake and Ohio Canal ran alongside the Potomac for 184.5 miles to Cumberland, Maryland, but it never went past that point.

19. *Liberator*, August 27, 1858.

20. Avis Thomas-Lester, "Tracking History on the Underground Railroad," *Washington Post*, February 23, 1991, D1, D7; Linda Wheeler, "Tracking the Underground Railroad," *Washington Post*, 1998.

21. Still, *Underground Railroad*, 477–78. Still's account included this description of her skin color.

22. Ibid., 188 (emphasis in original).

23. Ibid., 50.

24. Larry Gara, The *Liberty Line: The Legend of the Underground Railroad* (Lexington: University Press of Kentucky, 1967), 50–51.

25. Virginia Writers' Project, *The Negro in Virginia*, 138.

26. Letter from William Penn to William Still, April 3, 1856, in Still, *Underground Railroad*, 187–89.

27. William Penn to William Still, April 23, 1856, in Still, *Underground Railroad*, 188–89 (emphasis in original).

28. Still, *Underground Railroad*, 487–88.

29. *Washington Star*, October 12, 1858.

30. New-York Marine Register, 1858, Mystic Seaport.

31. *Washington Star*, October 12, 1858. Leverton was also the name of a Quaker family who had been known Underground Railroad operatives around Caroline County, Maryland, about that time. Jacob Leverton's widow Hannah still aided fugitives in 1849 when Harriet Tubman escaped through the area. One of the Levertons' daughters, Mary Elizabeth, married Anthony C. Thompson Jr., who lived near Tubman's aged parents, Ben and Rit Ross, and may have helped her in arranging their escape. In early January 1858, a group of seven runaways from Cambridge, Maryland, was caught trying to make their escape, and Hannah Leverton's son, Arthur Leverton, was immediately suspected along with his black neighbor, Daniel Hubbard. A mob formed to forcibly remove them to Cambridge for possible lynching, but Leverton and his friend got word of their plans and escaped to Philadelphia. Mary Elizabeth Leverton had been "disowned" by her local Quaker meeting in 1850 for marrying a non-Quaker and other offenses. During the 1850s she and Anthony Thompson lived for a time in Anne Arundel County and Dorchester County. See Kate Clifford Larson, *Bound for the Promised Land: Harriet Tubman: Portrait of an American Hero* (New York: Ballantine, 2004), 83–84, 329 n. 131, 149, 329–30 n. 133, 348–49 n. 102. Fergus M. Bordewich also has concluded that Hannah Leverton, the white mill owner's widow who was "part of a fragile network that linked Dorchester County Quakers with those farther north in Camden, Delaware, and beyond," probably arranged Tubman's flight in 1849. See Bordewich, *Bound for Canaan*, 349, 351, 376.

32. *Washington Star*, October 13–18, 1858.

Chapter 7. Still in Philadelphia

1. Sarah H. Bradford, *Scenes in the Life of Harriet Tubman* (Auburn, N.Y.: W. J. Moses, 1869), 19–20.

2. "Abolitionists at Niagara Falls, ca. 1860" (middle-plate ambrotype), in Jackie Napolean Wilson, *Hidden Witness: African-American Images from the Dawn of Photography to the Civil War* (New York: St. Martin's Griffin, 2002), 105.

3. Russell F. Weigley, ed., *Philadelphia: A 300-Year History* (New York: W. W. Norton, 1982), 386.

4. William Still (1821–1901), the foremost chronicler of the Underground Railroad, is still in need of a major biography. See William Still, *Still's Underground Railroad Records*, 3rd ed. (Philadelphia: William Still, 1883). Some of his papers are

located at the Historical Society of Pennsylvania. See also James Oliver Horton, "A Crusade for Freedom: William Still and the Real Underground Railroad," in *Passages to Freedom: The Underground Railroad in History and Memory*, edited by David W. Blight (Washington, D.C.: Smithsonian Books, 2004), 175–93.

5. Larry Gara, "William Still and the Underground Railroad," in *Blacks in the Abolitionist Movement*, edited by Bracey Meier Rudwick (Belmont, Calif.: Wadsworth, 1970), 44–51; Bordewich, *Bound for Canaan*, 355–59.

6. Journal of the Philadelphia Vigilance Committee, 1852–1857, Historical Society of Pennsylvania.

7. Still, *Underground Railroad*, 30.

8. Carton, *Patriotic Treason*, 249.

9. "MR. STILL: I take this opportunity of writing a few lines to you hoping that tha may find you in good health and femaly. i am well at present and doing well at present i am now in a store and getting sixteen-dollars a month; at the present. i feel very much o blige to you and your family for your kindnes to me while i was with you i have got along without any trub le a tal I am now in albany City. give my lov to mrs and mr miller and tel them I am very much a blige to them for there kind ns. give my lov to my Brother nore Jones tel him i should like to here from, him very much and he must write, tel him to give my love to all of my perticular frends and tel them i should like to see them very much. tel him that he must come to see me for I want to see him for sum thing very perticler. please ansure this letter as soon as posabul and excuse me for not writing sooner as i dont write myself. no more at the present. WILLIAM JONES." The Jones letter appears in Still, *Underground Railroad*, 47.

10. For the most extensive transcript of one of these interviews, see Still, *Underground Railroad*, 147–49.

11. Still, *Underground Railroad*, 487–88. Under the heading of "ARRIVAL FROM GEORGETOWN, D.C., 1858," Still spells Nalle's name phonetically as "Charles Nole," just as Charles likely said it. It's also possible but not likely that the trio was not escorted, but that they had been helped in some other way. For example, a letter from the same period instructed:

> April 12th 1858
> Robert M. Slattern
> Dear Sir
> The bearer of this letter is a fugitive slave. Just arrived from the eastern shore of Maryland he is on his way to Canada he comes to me recommended from a friend in Wilmington Delaware an I thought it best to send him to you will you please put him safe on board the rail road for Canada by the way of Albany or any way you think best the fare to Canada is eight dollars and I have given him one.
> Yours Respectfully
> George Fisher

Letter from George Fisher to Robert M. Slattern, April 12, 1858, Division of Rare and Manuscript Collections, Karl A. Kroch Library, Cornell University, Ithaca, New York.

12. Still, *Underground Railroad*, 487–88.

13. Twentieth-century psychoanalysts would later develop various theories to explain such thinking, calling it "identification with the aggressor." See, e.g., Karl Bettelheim, "Individual and Mass Behavior in Extreme Situations," *Journal of Abnormal and Social Psychology* 38 (1943): 417–52, describing the reaction of concentration camp survivors; and Anna Freud, *The Ego and the Mechanisms of Defense*, vol. 2 (Madison, Conn.: International Universities Press, 1966). In the 1970s, Swedish criminologist Nils Bejerot coined the term "Stockholm syndrome" to explain the puzzling reactions of several bank robbery victims in Sweden in 1973, who after their ordeal expressed loyalty to their captors. In the 1980s and '90s, more efforts were made to explore the dimensions of "posttraumatic stress." Attempts to encompass African American slaves within this framework have been more rare. One scholar has tried to account for the phenomenon of former slaves who remained loyal to their masters after emancipation, noting how some former slaves remained devoted to their American master despite the cruelty they had endured, saying: "Indeed, the regulation of behavior and the resultant adjustment that was made had a direct influence on the consequent formation of the slave's personality." Barbara Huddleston-Mattai, "The Sambo Mentality and the Stockholm Syndrome Revisited: Another Dimension to an Examination of the Plight of the African American," *Journal of Black Studies* 23, no. 3: 344–57. Her theory may be all the more interesting in Blucher Hansbrough's case because it appears that after emancipation, his former slave mistress Lucinda Wormly continued to maintain an intimate relationship with him.

14. William H. Seward, "The Irrepressible Conflict," Rochester, New York, October 25, 1859, in *The Works of William H. Seward*, edited by George Baker (Boston: Houghton Mifflin, 1884), vol. 5, 300–302.

Chapter 8. Farmed Out

1. Tom Calarco, *The Underground Railroad Conductor: A Guide for Eastern New York* (Schenectady, N.Y.: Travels through History, 2003), 191.

2. Nominating statement, Stephen Myers Residence, National Register of Historic Places, National Parks Service, n.d.

3. See Benjamin Quarles, *Black Abolitionists* (New York: Oxford University Press, 1969). Some of Myers's strongest interests involved efforts to expand Negroes' access to streetcars, schools, and the ballot box. See, e.g., a copy of a letter he wrote to Gerrit Smith, March 22, 1856, regarding his lobbying efforts to eliminate the property qualification for voting. *Black Abolitionist Papers*, vol. 4, 326–28.

4. Hoosick produced quite a number of prominent abolitionists and figures on the Underground Railroad. Laura Smith Haviland had married Charles Haviland,

a Quaker born in Hoosick in 1800; they were later involved in the UGRR in Ohio. Linneaus P. Noble (1802–73) was born in Hoosick and later became associated with Gerrit Smith, James C. Jackson, and Luther Myrick, and was founder and publisher from 1847–60 of the *National Era*, which first published *Uncle Tom's Cabin*; he was also a Baptist deacon in Fayetteville, New York, near Syracuse. See J. H. French, *Historical and Statistical Gazetteer of New York State* (Syracuse, N.Y.: R. Pearsall Smith, 1860).

5. Joel Munsell, *The Annals of Albany*, vol. 6 (Albany: J. Munsell, 1850), 198–99. "Colored People of Albany," 725. Jonathan Eights (1773–1848) and Alida Wynkoop Eights (1772–1849) were part of Albany's Dutch-English aristocracy. Jacobus Wynkoop (1725–95) had been a famous naval commander in the Revolution and the first to fly the American flag in battle at sea. "First American Battle Flag," *Washington Post*, July 25, 1926, p. SM4. Alida Koens Myers lived from 1736–94.

6. Thanks to Dr. Stefan Bielinski of the New York State Museum, an expert on colonial Albany, for sharing some of his research on the Eights family. Dr. Eights's only son, James, two years younger than Myers, grew up to be a protégé of his father's friend, Stephen Van Rensselaer, who was the patroon, or feudal lord of the region. As a young man James became a master surveyor and draftsman for such top scientists as Amos Eaton and Ebenezer Emmons and was an examiner at Van Rensselaer's Troy-based engineering school, which later became known as Rensselaer Polytechnic Institute. He was a great naturalist and painter, and would later become famous as one of the first Antarctic explorers. Char Miller and Naomi Goldsmith, "James Eights, Albany Naturalist: New Evidence," *New York History* 61, no. 1 (January 1980): 23–42.

7. Edgar J. McManus, *A History of Negro Slavery in New York* (Syracuse, N.Y.: Syracuse University Press, 1966).

8. David Lear Buckman, *Old Steamboat Days on the Hudson River* (New York: Grafton Press, 1907).

9. Samuel Ward Stanton, *American Steam Vessels* (New York: Smith & Stanton, 1895), 88.

10. Little is known about Harriet Myers, but C. Peter Ripley has identified her as one of the leading black women abolitionists and unacknowledged editor of her husband's black abolitionist newspaper. See Ripley, ed., "Black Women Abolitionists," in *Witness for Freedom: African American Voices on Race, Slavery, and Emancipation* (Chapel Hill: University of North Carolina Press, 1993), 96. One article that appeared in the *Northern Star and Freeman's Advocate* of March 3, 1842, criticized the existence of racial prejudice in the North, including bias among white abolitionists, saying: "And until abolitionists *eradicate prejudice from their own hearts*, they never *can* receive the unwavering confidence of the people of color. We do not ask them for money, neither do we wish them to educate our children; these we will endeavor to provide for by the sweat of our brow, but we *do* ask that their workshops may be opened to our youth, and that those of us who are already in business may be patronized" (emphases in original).

11. One of his early goals was to eliminate the state's $250 property qualification for black suffrage. See Gerrit Smith Papers, George Arents Research Library, Syracuse University, reprinted in C. Peter Ripley, ed., *The Black Abolitionist Papers* (Chapel Hill: University of North Carolina Press, 1991), vol. 4, 326–28.

12. Handbill, "Vigilance Committee Flyer," in American Antiquarian Society, Worcester, Massachusetts.

13. Ripley, *Black Abolitionist Papers*, vol. 4, 407.

14. Undated circular from 1858, reproduced in Tom Calarco, *The Underground Railroad in the Adirondack Region* (Jefferson City, N.C.: McFarlane, 2004), 192.

15. *New York Times*, March 1, 1858, reprinted in Calarco, *Underground Railroad Conductor*, 38.

16. Some of Myers's financial backers included Thurlow Weed, the editor of the *Albany Evening Journal* (who gave $100 a year); William H. Seward, a leading Republican politician; Simeon Draper, a prominent merchant; Robert B. Minturn, a shipping magnate; lawyer James W. Beekman; James Wadsworth, a large landowner in Livingston County; Governor John Alsop King; and John Jay, the grandson of a founding father. Stephen A. Myers to John Jay, 17 December 1858, reprinted in Ripley, *Black Abolitionist Papers*, vol. 4, 407–11.

17. Stephen A. Myers to John Jay, 17 December 1858, reprinted in Ripley, *Black Abolitionist Papers*, vol. 4, 407–8.

18. West Troy, known today as Watervliet, is located across the Hudson from Troy in Albany County. One of its early settlements included the original home of Ann Lee's Shaker religious sect, a religious group that supported antislavery. West Troy had also been home to Seth Concklin (1802–51), a member of the Underground Railroad who was killed in Indiana after his arrest for rescuing four Alabama slaves.

19. On the history of Sand Lake, see Nathaniel Bartlett Sylvester, *History of Rensselaer Co., New York* (Philadelphia: Everts & Peck, 1880), 518–28. The mill in question was Asa Barker's. Harriet Jacobs, a former slave, recalled receiving a linsey-woolsey dress each Christmas. "How I hated it! It was one of the badges of slavery." Jacobs, *Incidents in the Life of a Slave Girl*, 11.

20. George Baker Anderson, *Landmarks of Rensselaer County* (Syracuse, N.Y.: D. Mason & Co., 1897), 510–20. Cotton data and Sumner's quote are found in Liz Petry, "The Lash and the Loom: The Road to Fortune Was Lined with Cotton. What Matter If It Was Picked by Slaves?" *Hartford Courant*, Northeast, September 29, 2002, 30–31.

21. *Memoir of Rev. Abel Brown, by His Companion* (Worcester, Mass.: published by the author, 1849), 106–7. Brown served as pastor from March 1841 to December 1842.

22. Lovejoy, *Memoir of Rev. Charles T. Torrey*, 129.

23. "Our Village," an essay printed on the letterhead of H. F. Averill, Raymond City, Putnam County, West Virginia, undated, 2, copy in the office of the Sand Lake Town Historian.

24. Sylvester, *History of Rensselaer Co.*, 518–28. In 1852–53 the school's board of visitors included Emma Willard (a Troy educator); Reverend N. S. S. Beman of Troy's First Presbyterian Church; Thomas W. Blatchford, M.D., a Troy physician; Bradford R. Wood, a staunch abolitionist and temperance advocate with Thomas W. Higginson (of John Brown's "Secret Six"); and Susan B. Anthony, who was involved in the Kansas emigration. *First Annual Catalogue . . . Sandlake Collegiate Institute, 1853–54*, Troy Public Library.

25. United States Census, 1860, house #470, family #489. One of the teachers at the Sand Lake Collegiate Institute during this period was Charles H. Peck (1833–1917), who later became well known as one of the nation's leading mycologists. From 1859–63 he taught classics, mathematics, and botany at the school. He was an ardent Presbyterian and Republican. John Haines, "Charles Peck: Pioneer American Mycologist," New York State Museum. His brother, professor Henry E. Peck, was one of those arrested for the Oberlin slave rescue of 1858.

26. In a letter to the editor by John C. Nalle, reprinted in the *Troy Daily Times*, October 14, 1932, Nalle wrote that his father lived with Crosby's family in Sand Lake until about three weeks before the rescue. He cited as his source the *Troy Whig*, April 28, 1859 [1860].

27. Census of the United States, Sand Lake, New York.

Chapter 9. Family Pays a Heavy Price

1. *Troy Daily Arena*, May 26, 1860.

2. David K. Sullivan, "The District of Columbia Penal System, 1825 to 1875" (Ph.D. diss., Georgetown University, March 1973).

3. "Persecution of Negroes in the Capitol—Astounding Revelations," *Frank Leslie's Illustrated Magazine*, December 28, 1861.

4. The log has been published as Jerry M. Hyson, *District of Columbia, D.C. Department of Corrections Runaway Slave Book, 1848–1863* (Westminster, Md.: Willow Bend Books, 1999). A review of the records did not turn up any reference to Kitty Nalle, Kitty Simms, or Blucher W. Hansbrough. See Linda Wheeler, "D.C. Jail Log Unlocks History of Slave Era," *Washington Post*, January 10, 1971, pp. D1, D7.

5. John Hope Franklin, "Runaway Slaves," *American Visions* 6, no. 1 (February 1, 1991): n.p.

6. For example, in one case in 1849, the day after Eliza Williams was detained in the jail for running away, she gave birth to a baby girl, and the mother and child were released twenty-eight days later to a slave master who paid a fee of $11.20 for their keep. Jailers charged a daily fee for upkeep of slave men, women, and children. It apparently rose from about twenty cents a day in 1848 to eighty-two cents during the Civil War. Wheeler, "D.C. Jail Log Unlocks History of Slave Era," p. D1.

7. John Catesby Thom, Account Book, 1855–1858, Thom Family Papers, Virginia Historical Society.

8. *Troy Daily Arena*, May 26, 1860.

9. Robert C. Smedley, *History of the Underground Railroad in Chester and the Neighboring Counties of Pennsylvania* (Lancaster, Penn.: The Journal, 1883), 26–28.

10. Still, *Underground Railroad*, 736–39.

11. Willis L. Shirk Jr., "Testing the Limits of Tolerance: Blacks and the Social Order in Columbia, Pennsylvania, 1800–1851," *Pennsylvania History* 60, no. 1: 43–45, quoting *Lancaster Intelligencer*, January 28, 1851, p. 2; *Lancaster Saturday Express*, February 1, 1851, p. 2; *Lancaster Intelligencer*, February 11, 1851, p. 2.

12. "More Freedom Stories," http://muweb.millersville.edu/~ugrr/tellingstories/demosite/Columbia/stories/images/mor (accessed November 17, 2004).

13. "'Underground Railroad' Stop Holds Pre–Civil War Proof," *Lancaster Sunday News*, March 22, 1961.

14. "Stevens Stoked Underground Railroad," *Lancaster New Era*, August 15, 1991.

15. "Double-Agent's Reports Stopped 'Slave Catchers,'" *Lancaster New Era*, August 15, 1991.

16. One hint about the phenomenon of fugitive slaves and the lumber industry may be found in the offensive racist colloquial expression "there's a nigger in the woodpile" that originated in mid-nineteenth-century America, which was later rephrased by W. C. Fields as "Hmm. There's an Ethiopian in the fuel supply." Cartoonists of the era often depicted runaway slaves hiding under stacks of wood. What was less well known was that the lumber hauling industry was especially receptive to blacks, in part because several African Americans had assumed great success in the business.

17. Still, *Underground Railroad*, 386.

18. Drew, *North-Side View of Slavery*, 30.

19. Larson, *Bound for the Promised Land*, quote from Bradford, *Scenes in the Life of Harriet Tubman*, 20 (emphasis in original).

20. Franklin Sanborn, "Harriet Tubman," *The Commonwealth*, Boston, July 17, 1863; Larson, *Bound for the Promised Land*, 89–90.

21. Larson, *Bound for the Promised Land*, 90–91.

22. Sanborn, "Harriet Tubman."

23. Sanborn, "Harriet Tubman"; Larson, *Bound for the Promised Land*, 92–93; Douglass, *Life and Times of Frederick Douglass*, 101–2.

24. Larson, *Bound for the Promised Land*, chap. 6, 99.

25. Bradford, *Scenes in the Life of Harriet Tubman*, 61.

26. Drew, *North-Side View of Slavery*, 30.

27. Larson, *Bound for the Promised Land*, chap. 6, 143–45.

28. From an interview with Charles Nalle that appeared in the *Troy Daily Arena*, May 26, 1860.

Chapter 10. Meteors

1. *Troy Daily Times*, August 11, 1859.

2. Walt Whitman, "Year of Meteors (1859–60)," *Leaves of Grass* (New York: William E. Chapin, 1867), 51–52.

3. The constitution is reproduced in Richard S. Hinton, *John Brown and His Men* (New York: Funk & Wagnalls, 1904), 620–33.

4. There is a huge literature about John Brown. The best single source is Reynolds, *John Brown, Abolitionist.*

5. At the time, Reverend James N. Gloucester presided at Siloam Presbyterian Church in Brooklyn, one of New York City's (and the nation's) leading black congregations. On March 16, 1858, he had met with Henry Highland Garnet, Frederick Douglass, William Still, and a few others at Stephen Smith's home to hear John Brown outline some of his initial plans for his war of liberation. A few months later, Gloucester left Brooklyn to become pastor of the Liberty Street Presbyterian Church in Troy. Benjamin Quarles, *Allies for Freedom, and Blacks on John Brown* (New York: Oxford University Press, 1974), 39–41. Born in Philadelphia to a prominent Presbyterian minister, Gloucester later entered the ministry and served in New York, where he was also involved in the American Home Missionary Society and the Evangelical Association of the Colored Ministers of Congregational and Presbyterian Churches. Besides his close involvement with Garnet, N. S. S. Beman, Frederick Douglass, William Still, John Brown, Harriet Tubman, and Chester A. Arthur, his missionary activity may have brought him into contact with Minot Crosby. The most comprehensive information about Gloucester is in *Black Abolitionist Papers*, vol. 4, 377–81.

6. Letter from John Brown to John Brown Jr., April 8, 1858, Boyd B. Stutler Collection of John Brown, West Virginia Archives, Charleston, West Virginia.

7. Reynolds, *John Brown, Abolitionist*, 259.

8. I appreciate the information about Newby that was provided by Professor Phil Schwarz of Virginia Commonwealth University.

9. Douglass, *Life and Times of Frederick Douglass*, 314–20. Shields Green was hanged on December 16. Douglass's public appearance in Chambersburg was reported, very negatively, by the *Chambersburg Valley Spirit* on August 24, 1859.

10. William H. Johnson, *Autobiography of Dr. William Henry Johnson* (Albany, N.Y.: Argus Co., 1900), 195–96. Johnson's brief autobiography (which is very rare and often overlooked by scholars) includes one of the most interesting and potentially revealing accounts about the lead-up to John Brown's raid. Johnson's life also intersected with several of the persons and events described in this book about Charles Nalle, although it is unclear if they ever met. Late in Johnson's life he claimed to have trained under Gerrit Smith, Frederick Douglass, Stephen Myers, John C. Fremont, Bishop Logan, and Henry Highland Garnet. Johnson was born to free parents on March 4, 1833, in Alexandria, Virginia, and he left home at age twelve, equipped with a "Sunday school education," and moved to

Philadelphia where he spent four years until March 1850 learning the hairdressing trade. He moved to Albany in 1851 and worked for the Underground Railroad, as an assistant to Stephen Myers. He returned to Philadelphia in 1855 and in 1856 he attended the Republican National Convention in Philadelphia. In 1857 he became a member of the Banneker Literary Institute and helped to start a secret organization, the Proscribed American Council, designed to "revolutionize public opinion" in Philadelphia. He also was involved in the inner workings of the Underground Railroad in Philadelphia and claimed to have rooted out at least one informer within William Still's office. Johnson gave a public address in Philadelphia on July 4, 1859, and then experienced his first meetings with John Brown and Frederick Douglass. Very shortly after Brown's burial, he became a fugitive for alleged crimes he said were related to his aiding of fugitive slaves, and he hid out in Norwich, Connecticut—presumably utilizing some of the contacts he had developed through the Underground Railroad. He remained there until the outbreak of the Civil War, when he very early participated in the fighting and served in the first battle of Bull Run. After the war, in 1872, he claimed to have become the first black person elected to any office in New York State, when he was made janitor of the State Senate. Militant self-defense advocate J. J. Simmons, whom Johnson referred to as "general" but others called "captain," prophesied (quite accurately) that the time would come when Northern black military units would march through the South with "a bible in one hand and a gun in the other." Quoted in *Black Abolitionist Papers*, vol. 4, 319. For more about Simmons, see Jeffrey R. Kerr-Ritchie, "Rehearsal for War: Black Militias in the Atlantic World," *Slavery and Abolition* 26, no. 1 (April 2005): 1–34.

11. Reynolds, *John Brown, Abolitionist*, chap. 13. For an excellent and vivid account of the raid, also see Carton, *Patriotic Treason*, prologue.

12. See Renehan, *Secret Six*. The best analysis of Smith's response to Harpers Ferry is John R. McKivigan and Madeleine Leveille, "The 'Black Dream' of Gerrit Smith, New York Abolitionist," *Syracuse University Library Associates Courier* 20, no. 2 (Fall 1985), http://www.nyhistory.com/gerritsmith/dream.htm (accessed February 20, 2007).

13. "Non-Intervention—How It Works," *Richmond Enquirer*, October 28, 1859. I am grateful to Professor Philip J. Schwarz of Virginia Commonwealth University for bringing this article to my attention.

14. Reynolds, *John Brown, Abolitionist*, 380–81. Governor Wise later claimed to have received 3,600 letters threatening to rescue Brown. See *National Era*, February 9, 1860.

15. "Civil Disobedience" originated as a Concord Lyceum lecture Thoreau delivered on January 26, 1848. It was first published as "Resistance to Civil Government," in May of 1849, in Elizabeth Peabody's obscure periodical, *Aesthetic Papers*, but went on to become one of the most influential essays in world history. "Unjust laws exist," he wrote. "[S]hall we be content to obey them, or shall we

endeavor to amend them, and obey them until we have succeeded, or shall we transgress them at once? Men generally, under such a government as this, think that they ought to wait until they have persuaded the majority to alter them. They think that, if they should resist, the remedy would be worse than the evil. But it is the fault of government itself that the remedy *is* worse than the evil. It makes it worse. Why is it not more apt to anticipate and provide for reform? Why does it not cherish its wise minority? . . . Under a government which imprisons any unjustly, the true place for a just man is also a prison." Henry David Thoreau, *Walden and "Civil Disobedience"* (New York: New American Library, 1960), 228–30 (emphasis in original).

16. Henry David Thoreau, "A Plea for Captain John Brown" [read in Concord, Mass., on October 30, 1859], *The Writings of Henry David Thoreau* (Boston: Houghton Mifflin, 1893); excerpt, John L. Thomas, ed., *Slavery Attacked: The Abolitionist Crusade* (Englewood Cliffs, N.J.: Prentice Hall, 1965), 163–68.

17. Ralph Waldo Emerson, "Courage," *New York Times*, November 8, 1859.

18. Reynolds, *John Brown, Abolitionist*, 388.

19. Brown's courtroom speech was widely reprinted in many newspapers of the day. See Reynolds, *John Brown, Abolitionist*, 354–55.

20. Louis Ruchames, ed., *John Brown: The Making of a Revolutionary: The Story of John Brown in His Own Words and in the Words of Those Who Knew Him* (1969; New York: Grosset & Dunlap, 1971), 167.

21. Colonel J. T. L. Preston, "The Execution of John Brown," Boyd Stutler Archive, West Virginia Memory Project, http://www.wvculture.org.

22. Quoted in James M. McPherson, *Battle Cry of Freedom: The Civil War Era* (New York: Oxford University Press, 1988), 209–10.

23. *Weekly Anglo-African*, December 10, 1859; Daniel C. Littlefield, "Blacks, John Brown, and a Theory of Manhood," in *His Soul Goes Marching On: Responses to John Brown and the Harpers Ferry Raid*, edited by Paul Finkelman (Charlottesville: University Press of Virginia, 1995), 71.

24. *Troy Daily Arena*, December 2, 1859.

25. Johnson, *Autobiography of Dr. William Henry Johnson*, 31.

26. *Troy Daily Arena*, December 6, 1859.

27. Wendell Phillips (1811–84), a Boston patrician turned champion of common men and women, had last seen Brown in the company of Harriet Tubman when they visited his house. Sarah H. Bradford, *Harriet, the Moses of Her People* (New York: George R. Lockwood, 1886), 133–34.

28. *Troy Daily Arena*, December 6, 1859; *Troy Whig*, December 6, 1859.

29. "The Burial of John Brown," *New York Weekly Tribune*, December 17, 1859.

30. Quoted in Joanne Grant, *Black Protest* (New York: Fawcett Premier, 1983), 64–65. For more about Phillips, see James Brewer Stewart, *Liberty's Hero: Wendell Phillips* (Baton Rouge: Louisiana State University Press, 1998).

Chapter 11. Hooking Up

1. Slave letters are very rare and letters between fugitive slaves are exceedingly rare. A special collection of slave letters is located in the Rare Book, Manuscript and Special Collections Library at Duke University. Some sources that specifically address slave letters include Robert S. Starobin, ed., *Blacks in Bondage: Letters of American Slaves* (New York: Viewpoints, 1974); Janet Duitsman Cornelius, *"When I Can Read My Title Clear": Literacy, Slavery, and Religion in the Antebellum South* (University of South Carolina Press, 1991); John W. Blassingame, *Slave Testimony: Two Centuries of Letters, Speeches, Interviews, and Autobiographies* (Baton Rouge: Louisiana State University Press, 1977). Douglass, *Life and Times of Frederick Douglass*, chap. 11, talks about the danger of intercepted letters. The arrest of fugitive Anthony Burns in 1854 was attributed to a letter Burns had sent to his enslaved brother that had been intercepted even though it was sent through Canada. See Albert J. Von Frank, *The Trials of Anthony Burns: Freedom and Slavery in Emerson's Boston* (Cambridge, Mass.: Harvard University Press, 1998).

2. United States Census, Rensselaer County, New York, 1027, #78, taken June 14, 1860.

3. Averill had been summoned to appear in State Supreme Court in Westchester County. See *New York Times*, March 17, 1858. Most of this information about Averill has been pieced together from several sources including the James Knox Averill file, Horatio Franklin Averill file, Averill Family file, Horatio Averill Scrapbooks, Scram's Collegiate Institute file in the Sand Lake Historian's Office, Sand Lake, New York, and numerous contemporary newspaper accounts identifying Averill as the informer, particularly several stories that appeared in the *Troy Daily Arena*. After the rescue, Horatio Averill gave a brief statement defending himself. See *Troy Daily Arena*, April 30, 1860. He later issued another carefully worded account about his role in the incident shortly after Charles Nalle's obituary appeared in Troy on July 23, 1875, and revived the controversy about his actions. See *Troy Daily Press*, August 14, 1875. According to his version of the events, he never spoke with Nalle or knew him by sight until after his arrest on April 27, 1860, except that he later remembered having seen him driving a coach; he never wrote a letter for Nalle to Nalle's master or anyone else; he personally never wrote or saw Nalle's master until after the arrest; he was not a witness in the case or connected with it in any way except as an attorney for the parties and was retained by them in a regular professional capacity; he was regularly retained as an attorney and authorized to retain William A. Beach as counsel and did so; he did appear before the U.S. Commissioner, assisted by William Beach; the claimants informed him that letters written for Charles had been intercepted and his whereabouts ascertained through parties living in New York, who suggested Averill's name to them as an attorney, but Averill did not know the contents of these letters. On July 17, 1860, the *Troy Daily Times* pub-

lished what was in effect a retraction about the embezzlement charges against Averill, reprinting a letter of April 20, 1859, from three former plaintiffs who said they had respectfully countermanded and withdrawn all proceedings against him, including the orders for his arrest.

4. "The Slave Rescue at Troy," *New York Times*, May 1, 1860, p. 8. Several accounts reported that Nalle showed the letters to Averill. See, e.g., *Troy Daily Arena*, April 28, 1860, p. 3. Shortly after the rescue, Averill tried to blame the betrayal in Sand Lake on Minot Crosby, whom he said had known Nalle as a slave in Culpeper. To this accusation, (his former boss) Charles MacArthur of the *Troy Daily Arena* of April 30, 1860, responded: "We are authorized to say that Mr. Crosby never directly or indirectly gave any information of the character referred to, any statement by Mr. Averill or anybody else to the contrary notwithstanding."

"Will Mr. Averill inform us, whether he did not in the street, on Friday afternoon, in the presence of M. I. Townsend and Judge Robertson say, that he (Averill) was not the informer, but that Mr. Crosby of Sandlake was? And whether the plea of personal innocence now is any better than the charges against Mr. Crosby was then? Or if he did not write personally to the Virginia owner of Nalle, whether in order to fish 'a case,' he did not induce the New York parties to write to Virginia for him? And if he did not undertake to play the part of the informer, what was he hanging about Mr. Gilbert's a 'nigger-smelling' for?—And who, whether in Virginia, or anywhere else, would think of employing Mr. Averill for any services but that of a spy or informer? What else but his reputation for capacity in business of this sort ever placed him in a position which enabled him to speak of Hon. Wm. A. Beach as his 'associate counsel?'" *Troy Daily Arena*, May 1, 1860, p. 3.

5. *Troy Whig*, April 28, 1860.

6. Daniel J. Walkowitz, *Worker City, Company Town: Iron and Cotton Worker Protest in Troy and Cohoes, New York, 1855–84* (Urbana: University of Illinois Press, 1978), 20–25; Carole Turbin, *Working Women of Collar City: Gender, Class, and Community in Troy, New York, 1864–86* (Urbana: University of Illinois Press, 1992), chap. 1.

7. According to the 1860 census, Rensselaer County's population of 86,328 included 1,058 free colored persons, of which 331 were mulatto, whereas Troy's population of 39,235 included 322 free colored females and 289 free colored males.

8. See *Proceedings of the National Convention of Colored People, and Their Friends, Held in Troy, N.Y., on the 6th, 7th, 8th and 9th of October, 1847* (Troy: J. C. Kneeling, 1847).

9. The governor was Levi Lincoln. *Troy Daily Times*, November 22, 1880.

10. Sadly, he died in a Poughkeepsie insane asylum in 1881. *Troy Daily Times*, July 5, 1881.

11. *Troy Times*, February 6, 1913; *Troy Record*, February 7, 1913.

12. Calarco, *Underground Railroad in the Adirondack Region*, 199.

13. Martin I. Townsend to Wilbur Siebert, September 4, 1896, April 3, 1897, Siebert Papers; Larson, *Bound for the Promised Land*, 117.

14. Larson, *Bound for the Promised Land*, 340 n. 53.

15. Ibid., 90, 321 n. 30.

16. Ibid., 117.

17. Still, *Underground Railroad*, 399–401.

18. *Troy Daily Times*, October 6, 1857.

19. From a letter from Martin I. Townsend to Wilbur Siebert, written in 1896 or 1897, quoted in Wilbur H. Siebert, *The Underground Railroad: From Slavery to Freedom* (New York: Macmillan, 1898), 126. Townsend served as the lawyer for Charles Nalle in 1860.

20. James Oliver Horton, *Free People of Color: Inside the African American Community* (Washington, D.C.: Smithsonian Institution, 1993).

21. *Troy Daily Times*, May 29, 1860.

22. James McCune Smith, "Sketch of the Life and Labors of Rev. Henry Highland Garnet." Introduction to *A Memorial Discourse; Delivered in the Hall of the House of Representatives, Washington City, D.C., on Sabbath, February 12, 1865* (Philadelphia: Joseph M. Wilson, 1865).

23. Speech reprinted in Earl Ofari, *"Let Your Motto Be Resistance": The Life and Thought of Henry Highland Garnet* (Boston: Beacon Press, 1972), 149–50 (emphases in original).

24. Martin B. Pasternak, *Rise Now and Fly to Arms: The Life of Henry Highland Garnet* (New York: Garland Publishers, 1995), 38. Garnet lived in the Trojan Hardware Building at 137 Fourth Street, among other locations.

25. David Walker and Henry Highland Garnet, *Walker's Appeal and Garnet's Address to the Slaves of the United States of America* (1848; reprint, Nashville, Tenn.: James C. Winston, 1994).

26. Calarco, *Underground Railroad in the Adirondack Region*, 49.

27. Frederick Douglass, *Autobiographies* (New York: Library of America, 1994), 715.

28. Jeffrey Rossbach, *Ambivalent Conspirators: John Brown, the Secret Six, and a Theory of Slave Violence* (Philadelphia: University of Pennsylvania Press, 1982), 158.

29. For more about Garnet, see W. M. Brewer, "Henry Highland Garnet," *Journal of Negro History* 13 (January 1928): 36–52; Alexander Crummell, "Eulogium on Henry Highland Garnet, D.D.," in *Africa and America* (Springfield, Mass.: Willey & Co., 1891); Joel Schor, *Henry Highland Garnet* (Westport, Conn.: Greenwood Press, 1977).

30. Martin I. Townsend, *Proceedings of the Centennial Anniversary of the First Presbyterian Church, Troy, N.Y., December 30, 31, 1891* (Troy, N.Y.: Troy Times, 1892), 24.

31. *Brief Account of the Origins and Progress of the Divisions of the First Presbyterian Church in the City of Troy: Containing also Strictures upon the New Doctrines Preached by the Rev. C. G. Finney and N. S. S. Beman, with a Summary Relation of the Trial of the Letter before the Troy Presbytery, by a Member of the Late Church and Congregation* (Troy, N.Y.: Tuttle & Richards, 1827), 32–35. The bill of sale is in the Benjamin C. Yancey Papers, Southern Historical Collection, University of North Carolina Library, Chapel Hill.

32. *Anti-Slavery Record* 1, no. 7 (July 1835): 81; see also Owen Peterson, *A Divine Discontent: The Life of Nathan S. S. Beman* (Macon, Ga.: Mercer Press, 1986), chap. 6.

33. John Witherspoon DuBose, *Life and Times of William Lowndes Yancey*, 2 vols. (New York: Peter Smith, 1942); Peterson, *Divine Discontent*, chap. 5.

34. Nathan S. S. Beman, *Antagonisms in the Moral and Political World* (Troy, N.Y.: A. Scribner & Co., 1858), 35.

35. Eaton & Gilbert coaches are featured in Mildred V. Frizzell, "Anatomy of American Stagecoaches," *Persimmon Hill* 1 (1970): 16–18.

36. *Troy Daily Arena*, May 28, 1860.

37. David Hackett Fischer, "The Original Uncle Sam," in *Liberty and Freedom: A Visual History of America's Founding Ideas* (New York: Oxford University Press, 2005), 228–32.

Chapter 12. Caught

1. The writ of personal replevin (writ *de homine replegiando*) had been handed down in English common law along with trial by jury and writ of habeas corpus, allowing men to invoke legal processes to challenge their confinement, under the assumption that all men were presumed to be free. This type of writ commonly involved instances in which someone had allegedly taken property from an individual wrongfully in possession of it and sought to return it to its rightful owner. Unlike the writ of habeas corpus, it was designed to be served on private individuals rather than on government officials. Anciently recognized but seldom used, it had survived in Massachusetts as a right to every person in the state "who shall be imprisoned, confined or held in duress." It offered the advantage of securing a jury trial rather than a hearing before a judge. Thomas D. Morris, *Free Men All: The Personal Liberty Laws of the North, 1780–1861* (Baltimore: Johns Hopkins University Press, 1974), 11–12.

2. Tom Foran Clark, "The Kidnapping of Frank Sanborn," *Concord Magazine*, June 1998.

3. Franklin and Schweninger, *Runaway Slaves*, 156.

4. *Troy Daily Times*, April 30, 1860.

5. Madden, *We Were Always Free*, 97. In a personal interview with the author on

October 1, 1994, Madden reiterated his belief that he was a descendant of "Jack Wale, the slave trader."

6. Section 6, Fugitive Slave Act.

7. A copy was reprinted in the *Troy Daily Budget*, April 30, 1860.

8. Blucher W. Hansbrough's affidavit, reprinted in the *Troy Daily Budget*, April 30, 1860.

9. From the affidavit of William Stout, dated April 21, 1860, reprinted in the *Troy Daily Budget*, April 30, 1860.

10. Alfred L. Ashby's affidavit of April 21, 1860, reprinted in the *Troy Daily Budget*, April 30, 1860. After the Civil War, Stout and Ashby would become two of Culpeper's first post-war judges. Eugene M. Scheel, *Culpeper*, 417–30.

11. From the affidavit of Henry J. Wale dated April 20, 1860, reprinted in the *Troy Daily Budget*, April 30, 1860.

12. For William A. Beach's obituary, see the *Troy Observer Budget*, August 26, 1886.

13. Miles Beach's early career is described in the *New York Times*, June 1, 1860.

14. *Troy Daily Budget*, April 30, 1860.

15. This was reprinted in the *Troy Daily Times*, April 30, 1860.

16. Frederick S. Calhoun, *The Lawmen: United States Lawmen and Their Deputies* (Washington, D.C.: Smithsonian Press, 1989).

17. Martin Scorsese chose Washington Park as a setting for his period film, *The Age of Innocence*.

18. Frances Ingraham Heins, "Splendor on the Park," *Albany Times Union*, April 29, 2001, pp. H1, H10.

19. 1860 census, Troy.

20. *Albany Evening Journal*, April 27, 1860.

21. George Holeur, thirty-four, a French baker, lived with his family and employees close to William Henry's grocery. Shortly after the rescue, the street directly outside Holeur's bakery may have been the target of some vandalism, and a curious newspaper column printed immediately after Nalle's arrest indicates that Holeur may have been singled out as a "spy" or informant for one side or the other; the same column also contained an apparent reference to William Henry. The following is the text of the apparently coded message that appeared in the *Troy Daily Arena* of May 1, 1860, p. 3:

> "BROKE DOWN—The axle-tree of the baker wagon belonging to G. Holeur of SecondSt., gave way this morning on the corner of Second and Ferry, letting down the entire institution. No particular damage was done.— Evening paper.
>
> "It is a lamentable coincidence that at one hour and 31 minutes afterward, a darkey upset a wheelbarrow at precisely the same point. On the wheelbarrow was a pail of swill, and a pail of white-washing preparation. The swill

is a dead loss for the darkey—The white-wash was partially insured. How true it is as disasters, "not to single spies, but in battalions."

P.S.—we are informed, just as we go to press, that four bottles of root beer burst in a corner-grocery store uptown, about 5 yesterday afternoon—cause, unusual warmth of the atmosphere and the neglect of the proprietor to surround the bottles with ice. Two of the bottles were destroyed; but the corks only were drawn out of the others. Beer a total loss."

22. *Troy Daily Times*, April 30, 1860.

23. *New-York Tribune*, quoted in *Weekly Afro-American*, May 5, 1860.

24. *Troy Daily Times*, April 30, 1860. Transcripts of most of the legal papers also appeared in the *Troy Daily Budget*, April 30, 1860.

25. After the rescue, Miles Beach issued a public statement defending his official actions. "I endeavoured to act officially with calmness and deliberation, and did so, but with the determination to perform the duties of my office," he wrote. "After a review of the circumstances I am satisfied that I did no more and no less than was my duty. I have thereby retained my self-respect, and I trust the respect of the conservative and thinking portion of the community in which I live. . . ." *Troy Daily Budget*, April 30, 1860.

26. Although many of the Nalle case records were reprinted in the newspaper, the official court records appear to have been lost or destroyed. The National Archives and Records Administration, Northeast Region, Record Group 21, contains some records for slave cases from the Southern District of New York for this period (1837–60) but none for the Northern District. Likewise, the records for the U.S. marshal are also missing.

27. Reprinted in the *Troy Daily Times*, April 30, 1860.

Chapter 13. Busting Out

1. *Troy Whig*, April 28, 1860, in Bradford, *Scenes in the Life of Harriet Tubman*, 94.

2. *New York Times* in *Weekly Anglo-African*, May 5, 1860.

3. *Troy Daily Times*, April 30, 1860; *Troy Observer*, September 29, 1907.

4. From Harden's firsthand account, in the *Troy Observer*, September 29, 1907.

5. *Troy Observer*, September 29, 1907.

6. The *Troy Daily Arena* newspaper office was located at 1 First Street, the first door south of Troy House, just down the street from the Mutual Building. It was edited by Charles L. MacArthur.

7. The Antonio Lewis case is mentioned in the *Troy Times*, March 16, 1903.

8. A lengthy biography of Townsend appears in *Landmarks of Rensselaer County*, 575–79. His statement attesting to Tubman's version of the rescue was included in Bradford, *Scenes in the Life of Harriet Tubman*, 101–4. Bradford wrote (92) that Townsend also gave a "rich narration" to the Reverend Henry Fowler for the

book, and was scheduled to write up a detailed version, but he took ill and apparently never completed the project.

9. *Weekly Anglo-African*, May 5, 1860.

10. *National Anti-Slavery Standard*, January 6, 1859.

11. Campbell, *Slave Catchers*, 86–87; New York State Legislature, Select Committee on the Petition to Prevent Slave Hunting, *Report of the Select Committee on the Petitions to Prevent Slave Hunting in the State of New York, Assembly Report No. 72* (Albany, N.Y.: V. Van Benthuysen, February 11, 1860). See Morris, *Free Men All*.

12. *New York Assembly Document No. 100*, 1860.

13. See *New York Assembly Journal*, 1860: pp. 531, 544, 647, 651, 748–49, 815.

14. *Troy Whig*, April 28, 1860.

15. Campbell, *Slave Catchers*, 175.

16. The author discovered and explored this vault in the building in April 2001 while being interviewed on camera by Dan DiNicola of WRGB-TV.

17. *Weekly Anglo-African*, May 5, 1860.

18. *Troy Daily Times*, April 30, 1860.

19. Bradford, *Scenes in the Life of Harriet Tubman*, 94–95.

20. Ibid., 95; *Troy Observer*, September 29, 1907.

21. *Troy Whig*, April 28, 1860, in Bradford, *Scenes in the Life of Harriet Tubman*, 95.

22. *Troy Daily Times*, April 30, 1860.

23. *Troy Whig*, April 28, 1860.

24. This description of Tubman comes from Earl Conrad, "'General' Tubman at Troy," *The Crisis*, March 1941, 78.

25. Bradford, *Scenes in the Life of Harriet Tubman*, 88.

26. *Troy Whig*, April 28, 1860, in Bradford, *Scenes in the Life of Harriet Tubman*, 89, 95; *Troy Daily Times*, April 30, 1860.

27. One contemporary account reported, "Near the window opening upon State Street from the hall was a somewhat antiquated colored woman, who at a later period became an active spirit of the *melee*, and who was said to be in some way related to the prisoner. She was provided with a signal to prepare those on the outside for an attack, when the prisoner should be brought forth." *Troy Daily Times*, April 30, 1860.

28. Bradford, *Scenes in the Life of Harriet Tubman*, 88–89. Shortly after the incident, the American Anti-Slavery Society reported, "In this rescue, a colored woman was prominent, very active and persevering, until success crowned their efforts—a woman known among the colored people extensively as 'Moses,' because she has led so many of their number out of worse than Egyptian bondage into the goodly land of freedom." *National Anti-Slavery Standard*, May 5, 1860; Samuel May, *The Fugitive Slave Law and Its Victims*, Anti-Slavery Tracts, No. 15, new series (New York: American Anti-Slavery Society, 1861), 134–35.

29. His family owned a cotton mill in Sand Lake.

30. *Troy Daily Times*, April 30, 1860. Quin was a gas fitter at 16 Congress Street and lived at 144 Fifth Avenue. A. J. Weise, *History of the City of Troy* (Troy, N.Y.: William H. Young, 1876), 225.

31. See Gary Collison, *Shadrach Minkins: From Fugitive Slave to Citizen* (Cambridge, Mass.: Harvard University Press, 1997); *Abstract of the Argument on the Fugitive Slave Law Made by Gerrit Smith in Syracuse, June, 1852 on the Trial of Henry W. Allen, U.S. Deputy Marshal, for Kidnapping* (Syracuse, n.d.), excerpted in John L. Thomas, ed., *Slavery Attacked: The Abolitionist Crusade* (Englewood Cliffs, N.J.: Prentice-Hall, 1965), 137–41.

32. *Troy Daily Times*, April 30, 1860; Bradford, *Scenes in the Life of Harriet Tubman*, 95.

33. Bradford, *Scenes in the Life of Harriet Tubman*, 96.

34. Ibid., 89.

35. *Troy Daily Times*, April 30, 1860.

36. Ibid.

37. Ibid.; *New York Times*, reprinted in *Weekly Anglo-African*, May 5, 1860. Bradford, *Scenes in the Life of Harriet Tubman*, 95–96.

38. Bradford, *Scenes in the Life of Harriet Tubman*, 89.

39. Ibid., 96. The affidavit on which the writ was based later mysteriously disappeared from Judge Gould's table when the mob was about his office. *Troy Daily Budget*, April 27, 1860.

40. *Troy Daily Times*, April 30, 1860.

41. Bradford, *Scenes in the Life of Harriet Tubman*, 90–91.

42. *Troy Daily Times*, April 30, 1860.

43. Ibid.

44. *Troy Whig*, April 28, 1860; Bradford, *Scenes in the Life of Harriet Tubman*, 96–97.

45. *Troy Observer*, September 29, 1907.

46. Baltimore's firsthand account was included in the *Troy Observer*, September 29, 1907.

47. *Troy Observer*, September 29, 1907.

48. *Troy Daily Times*, April 30, 1860.

49. Ibid.

50. Ibid.

51. Bradford, *Scenes in the Life of Harriet Tubman*, 97.

52. *Troy Daily Times*, April 30, 1860.

53. Bradford, *Scenes in the Life of Harriet Tubman*, 90.

54. Ibid. The *Troy Daily Times*, April 30, 1860, reported, "Nalle's hands and wrists were badly mangled by the shackles in pulling and hauling him to and fro."

55. *Troy Daily Times*, April 30, 1860.

56. *Albany Evening Journal*, April 28, 1860.

57. *Frederick Douglass' Monthly* 3, no. 1 (June 1860): 282; *Albany Evening Journal,* April 28, 1860.

58. Bradford, *Scenes in the Life of Harriet Tubman,* 98; *Troy Observer,* September 29, 1907.

Chapter 14. Rescue

1. Bradford, *Scenes in the Life of Harriet Tubman,* 98.

2. Ibid., 91.

3. *Frederick Douglass' Monthly* 3, no. 1 (June 1860): 282, quoting the *Troy Daily Arena.* During the Civil War, as a captain of Company A Thirty-fourth New York Infantry, Oswald was drummed out of the army for treason—a highly unusual distinction.

4. *Troy Daily Arena,* quoted in *Frederick Douglass' Monthly* 3, no. 1 (July 1860): 282. *Troy Whig,* April 28, 1860, in Bradford, *Scenes in the Life of Harriet Tubman,* 98. Today the site, at Broadway and Sixteenth Street, houses a McDonald's restaurant and in 2009 a historical marker was erected to indicate what happened there in 1860.

5. The newspaper decried the fact that West Troy had been made by the Fugitive Slave Law into a slave-hunting ground. "The Slave Rescue," *West Troy Advocate,* May 2, 1860.

6. *Troy Observer,* September 29, 1907.

7. *Troy Daily Times,* April 30, 1860.

8. Ibid.

9. *Albany Evening Journal,* April 28, 1860; *Troy Whig,* April 28, 1860, in Bradford, *Scenes in the Life of Harriet Tubman,* 99; *Troy Observer,* September 29, 1907.

10. *Troy Daily Times,* April 30, 1860.

11. *Troy Whig,* April 28, 1860, in Bradford, *Scenes in the Life of Harriet Tubman,* 99; *Troy Daily Times,* April 27, 1860.

12. *Troy Daily Arena* reprinted in *Frederick Douglass' Monthly,* June 1860. Deputy Sheriff Morrison later said over twenty shots were fired during the melee, the officers reloading their revolvers. That nobody was killed was attributed to an astounding lack of accuracy. The man who received a hole in his hat was reported to be a barber from Peter Baltimore's shop.

13. *Troy Observer,* September 29, 1907.

14. *Troy Whig,* April 28, 1860, in Bradford, *Scenes in the Life of Harriet Tubman,* 99.

15. *Troy Observer,* September 29, 1907.

16. Bradford, *Scenes in the Life of Harriet Tubman,* 99.

17. *Troy Daily Times,* April 30, 1860; *Weekly Anglo-African,* May 5, 1860.

18. *Troy Daily Times,* April 30, 1860.

19. *Troy Daily Arena,* reprinted in *Frederick Douglass' Monthly,* June 1860.

20. *Frederick Douglass' Monthly*, June 1860, quoting *Troy Daily Arena*.

21. *Troy Daily Times*, April 30, 1860. *Troy Daily Arena*, reprinted in *Frederick Douglass' Monthly*, June 1860.

22. *Troy Daily Arena*, reprinted in *Frederick Douglass' Monthly*, June 1860. *Troy Whig*, April 28, 1860, in Bradford, *Scenes in the Life of Harriet Tubman*, 99.

23. *Troy Observer*, September 29, 1907.

24. Ibid.

25. Bradford, *Scenes in the Life of Harriet Tubman*, 91. The *Weekly Anglo-African*, May 5, 1860, reported that the charge was "led by one heroic colored woman, who 'facing the cannon's mouth,' rushed frantically on, pressed upward by the surging billows below."

26. *Troy Whig*, April 28, 1860, in Bradford, *Scenes in the Life of Harriet Tubman*, 99–100; *Frederick Douglass' Monthly*, May 1860, quoting *Troy Daily Arena*.

27. *Troy Daily Times*, April 30, 1860.

28. *Weekly Anglo-African*, May 5, 1860.

29. *Frederick Douglass' Monthly*, July 1860, quoting *Troy Daily Arena*; *Troy Daily Times*, April 30, 1860; *Troy Observer*, September 29, 1907.

30. *Troy Daily Times*, April 30, 1860.

31. After entering West Point at age fifteen, Alfred Mordecai had graduated first in his class and served with distinction in the Mexican War, but was now at the end of his career. A native North Carolinian, he struggled to stay neutral in sectional conflicts and would even opt out of serving in the Civil War, although all four of his sons would later serve in the Confederate army. Alfred Mordecai's official correspondence is in RG 156, Office of the Chief of Ordnance, National Archives. Large collections of personal papers are at the Manuscript Division, Library of Congress; Syracuse University Library, Syracuse, New York; and the American Jewish Historical Society, Waltham, Massachusetts. See Stanley L. Falk, "Soldier-Technologist: Major Alfred Mordecai and the Beginnings of Science in the United States Army" (Ph.D. diss., Georgetown University, 1959).

32. The Watervliet Arsenal Museum allowed me to examine the letter books and other arsenal records from this time period, but none contained any information about this incident.

33. *Frederick Douglass' Monthly*, June 1860, quoting *Troy Daily Arena*. "The Slave Rescue," *West Troy Advocate*, May 2, 1860.

34. *Troy Daily Times*, April 30, 1860.

35. Ibid. Thirty years later, the *New York Sun* reported that somebody had recovered from the river a pair of broken slave shackles that had been broken from Charles Nalle's wrists near West Troy on April 27, 1860. The article did not say precisely where they had been discovered, nor did it provide other information enabling the author to verify its accuracy. The article was reprinted in the *Madisonville* (Tennessee) *Democrat*, June 18, 1890.

36. Hank York, in the *Troy Observer*, September 29, 1907.

37. *Troy Daily Arena*, May 26, 1860; *Troy Daily Times*, April 26, 1860.

38. *Troy Daily Arena*, May 1, 1860, May 2, 1860; Arthur J. Weise, *City of Troy and Its Vicinity* (Troy, N.Y.: E. Green, 1886), 227.

39. Douglass, for example, was criticized for allowing himself to be freed in this manner. Gara, *Liberty Line*, 72–73.

40. *National Anti-Slavery Standard*, November 21, 1844; Gara, *Liberty Line*, 74.

41. *Troy Daily Arena*, May 26, 1860.

42. On June 16, 1860, "Charles Nalle, age 35, coachman," was counted by the census taker, none other than assistant U.S. marshal John L. Holmes, as living at William Henry's. United States Census, 1–WD Troy, New York, series M653, roll 846, p. 37.

43. *Troy Daily Arena*, May 10, 1860.

44. Ibid.

45. *Troy Daily Times*, July 18, 1860.

46. *Troy Daily Times*, July 28, 1860.

47. *Lansingburgh Gazette*, August 21, 1860.

Chapter 15. Aftermath

1. Townsend, the lawyer involved in the rescue, was one of those who described her as having been "repeatedly beaten over the head with policemen's clubs" and suffering other injuries, from which she was "partially disabled." Bradford, *Scenes in the Life of Harriet Tubman*, 102.

2. *Weekly Anglo-African*, May 12, 1860; Benjamin Quarles, "Harriet Tubman's Unlikely Leadership," in *Black Leaders of the Nineteenth Century*, edited by Leon F. Litwack and August Meier (Urbana: University of Illinois Press, 1991), 49.

3. May, *Fugitive Slave Law and Its Victims*, 135.

4. Quoted in Jean M. Humez, *Harriet Tubman: The Life and the Life Stories* (Madison: University of Wisconsin Press, 2004), 32.

5. Letter from John Brown to John Brown Jr., April 8, 1858, Boyd S. Stutler Collection of John Brown, West Virginia Archives, quoted in Sanborn, *Life and Letters of John Brown*, 452.

6. Letter from Phillips, published in Bradford, *Harriet, the Moses of Her People*, 133–34.

7. Larson, *Bound for the Promised Land*, 178.

8. Ibid.; "A Fugitive Slave from Harper's Ferry at Auburn—Narrow Escape from a United States Marshall," *New York Herald*, January 21, 1860. Anderson later published his own memoir about the raid. See Osborne P. Anderson, *A Voice from Harper's Ferry: A Narrative of the Events at Harper's Ferry with Incidents Prior and Subsequent to Its Capture by Captain John Brown and His Men* (Boston: printed

for the author, 1861). Anderson had first met Brown in April 1858 at Chatham when he was with Harriet Tubman. He later served in the Union army.

9. An interesting sidelight to Brackett involves Edmonia Lewis (1840–1909), a black woman sculptor who had started under him at about this time. Born in Greenbush, New York, only a few miles from Sand Lake and Troy, to a Chippewa mother and an African American father, Lewis had been a student at Oberlin College at the time of the Wellington rescue there, but was accused (apparently falsely) of poisoning two students. She later moved to Boston, studied with Brackett, and began clay and plaster medallions of John Brown, Garrison, and other abolitionists and freedom seekers. See Stephen May, "The Object at Hand," *Smithsonian*, September 1996, 16, 18, 20.

10. Franklin Sanborn to Sarah Bradford, 1868, in *Scenes in the Life of Harriet Tubman*, 54. Edward Augustus Brackett (1819–1908) was a prominent New England sculptor who made busts of Brown, William Lloyd Garrison, Wendell Phillips, William Seward, Charles Sumner, Richard Henry Dana, and other leading abolitionists.

11. Sanborn, "Harriet Tubman."

12. Larson, *Bound for the Promised Land*, 177.

13. Ednah Dow Littlehale Cheney, "Moses," *Freedmen's Record*, March 1865.

14. *The Liberator*, June 8, 1860; Conrad, "'General' Tubman at Troy," 145.

15. *The Liberator*, June 8, 1860; see also Humez, *Harriet Tubman*, 41.

16. Conrad, "'General' Tubman at Troy," 147; *The Liberator*, July 6, 1860; Humez, *Harriet Tubman*, 41.

17. John Bell Robinson, *Pictures of Slavery and Anti-Slavery: Advantages of Negro Slavery and the Benefits of Negro Freedom, Morally, Socially, and Politically Considered* (Philadelphia: published by the author, 1863), 322–27.

18. Douglas W. Jaenicke, "The Rupture of the Antebellum Democratic Party," *Party Politics* 1, no. 3 (1995): 347–67.

19. Yancey on October 26, 1860, quoted in George M. Frederickson, *The Black Image in the White Mind: The Debate on Afro-American Character and Destiny, 1817–1914* (New York: Harper & Row, 1971), 61.

Chapter 16. The War Hits Home in Culpeper, 1861–65

1. A fine history about Civil War Culpeper is Daniel E. Sutherland, *Seasons of War: The Ordeal of a Confederate Community, 1861–1865* (New York: Free Press, 1995). For an excellent overview and maps, see Scheel's authoritative *Culpeper* and Historic-Site Survey and Archaeological Reconnaissance of Culpeper County. During the Union occupation, Custer spent his honeymoon in Stevensburg.

2. Alfred Townsend, *Rustics in Rebellion* (1866; reprint, Chapel Hill: University of North Carolina, 1950), 217–18.

3. Townsend, *Rustics in Rebellion*, 226.

4. Sutherland, *Seasons of War*, 157–58; William Nalle, *Tales of Old Culpeper* (Culpeper, Va.: Culpeper Historical Society, 1974), 30–31; David H. Strother, "Personal Recollections of the War, Part 8," *Harper's Magazine* 35 (August 1867): 287–88; Mrs. Berkeley G. Calfee, *Confederate History of Culpeper County in the War Between the States* (Culpeper, Va.: Culpeper Chapter United Daughters of the Confederacy, 1984), 3.

5. Sutherland, *Seasons of War*, 158.

6. William Nalle, *Notes on the Nalle Family of Culpeper County, Virginia* (Culpeper: published by the author, 1970), 70–71; Sutherland, *Seasons of War*, 139–40, 368–69.

7. William Nalle Diary, December 24–31, 1864, Virginia Historical Society, Richmond; Sutherland, *Seasons of War*, 369–70.

8. Interview with former Virginia slave William Yager, quoted in Perdue et al., *Weevils in the Wheat*, 335.

9. Madden, *We Were Always Free*, 103–6.

10. Cases of Slaughter Madden and Willis Madden (No. 128), Southern Claims; this incident is recounted in Madden, *We Were Always Free*, 108–10.

11. The Virginia Department of Historic Resources Inventory has designated the place as a potential National Register Site.

12. Allison Brophy Champion, "Stevensburg: Civil War Central: Culpeper Farmer Befriends Gen. Custer during Winter Encampment," *Culpeper Star-Exponent*, July 23, 2006, p. A4; General George A. Custer, *My Life on the Plains, or Personal Experiences with Indians* (New York: Sheldon & Co., 1874).

13. Walt Whitman, *Memoranda during the War*, edited by Peter Coviello (New York: Oxford University Press, 2004), 52.

14. Drew Gilpin Faust, "Evangelism and the Meaning of the Proslavery Argument: The Reverend Thornton Stringfellow of Virginia," *Virginia Magazine of History and Biography* 85 (January 1977): 11; Thomas and Green, *Early Churches of Culpeper County*, 235–36.

15. William Alexander Thom to Ella Tazewell, in Bartlett, *"My Dear Brother,"* 126.

16. Bartlett, *"My Dear Brother,"* 67; Sutherland, *Seasons of War*, 123, 126.

17. Quoted in Sutherland, *Seasons of War*, 126.

18. *Washington Evening Star*, July 28, 1862, p. 2; Frederic Denison, *Sabre and Spurs: First Regiment, Rhode Island Cavalry in the Civil War, 1861–1865* (Central Falls, R.I.: n.p., 1876), 117; *Richmond Enquirer*, August 8, 1862, p. 4, quoted in Sutherland, *Seasons of War*, 126.

19. George T. Fleming, ed., *Life and Letters of Alexander Hays, Brevet Colonel United States Army* (Pittsburgh: n.p., 1919), 516; Sutherland, *Seasons of War*, 305.

20. Margaret Jeffries, "Rose Hill," Works Progress Administration of Virginia, Historical Inventory for Culpeper County, Virginia, Culpeper County Court-

house, p. 2; Edward G. Longacre, *Mounted Raids of the Civil War* (South Brunswick, N.J.: 1975), 227–38; V. C. Jones, "The Kilpatrick-Dahlgren Raid: Badly Planned . . . Timidly Executed," *Civil War Times* 4 (April 1965): 12–21; Scheel, *Culpeper*, 212; Sutherland, *Seasons of War*, 335.

21. George R. Agassiz, ed., *Meade's Headquarters, 1863–65: Letters of Colonel Theodore Lyman from the Wilderness to Appomattox* (Boston: Massachusetts Historical Society, 1922), 85–87; Sutherland, *Seasons of War*, 359. Historic interest in Hansbrough's Ridge has increased in recent years due to its strategic role in Civil War battles and encampments. See, e.g., Scheel, Historic-Site Survey and Archaeological Reconnaissance of Culpeper County, pp. CE-16–CE-17.

Chapter 17. Moving On

1. The paternalistic Thoms were shocked that their faithful servant Winny would escape. Neff, *The Thom Family of Culpeper County, Virginia*, pp. 152–54. Pembroke Thom's sister-in-law Mary Helmsley wrote from Maryland's Eastern Shore on February 21, 1863: "Winny has been heard from twice and Papa answered the letter. She was living in Troy where she 'persuaded her husband to go that she might oftener hear from the children.'" Enclosed with this letter was a letter from Winny herself, dated January 24, 1863, in which she said she had moved from Canada to Troy: "tel De Cozecy to remember me to all the servants— please write me word where mazter Pem is well no more at present but remain Your faithful servant winny Ann Burrell direct Your letter Troy third street in care of mr Charles Nalle." Quoted in Bartlett, *"My Dear Brother,"* 85–86. Bartlett continues in her Thom family history: "As her [Winny's] destination was the home of Charles Nalle in Troy, New York who was an ally of the Maryland ex-slave Harriet Tubman, famous 'Moses of Her People,' it is likely that there was contact between Winny and that amazing woman." Bartlett, *"My Dear Brother,"* 216 n. 4. A few months later, Winn's daughter Mary also tried but failed to escape, prompting her master Alexander Thom to write to his brother Pembroke: "It seems most prudent to sell her, but knowing how you feel about her I hesitate to it. I think after further investigation, if I consider it was an attempt to get away, I shall sell her anyway." Bartlett, *"My Dear Brother,"* 92.

2. *Troy Daily Times*, July 23, 1875.

3. Weise, *History of the City of Troy*; Thomas Phelan, *The Hudson Mohawk Gateway: An Illustrated History* (Northridge, Calif.: Windsor Publications, 1985). Thanks to Jim Corsaro at the Rensselaer County Historical Society for sharing newly discovered correspondence about the Troy draft riot.

4. The Washington, D.C., Census of 1870 listed Charles Nolle, age forty-seven, as a "domestic," and Catherine, forty-six, as a "dressmaker." Also living in their household were their children Annie, nineteen; Lucy, eighteen; Agnes, sixteen; John, fourteen; Mary, eleven; Edward, eight; and Katie, four years old, as well as

Kitty's aged mother, Fanny Simms, sixty-eight. The family's property was valued at only $100, yet everyone but Fanny Simms was listed as being able to read or write—an extraordinary accomplishment.

5. *Troy Press*, October 4, 1870. The newspaper reported, "Nalle was almost white in complexion, and had a daughter, named Alice, whom it would be difficult to distinguish as a colored girl. Her complexion was light and freckled, and her hair straight and tinged with red." George Thompson Ruby (1841–82) was one of the most prominent black Republicans in Texas during radical reconstruction. On one occasion in Galveston, whites saw him walking arm in arm with his wife and assumed she was white, for which he was almost lynched. "Ruby, George Thompson," the Handbook of Texas Online. http://www.tsha.utexas.edu/hand-book/online/articles/view/RR/fru2.html (accessed April 1, 2004).

6. A search by the Department of Health of the District of Columbia, as certified on November 2, 2004, failed to find any vital records about his death. Extensive efforts to find his grave were also not successful, as it appears that his remains were later disturbed by excavation for a new highway.

7. *Troy Daily Press*, July 23, 1875.

8. *Troy Daily Times*, July 23, 1875.

9. "To a Most Heroic Negress. Fitting Memorial of Harriet Tubman Is Appropriately Unveiled," Auburn (New York) *Citizen*, June 13, 1914; Larson, *Bound for the Promised Land*; David W. Blight, *Race and Reunion: The Civil War in American Memory* (Cambridge, Mass.: Harvard University Press, 2001), 332, 393.

10. *Troy Times*, October 14, 1932.

Chapter 18. The Search for Charles Nalle

1. Billed as "probably the largest group of dinosaur tracks ever found in the world," the prints were uncovered near Stevensburg in 1989 by the Culpeper Stone Company and some slabs were later removed and donated to the Smithsonian Institution. Some tracks ended up on display in the Triassic Gallery at the Museum of Culpeper History.

2. See John Smith, *The Generall Historie of Virginia . . . in Travels and Works of Captain John Smith*, edited by Edward Arber II (Edinburgh: John Grant, 1910), 421–29.

3. Scheel, *Culpeper*, 29, 384 n. 4. Washington's surveys appear in *The George Washington Atlas*, edited by Lawrence Martin (Washington, D.C.: George Washington Bicentennial Commission, 1932).

4. Scheel, *Culpeper*, 55–56, 389 n. 8.

5. Ibid., 158.

6. See Sutherland, *Seasons of War*.

7. See Thom Family Papers, 1670–1924, Virginia Historical Society Manuscript Collection, Richmond, Virginia; Thom Family Papers, Maryland Historical So-

ciety Manuscript Collection, Baltimore, Maryland; Wright-May-Thom Family Papers, Maryland Historical Society Manuscript Collection, Baltimore, Maryland; Cameron E. Thom Papers, 1785–1923, Huntington Library Manuscript Collection, San Marino, California. Also, Bartlett, *"My Dear Brother,"* based on correspondence between William Alexander Thom and his brother Joseph Pembroke Thom; David Pembroke Neff, "The Thom Family of Culpeper County: The Rise, Fall, and Restoration of a Nineteenth-Century Virginia Planter Family, 1746–1935" (PhD diss., George Mason University, 2004).

8. Some of the more notable relevant historiography regarding slave women includes Mary Ellison, "Resistance to Oppression: Black Women's Response to Slavery in the United States," *Slavery and Abolition* 4 (March 1983): 56–63; Elizabeth Fox-Genovese, *Within the Plantation Household: Black and White Women of the Old South* (Chapel Hill: University of North Carolina Press, 1988); Paul Finkelman, ed., *Women and the Family in a Slave Society* (New York: Garland, 1989); Herbert Gutman, *The Black Family in Slavery and Freedom, 1750–1925* (New York: Pantheon, 1976); Thelma Jennings, "'Us Colored Women Had to Go through a Plenty': Sexual Exploitation of African-American Slave Women," *Journal of Women's History* 1 (Winter 1990): 45–74; Elizabeth Keckley, *Behind the Scenes, or, Thirty Years a Slave, and Four Years in the White House,* with an introduction by James Olney (1868; reprint, New York: Oxford University Press, 1988); Wilma King, *Stolen Childhood: Slave Youth in Nineteenth-Century America* (Bloomington: Indiana University Press, 1995); Carole Shammas, "Black Women's Work and the Evolution of Plantation Society in Virginia," *Labor History* 26 (Winter 1985): 5–28; Deborah Gray White, "Female Slaves: Sex Roles and Status in the Antebellum Plantation South," *Journal of Family History* 9 (Fall 1983): 248–61; White, *Ar'n't I a Woman?*; and Jean Fagan Yellin, *Harriet Jacobs: A Life* (New York: Basic Books, 2003).

9. For a powerful revisionist consideration of slave women in the American South, see White, *Ar'n't I a Woman?*

10. Madden, *We Were Always Free,* 97–98; interview with T. O. Madden Jr. at his home, October 1, 1994.

11. *Troy Daily Arena,* May 26, 1860.

12. Still, *Underground Railroad,* 487–88.

13. Harrold, *Subversives,* 73.

14. Franklin and Schweninger, *Runaway Slaves.*

15. See, e.g., Still, *Underground Railroad,* and Still's *Underground Railroad Records* (Philadelphia: William Still, 1883); Robert C. Smedley, *History of the Underground Railroad in Chester and the Neighboring Counties of Pennsylvania* (Lancaster: the Journal, 1883); Siebert, *Underground Railroad from Slavery to Freedom;* Charles L. Blockson, *The Underground Railroad: Dramatic Firsthand Accounts of Daring Escapes to Freedom* (New York: Berkley Books, 1994); Harrold, *Subversives;* Blight, *Passages to Freedom;* and Bordewich, *Bound for Canaan.*

16. Bordewich, *Bound for Canaan*, 4 (emphasis in original).

17. Blight, *Passages to Freedom*, 3.

18. Gara, *Liberty Line*, 112–14.

19. Bordewich, *Bound for Canaan*, 5.

20. They include: Shadrach (Boston, 1851); two unspecified fugitives (Christiana, Pennsylvania, 1852); Jerry (Syracuse, 1852); three unspecified fugitives (Sandusky, Ohio, 1852); Joshua Glover (Racine, Wisconsin, 1854); John Anderson (Boston, 1855); George Clark (Norristown, Pennsylvania, 1855); unspecified fugitive (Dayville, Connecticut, 1855); unspecified fugitive (Syracuse, 1857); unspecified fugitive (Blairsville, Pennsylvania, 1858); unspecified fugitive (Sandusky, Ohio, 1858); John (Oberlin, Ohio, 1858); Jim (Ottawa, Illinois, 1859); Charles Nalle (Troy, 1860); two unspecified fugitives (Iberia, Ohio, 1860); and Eliza (Chicago, 1860). Campbell, *Slave Catchers*, appendix.

21. See, e.g., *Trial of Henry W. Allen, U.S. Deputy Marshal, for Kidnapping, With Arguments of Counsel & Charge of Justice Marvin, on the Constitutionality of the Fugitive Slave Law in the Supreme Court of New York* (Syracuse, N.Y.: Daily Journal Office, 1852); Jacob R. Shipherd, *History of the Oberlin-Wellington Slave Rescue* (Boston: John P. Jewett, 1859); Nat Brandt, *The Town That Started the Civil War* (Syracuse, N.Y.: Syracuse University Press, 1990); Earl Evelyn Sperry, *The Jerry Rescue, October 1, 1851 . . . Additional Jerry Rescue Documents and Rescue of Harriet Powell in Syracuse, September 1839*, compiled and edited by Franklin H. Chase (Syracuse, N.Y.: Onondaga Historical Association, 1924); Collison, *Shadrach Minkins*; von Frank, *Trials of Anthony Burns*; H. Robert Baker, *The Rescue of Joshua Glover: A Fugitive Slave, the Constitution, and the Coming of the Civil War* (Athens: Ohio University Press, 2006). See also Benjamin Franklin Prince, "The Rescue Case of 1857," *Ohio Archaeological and Historical Society Publications* 16 (January 1907): 293–306; Stanley Harrold, "John Brown's Forerunners: Slave Rescue Attempts and the Abolitionists, 1841–1851," *Radical History Review* 55 (Winter 1992): 89–112.

22. Larson, *Bound for the Promised Land*; Humez, *Harriet Tubman*; Catherine Clinton, *Harriet Tubman: The Road to Freedom* (Boston: Little, Brown, 2004); Reynolds, *John Brown, Abolitionist*; and Carton, *Patriotic Treason: John Brown and the Soul of America*.

23. W. E. B. DuBois, *The Gift of Black Folk: The Negroes in the Making of America* (New York: Washington Square Press, 1970), 146.

24. Genovese, *Roll, Jordan, Roll*, 419.

25. See Alison Brophy Champion, "Half Brother, Fully Enslaved," a three-part series in the Culpeper *Star-Exponent*, July 22–23, July 27, 2006.

26. Remarks of Senator Barack Obama, "A More Perfect Union," Constitution Center, Philadelphia, March 18, 2008.

27. See esp. Pierre Nora, *Realms of Memory: Rethinking the French Past*, 3 vols., trans. by Arthur Goldhammer (New York: Columbia University Press, 1996–98).

28. See, e.g., Annette Gordon-Reed, *Thomas Jefferson and Sally Hemmings: An American Controversy* (Charlottesville: University of Virginia Press, 1998).

Appendix

1. Brodie S. Herndon (1810–86) was a graduate in medicine of the University of Maryland and received his M.D. at age twenty. He practiced medicine in Culpeper for at least ten years, from 1830 to 1840, before removing to his native town of Fredericksburg, Virginia. Besides his Civil War medical service, Dr. Herndon also became famous for performing an early Caesarean operation in the nation. See Hansborough, *History and Genealogy of the Hansborough-Hansbrough Family*, 123–24; John W. Herndon, Genealogy of the Herndon Family; *Virginia Magazine of History and Biography*, Broderbund Software, Inc., Genealogics of Virginia Families IV, He-S, CD No. 162 (1997), 34.

2. Vol. 1, Diary in Brodie S. Herndon Papers, University of Virginia, Charlottesville, also quoted in *Hansbrough, History and Genealogy of the Hansborough-Hansbrough Family*, 116. The "Kitty" referred to is likely one of Herndon's daughters and Jacob is one of the slaves who had been seized with Charles.

3. Brodie S. Herndon Diary, vol. 2, transcription by Waterhouse Herndon, MSS 4107 Box 103, University of Virginia Library.

4. Brodie Strachan Herndon Jr. (1834–90) graduated from New York Medical College in 1855. See Brodie Strachan Herndon Sr. Letters, Library of Virginia, Richmond; Brodie S. Herndon Diary, University of Virginia Library, Charlottesville; Thomas C. Reeves, *Gentleman Boss: The Life of Chester Alan Arthur* (New York: Alfred A. Knopf, 1975), 31.

5. Brodie S. Herndon Diary, vol. 2.

6. About Dabney Herndon, see Herndon, *Genealogy of the Herndon Family*, 31. See George Frederick Howe, *Chester A. Arthur: A Quarter-Century of Machine Politics* (New York: Frederick Ungar, 1957); Reeves, *Gentleman Boss*. Chester A. Arthur (1829–86) was born in Vermont near the Canadian border and his father was an Irish-Canadian immigrant who served as a Baptist minister throughout Vermont and upstate New York. While attending Union College in Schenectady, Arthur taught school in Rensselaer County. He went to New York City in 1853 and started his legal career as a law clerk for Erastus D. Culver's law firm in Brooklyn. Culver, a former antislavery member of Congress, and Gerrit Smith were both abolitionist friends of Chester Arthur's father in Washington County, New York. Dabney Herndon, M.D., was born in Fredericksburg on September 22, 1831. One can also speculate whether Dabney Herndon or Brodie Strachan Herndon Jr. knew another fellow New York medical student from that era, Alexander Milton Ross, the "secret abolitionist" who had trained under Dr. Valentine Mott. The addresses mentioned are found in the New York City directory of 1859. Kit Herndon's slave continued to live in her household even after Chester Arthur and his new wife Nell

moved into the home in 1859. See *New York State Census of 1860*, Third Division, Eighteenth Ward, 203.

7. Brodie S. Herndon Diary, vol. 2, University of Virginia Library, Charlottesville.

8. Edwin G. Burrows and Mike Wallace, *Gotham: A History of New York City to 1898* (New York: Oxford University Press, 1999), 856–57. Jennings's account of her experience appeared in the *New York Times*, July 19, 1854; *Black Abolitionist Papers*, vol. 4: 230–32; Ripley, *Witness for Freedom*, 60–61.

9. Reeves, Gentleman Boss, chap. 1; Warren F. Broderick, "President Arthur's Father Lived in Area," *Record Newspapers* (Troy, New York), October 16, 1971. The Reverend Henry Highland Garnet was a Presbyterian minister in Manhattan and his friend the Reverend James N. Gloucester was a Presbyterian minister in Brooklyn.

10. May, *Fugitive Slave Law and Its Victims*, 24. See also Calarco, *Underground Railroad in the Adirondack Region*, pp. 136–37. While working on the Lemmon appeal for Culver, Arthur's legal assignments often brought him to Albany for his court appearances and lobbying regarding matters of Negro access to public transportation—a cause that likely put him in contact with Stephen Myers, who was also one of the state capitol's leading lobbyists on the subject. At the time, Arthur's father also served as pastor of the Calvary Baptist Church in Newtonville, just a couple of miles from Myers's Underground Railroad office. Culver also served as judge in another important fugitive slave legal case in New York that occurred about the same time, involving a light-colored fugitive who was seized aboard ship in Brooklyn harbor. See "The Brooklyn Fugitive Slave Case," *New York Times*, December 4, 1857, p. 1.

11. Some documents can be found in the Chester A. Arthur Papers, Library of Congress.

INDEX

The New Black Studies Series

SCOTT CHRISTIANSON is a prominent independent scholar whose work has appeared in the *New York Times, Washington Post, The Nation,* and *Journal of American History.* He is the author of several books including *With Liberty for Some: 500 Years of Imprisonment in America* and *Condemned: Inside the Sing Sing Death House.*

The University of Illinois Press
is a founding member of the
Association of American University Presses.

Composed in 9.75/13 Janson Text
with Memphis display
by Celia Shapland
at the University of Illinois Press
Designed by Kelly Gray
Manufactured by Cushing-Malloy, Inc.

University of Illinois Press
1325 South Oak Street
Champaign, IL 61820-6903
www.press.uillinois.edu